Key Concepts in Writing and Rhetoric

The Program in Writing and Rhetoric

Department of English
Columbia College Chicago

Edited by
Pegeen Reichert Powell and Jennie Fauls

Written by
Jennifer Ailles, Kenneth Daley, Jennie Fauls, Matthew McCurrie, Nita Meola, Pegeen Reichert Powell, Jonn Salovaara, Hilary Sarat-St. Peter, and Ryan Trauman

Our "green" initiatives include:

Electronic Products
We deliver products in nonpaper form whenever possible. This includes PDF downloadables, flash drives, and CDs.

Electronic Samples
We use a new electronic sampling system, called Xample. Instructor samples are sent via a personalized Web page that links to PDF downloads.

FSC Certified Printers
All of our printers are certified by the Forest Service Council which promotes environmentally and socially responsible management of the world's forests. This program allows consumer groups, individual consumers, and businesses to work together to promote responsible use of the world's forests as a renewable and sustainable resource.

Recycled Paper
Most of our products are printed on a minimum of 30% post consumer waste recycled paper.

Support of Green Causes
When we do print, we donate a portion of our revenue to Green causes. Listed below are a few of the organizations that have received donations from Fountainhead Press. We welcome your feedback and suggestions for contributions, as we are always searching for worthy initiatives.

Rainforest 2 Reef
Environmental Working Group

Cover design: Doris Bruey
Cover art: Lauren Nieves
Book Layout: OffCenter Concept House

Books may be purchased for educational purposes.

For information, please call or write:

1-800-586-0330

Fountainhead Press
Southlake, TX 76092

Web site: www.fountainheadpress.com
E-mail: customerservice@fountainheadpress.com

ISBN: 978-1-59871-536-1

Printed in the United States of America

Acknowledgements

This textbook was conceived of and written by a committee of instructors in the Program in Writing and Rhetoric. We are grateful to each other for the collaborative spirit that pervaded this project. We also want to acknowledge the support of Jennifer Loeb, Coordinator of Services in the Department of English, and Ken Daley, Chair of the Department of English. Thanks, too, to the staff at Fountainhead Press.

This edition of the textbook was revised in response to feedback from instructors and students in Writing and Rhetoric I in previous years. Thank you everyone who provided suggestions!

The cover image, *Interconnecting,* is provided by Lauren Nieves, Photojournalism, Class of 2019.

No individual author profits from the sale of this textbook.

What Is Writing in the 21st Century?

A welcome to Writing and Rhetoric I from the director of the Program in Writing and Rhetoric

Pegeen Reichert Powell

The very nature of writing is in tremendous flux. We are not in a stage of transition from an era of print to the digital era, as some might believe; rather we are entering an era when change itself is the dominant characteristic, when it is impossible to define or describe, with any certainty or finality, what writing in the 21st century is.

Teaching writing in this era of constant flux, when technologies for producing and consuming writing are evolving faster than ever before, when everything we know about writing is up for grabs, can be daunting. And it might seem strange to begin a textbook for a writing course with the statement that it is impossible to describe or define our subject.

In fact, though, what we are saying about the nature of writing is true of many areas of human experience. Consider the comments of the President of Columbia College Chicago, Dr. Kwang-Wu Kim:

> The idea of educating people for a specific profession is a very obsolete model. It assumes that the world is fairly static, and that you can bring young people in and four or five years later they will have whatever

> they need to succeed in a career as if that career hasn't changed. Today's college graduate will have five to eight different careers. . . not different jobs, different careers.
>
> So, the question then is how is an undergraduate education helping to prepare students for careers that *they are not even imagining at the time*? You're not doing that by giving them specific skills. You're doing that by giving them proficiencies and capacity, and that can only be done through a broader way of educating students, which is not so much about content, but more about *learning how to learn*—learning how to transfer knowledge. (emphasis mine) (White)

Our goal in Writing and Rhetoric I, then, is to teach students *how to learn about writing*, so that they are prepared to produce and consume the genres and texts that none of us are even imagining at this time.

And we instructors do know a lot about *how to learn about writing*, because we have made careers of mastering this task. We know the vocabulary, the reading and writing practices, and the habits of mind that inform the project of learning about writing, and the goal of Writing and Rhetoric I is to teach students these.

This course is centered on ten key concepts that will guide students as they encounter new writing scenes and tasks throughout their education, their careers, and their lives as citizens.

Key concepts in writing and rhetoric:

- affordances
- alphabetic text
- arrangement
- circulation
- ethos
- field
- genre
- image
- kairos
- remix

Writing and Rhetoric I will introduce students to these concepts, and the concepts themselves form the content and practice of the course. They are drawn from classical rhetoric and theories about digital and multimodal writing. One could argue that none of the concepts is new. However, each becomes richer and more complicated in the context of the networked, digital, multimodal composition that dominates the communication landscape today.

Each concept will be the basis for both reading and writing: students will learn to recognize these concepts in the work of others, and practice explaining their own choices in the texts they compose using this vocabulary. These concepts are not discrete vocabulary items to be memorized, but interrelated strategies for navigating the world as readers and writers.

Assignments and projects will practice, or enact, the key concepts of the course. This is perhaps a rather obvious statement, but the implications are far-reaching in this case. For example, one of the key concepts is ethos, which refers to how other people view us based on what we write and say (see the chapter on ethos for a full discussion). Ethos is not a new concept in writing courses. However, if we are to help students fully understand this concept in the context of digital, networked writing, we must address how ethos is constructed not just in words, but in all decisions that go into composing: the images (another key concept), music, fonts, colors, video one includes, and the arrangement (yet another key concept) of these various pieces, all contribute to one's ethos. If students are to practice constructing a positive ethos in this environment, then they must have the opportunity to create a multimodal text. Other key concepts, such as circulation and kairos, entail experimenting with ways to reach readers outside of the class and so may involve a variety of social media, for example.

Underlying this course are two basic assumptions about writing. First, writing no longer means solely alphabetic text in print. When we say "writing," we mean writing writ large, all the resources involved in producing and consuming a variety of texts, both digital and print. Second, alphabetic text is not going away soon, and this remains the focus of our program. In a world dominated by digital networked communication, if one is truly going to learn how to learn about writing, one must study the juxtaposition of alphabetic texts with other forms of communication (image, video, music, and so on). At Columbia, however, we are fortunate that our students are immersed in an academic environment marked by expertise in producing and consuming a variety of other media (for example, film, music, photography, graphic design, dance, sound, and so on). We can therefore focus on alphabetic text and rhetoric in relation to these other media.

In this era of tremendous flux, we see students as co-investigators into the question "What is writing in the 21st Century?" This is an important question! Arguably, writing scholars have always been investigating the nature of writing, but we are in an historical moment when the urgency of this question is felt keenly by scholars in composition and rhetoric, and also by other academics and the general public. Because change is happening so fast, the difference among generations when it comes to daily reading and writing practices is far greater than it has been in previous eras. We in the Program in Writing and Rhetoric have a lot to learn from our students about what writing is for their generation. Therefore, in the process of teaching the course, instructors may ask their students to submit work as examples for future students in Writing and Rhetoric I. Even this textbook will be revised regularly, and we may solicit some help from students with this task, too. In other words, I'd like to welcome you not just to a Writing and Rhetoric I course, but to a collaborative, ongoing project to study what writing in the 21st century is!

The textbook

A group of eight instructors in the Program in Writing and Rhetoric wrote this textbook especially for students in Writing and Rhetoric I at Columbia College Chicago. It has been revised with input from students and instructors who participated in Writing and Rhetoric I in previous years. There are chapters for each key concept, where students will be introduced to the definition, history, and examples of the concept. Students will want to read the textbook alongside the companion website, which will provide examples referred to in the chapters, as well as additional examples, resources, and suggestions for further reading. Following the chapters about the key concepts, there are several essays and articles about writing in the 21st century.

Learning outcomes for Writing and Rhetoric I

Students who successfully complete Writing and Rhetoric I should be able to

- Define and explain key concepts in writing and rhetoric, and use those concepts to describe their own rhetorical goals and choices and those of other authors
- Recognize the affordances of a variety of genres, media, platforms, and technologies, and compose texts that take advantage of these affordances to meet their own rhetorical goals
- Identify, question, and extend the narratives and arguments in a wide range of texts, images, and other media
- Explain why conventions for structure, arrangement, paragraphing, and mechanics vary across contexts, and practice composing texts with conventions appropriate to their contexts

1

Affordances

Affordances refers to what one thing can do, or allow us to do, that other things can't. In the context of writing and rhetoric, we talk about the affordances of different modes of communicating (**alphabetic text**, still **image**, moving image, sound, gesture, etc.), as well as the affordances of different technologies, platforms, **genres**, or media. Likewise, we must consider the constraints or limitations of each of these. When we want to communicate with other people, we make decisions based on the affordances and constraints of the various resources we have available to us.

History of affordances

Affordances is a relatively new word. According to the *Oxford English Dictionary*, the term was coined in 1966 by James J. Gibson, a psychologist who specialized in visual perception. The concept has since been used in fields related to design, and Donald Norman is credited with bringing it to theories about the design of objects. A common example is the design of the teacup. We intuitively know to grasp the teacup by the handle, because the affordances of the handle—the right size and shape for a couple of fingers to go through—makes it work. (For an example of human computer interface and affordances, check out the article, "Affordances Matter," on our course website.)

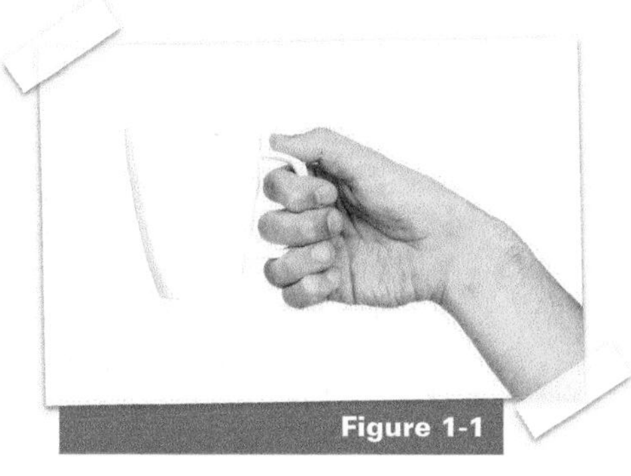

Figure 1-1

Gunther Kress has brought the concept of affordances to theories of multimodal communication. Kress uses the term "**mode**" to refer to the material resources we have available to us as we make decisions about how to communicate with others—**alphabetic text**, still **image**, moving image, sound, gesture, etc. Each of these modes has different affordances and constraints. Kress has emphasized the point that the affordances of different modes are not just material, but also social (*Multimodality* 79-83). What one group of people might communicate with gesture, another will communicate with spoken word. The affordances of gesture and spoken word lay both in their materiality (gesture uses parts of the body in space, while spoken word uses sound waves in sequential order), but also in what the people who use these modes recognize as meaningful. See our course website for a video of Kress discussing this subject in greater depth and refer to the chapter on Additional Key Concepts for a longer discussion of the concept of "modes."

Affordances today

Figure 1-2

It may be that game designers think more deliberately about the concept of affordances than any other creative individuals, because they are creating a world from scratch. It is the game designer's challenge to consider how the affordances of shape, color, light and dark, and movement will communicate to players how the invented world works. In an interview, Brian Block, a Columbia graduate and current instructor, offered his insights on how game designers think about affordances. According to Block, the ultimate goal when designing a game is for the player to be immersed in this world, to think of it as a real space. In a game, though, nothing is real, and the player is not really there, so nothing about the world can be assumed. When encountering a new game world, players don't know where they can move, what they're supposed to do, what objects in the world they can interact with, and the flipside of all of these: they don't know what is *not* possible in this world.

Block points out that some design elements that game designers have used repeatedly have become a part of the communicative framework for games, a kind

Figure 1-3

of language. Players know that red barrels always explode, and if a door has a handle on it you can probably go through it, otherwise it's there for decoration. However, the original designers of games were using the affordances of color—red is bad! green is good!—to help players navigate these wholly invented worlds.

For example, if you've ever played Super Mario Bros., you may remember that in the first moment on the first level of the game, there are gold question blocks floating on the screen and when Mario jumps, his fist is up. Using the affordances of color (it's shiny and gold! I want that!), symbol (hmm, questions are usually something that requires a response), and the shape of Mario's body (his fist is in just the right position to bump something!), the game designer is communicating to players what they need to know in this world: make Mario jump and bump those gold blocks.

The Half Life series creates a very realistic-seeming world, compared at least to the pixilated world of those early Mario Bros. games. Nevertheless, this world is still entirely imaginary and so must rely thoroughly on the concept of affordances to help players navigate. In fact, in this world where everything seems real, the designers must be even more thoughtful about indicating which elements can actually be manipulated or where the player needs to go. For example, notice how the designers of these games use the affordances of light to indicate which doors you could go through, which parts of a room you should investigate, where the next action might occur.

Figure 1-4

The challenge of game designers is multiplied by the fact that players' movements have to be interpreted through a device, a controller that must translate the players' actions in the real world (pressing a button or computer key, moving a lever, and so on) into actions in the game world (shooting, running, grabbing, and so on). The designers of game controllers are also thinking about affordances. (See the video on our website about affordances in game design.)

If you don't notice these things when you're playing games, Block argues, then the game designer has done his or her job well. Using the affordances of the visual elements they have to work with—color, light, shape, and so on—they invite you into the game and communicate to you what you want to do and how to do it.

Just as game designers rely on the concept of affordances to communicate what they need to about a complicated new world, we all need to consider affordances as we approach any rhetorical task. We need to think about the resources that we have available to us and which resources work best to do what we want to do. (See the section about **modes** in the chapter on Additional Key Concepts, in this textbook.) The

Figure 1-5

most effective communication will use the modes that work best. **Alphabetic text**, **image**, video, sound, each of these modes does some things better than others and each has constraints that need to be considered as well. Likewise, we choose which **genre**, technology, platform, or media allow us to do what we want to do.

Consider the choices that Eddie Seitz and Liz Zaroogian made when composing these images. (Seitz and Zaroogian were students in Dr. Jennifer Ailles's Writing and Rhetoric I in Fall 2014.) Both **remixes** of fairy tales, these memes update the moral of the traditional stories to communicate a feminist message. In a reflection on the "Don't Sleep Your Life Away" image, a remix of *Sleeping Beauty,* Seitz explains that the purpose is to "promote women's independence and dismiss the societal ideology that men need to be the ones to sweep women off their feet." Because the audience is young women, he considered the affordances of the methods of **circulation**, and opted to create a text that could be distributed via various social networks such as Facebook, Twitter, and Tumblr. He also considered the affordances of the font he chose ("simplistic and easy to read") and the color and layout ("a dark red border so the eye is drawn to the center of the image"). Finally, he considered the affordances of **image** and **alphabetic text**. The text is able to succinctly communicate the message he is trying to get across. The image of the old woman "serves as a 'woman of wisdom' to the audience," as well as adding "a little bit of comedy and sarcasm"; in other words, Seitz understood that one of the affordances of image in this case is to communicate a range of emotions that the words alone couldn't do.

Figure 1-6

Zaroogian's powerful meme, though visually quite simple, is actually the result of a series of complex choices. Zaroogian intends to address "victims of rape, telling them that no matter what they were wearing it was not their fault." The affordances of the **image** of Little Red Riding Hood's cape here are important, because Zaroogian recognized that the red cloak could accomplish two things: it engages the viewer and it is part of the content of the message. She explains, "Visually, it attracts the eye and draws attention with the red cloak in the center of the poster. . . [I]t is an example of a rape victim whose fate was blamed on her clothing (and is a widely-enough known tale that it is relatively universally recognizable)." However, the **alphabetic** text, according to Zaroogian, carries the most significant load in this piece of communication, the message that "it's not your fault." As such, she considered the affordances of the font choice, which she describes as "minimalistic, sans-serif. . .that would appear simple and inviting," and the affordances of **circulating** the text on various social media sites with a hashtag #itsnotyourfault.

These excellent examples illustrate that even seemingly straightforward texts require thoughtful, deliberate choices about the affordances of the various resources available to us.

Affordances and other concepts

All of the decisions that go into communicating a message must take into account the affordances of different resources. We have a large array of **genres** that we are familiar with, for example, and we determine the affordances of each when we decide which one to write with. Likewise, different **circulation** methods have different affordances. The constraints of a tweet, its 140 character limit, may not be as significant as the affordances, its potentially wide reach as it goes to all of one's followers simultaneously and the ease with which it can be retweeted. The affordances of an email include the ability of a user to format the message using varying fonts, bulleted lists, and highlighting, and the fact that, as long as we have an address, we can send the message to the intended reader (there are no privacy settings on email programs that deflect messages from unknown senders). When these features are important, one might choose email over a Facebook message.

Affordances become important, too, when working on **arrangement**. Go to Wordpress.com (link available on our course website) and browse the wide variety of themes. Each theme provides different templates for bloggers to choose among as they create their own site. In addition to different fonts and colors (which all have different affordances), each template arranges the **alphabetic text** and **images** and menus in different ways. Writers will choose the theme that best fits their intended purpose for the blog, considering the affordances of the different arrangements.

Alphabetic text has been used as the dominant mode for communication in Western culture for generations, the mode in which people conduct their most important affairs (economic, religious, political). However, Kress and Theo van Leeuwen argue that we are witnessing a weakening of the assumption that alphabetic text is preferable and an increasing reliance on **image** in our culture (*Reading Images* 23). While the material affordances of the two modes have not really changed, this transition demonstrates Kress's point that a mode's affordances are not just material, but also social.

For examples referred to in the textbook, additional resources, and further reading, please visit the course website: www.fountainheadpress.com/keyconcepts.

Writing with affordances

When we have the occasion to compose using different modes, **genres,** technologies, or platforms, we have to take great care with our decisions by considering the affordances and constraints associated with our different options.

Our decisions should take into account not just the materiality of the modes, **genres**, technologies, and platforms, but also the social relationships implied by these different options. So we need to ask:

- What can this option do?
- What does it allow me as a writer to do and communicate?
- What does it allow my readers to do?
- How is this option perceived by those with whom I am trying to communicate—is it meaningful for them in the same way it is for me?
- Does this option communicate the level of seriousness or authority I want?
- And for each option we need to ask what it cannot do or communicate? What are the constraints that may make this option less useful?

Each of our decisions forecloses on other options, and it's worth pausing long enough to consider those other options. While many of our decisions may be intuitive or instinctive (you don't have to think too long about sending an email to a professor to make an appointment to meet with him or her), our options today are virtually limitless and considering affordances is important.

2

Alphabetic Text

Alphabetic text refers to the letters and words we use when we're communicating in writing. This key concept may seem obvious, but that is because it has been the dominant form of communication in Western culture for centuries and we tend to take it for granted. It is actually more complicated than we might think. First of all, we tend to forget that alphabetic text is a visual mode, so we must consider how it looks. It's also worth noting that our alphabet represents the sounds of our spoken language, which distinguishes it from writing systems that rely on characters that represent ideas and objects (such as Chinese and Japanese).

Alphabetic text is just one resource we have for communicating our ideas—we can communicate with **image**, the sound of our voice, video, animation, or music, among many other modes (see the chapter on Additional Key Concepts for a longer discussion of **modes**), and our electronic devices and the internet make it easier than ever before to use these other modes to communicate with a wide audience. Distinguishing among these various resources, and using one instead of another, becomes one of the many rhetorical choices we make whenever we face a situation when we are trying to communicate with others. Therefore, it's important to study what makes alphabetic text unique and how it relates to all other modes.

History of alphabetic text

Although it might be hard to imagine our world without some form of writing, the fact is that writing evolved (or was invented) relatively late in human history. This is worth remembering because while spoken language is innate and biologically determined, every person has to learn how to write and read.

Figure 2-1

Scott McCloud provides a brief history of the evolution of writing systems in "Show and Tell," a reading included in this textbook. As he explains, writing likely evolved out of cave drawings and other instances of pictographic writing, and gradually, the images became increasingly abstract to evolve into writing systems based on a complex system of characters. Our writing system derived from the Greek alphabet, which developed hundreds of years BC. It wouldn't begin to be standardized until centuries later, after the invention of moveable type and the printing press in the 15th and 16th centuries AD.

The printing press also gave rise to the **affordances** of the visual nature of alphabetic text. A page of writing used to be an uninterrupted string of letters that relied on the reader, usually reading out loud to other people, to determine where one word or idea ended and the other began. When the printing press made books available to more people, reading became a solitary and silent activity. At the same time, visual conventions were introduced to help people make sense of the alphabetic text on the page. For example, we have capital letters to mark the beginning of a sentence and punctuation that marks the end of the sentence. We also have paragraph breaks that help communicate where subtle shifts in ideas occur.

As alphabetic text became standardized, readers grew accustomed to these visual clues; it is likely that after you learned these conventions, you have taken them for granted as both a writer and reader. In fact, many texts are designed so that you don't really look *at* the alphabetic text, but rather look *through* it, straight to the ideas it contains. (See Richard Lanham, in his reading "Economists of Attention" included in this textbook, for more on this point.)

However, writers today have far more options for working with the visual affordances of alphabetic text. From fonts and sizes to colors to the **arrangement** of chunks of text on a page or screen, we have a lot more choices to make when we use alphabetic text, which requires us to look at this resource in a new way.

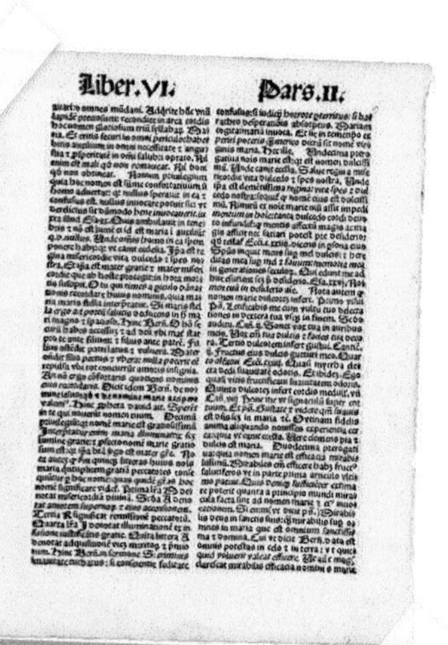

Liber.VI. Pars.II.

Figure 2-2

Alphabetic text today

Alphabetic text has served as the dominant mode for communication in Western culture for centuries, the mode in which people conduct their most important affairs: think of the religious documents that spell out how one is to worship, the contracts that determine who owes whom what, the political treatises that establish laws, and educational texts like this one. Because alphabetic text has been so pervasive, and therefore taken for granted, we often aren't even aware of how it works.

We all know that writing happens by **arranging** words into phrases and sentences that convey meaning, but if we pause long enough to consider what's involved in that action, it can be fascinating. Each time we put one word after another after another, we are making choices about which words we use, from the countless words available in our language, and each choice excludes all the other words we could have used instead. There are some principles that govern the order in which we have to arrange the words, but even here, our options are overwhelming. The resources available to us when we are working with alphabetic text are virtually limitless.

Consider the following, all headlines and the first paragraphs of articles that appeared on August 10th or 11th in 2014, about an incident that dominated the news for several months that year.

Unarmed black Mo. teen shot after altercation, police say
CBS 8/10

An unarmed 18-year-old black man was shot and killed by police in suburban St. Louis after an altercation that involved two people and an officer, authorities said Sunday while hundreds of protesters demanded answers outside.

Police Say Mike Brown Was Killed After Struggle for Gun in St. Louis Suburb
New York Times, August 10, 2014

The fatal shooting of an unarmed black teenager Saturday by a police officer in a St. Louis suburb came after a struggle for the officer's gun, police officials said Sunday, in an explanation

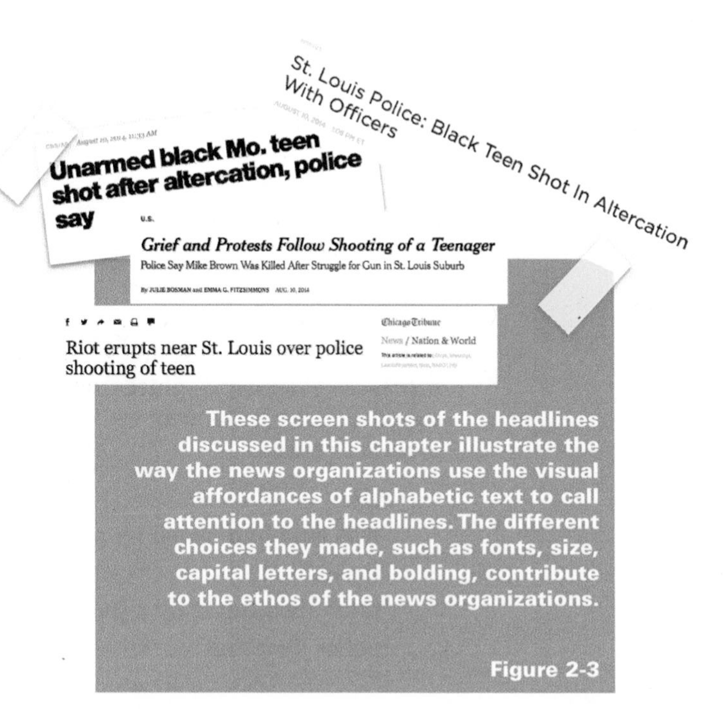

These screen shots of the headlines discussed in this chapter illustrate the way the news organizations use the visual affordances of alphabetic text to call attention to the headlines. The different choices they made, such as fonts, size, capital letters, and bolding, contribute to the ethos of the news organizations.

Figure 2-3

that met with outrage and skepticism in the largely African-American community.

Riot erupts near St. Louis over police shooting of teen
Chicago Tribune, August 11, 2014

Rioting and looting erupted in Ferguson, Missouri, late on Sunday as protests over the killing of an unarmed black teenager by a police officer turned violent, law enforcement officials and media reports said.

St. Louis Police: Black Teen Shot In Altercation With Officers
NPR.org, August 10, 2014

The chief of the St. Louis County Police says a black teenager fatally shot by officers Saturday was killed during an altercation with authorities.

Each news organization attempted to describe an event, but the range of choices they made are significant. Notice the various ways that the victim, Michael Brown, was identified:

- unarmed black Mo. teen
- unarmed 18-year-old black man
- Mike Brown
- unarmed black teenager
- teen
- Black Teen
- a black teenager

It is worthwhile to discuss with friends and classmates the implications of referring to Michael Brown as a teen or teenager instead of as a man, for example. Half of these phrases include the detail that he was unarmed, five of them include the detail that he was black. Why might those differences matter? Most of the news media came to use the name "Michael"; what does the use of "Mike" instead contribute to the story?

How we use the resources available to us in alphabetic text to represent the people, places, or things involved in events is extremely significant, as is the way we depict the actions. Again, look at the range of choices made:

- shot
- was shot and killed by police
- was killed
- fatal shooting. . .by a police officer
- police shooting

- the killing. . .by a police officer
- fatally shot by officers

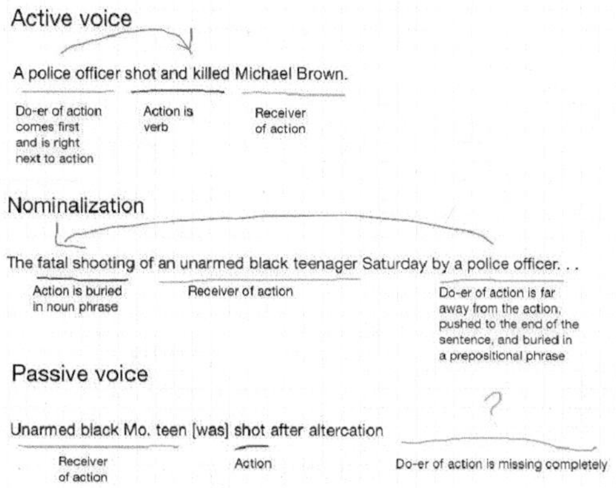

Figure 2-4

You might discuss the difference between identifying the verb as "shoot" or "kill." Both, of course, are accurate, but they mean different things. Moreover, in none of these examples, is the active voice used. The active voice would read like this: A police officer shot/killed Michael Brown. Instead, nominalizations or passive voice are used. A nominalization is when you take an action, typically represented as a verb, and turn it into a noun phrase instead. For example, "fatal shooting" or "the killing" removes the action from the event and kind of hides it inside a noun phrase.

The passive voice, as in "was killed" or "shot," distances the actor (the police officer) from the action itself (killing, shooting) by pushing the actor to the end of the sentence, or removing the actor altogether. Notice how the first and third example in the bulleted list above doesn't name the actor at all, whereas some of them name the shooter/killer in the "by-phrase," so we have "shot by officers," for example.

This brief analysis doesn't even begin to cover the way the authors of these words drew on the resources of alphabetic text to communicate the meaning of this event. Other questions you might discuss with friends and classmates: What words or phrases are missing from these headlines and paragraphs? Why, for example, do none of them identify the race of the police officer? What is the difference between referring to the response by the citizens of Ferguson as a "riot" or a "protest" and what are the implications of the verb "erupts" in the *Chicago Tribune* headline?

When we talk about the **affordances** of the different modes, it is worth remembering the vast array of resources we have available to us each time we put even a few words together using alphabetic text. It's no wonder, then, why alphabetic text has been the dominant mode in our culture for centuries. However, Gunther Kress and Theo van Leeuewen, among others, argue that we are witnessing a period in history in which the prominence of alphabetic text is weakening, and we are increasingly relying on image to communicate in our culture (*Reading Images* 23). The extent to which this is true is up for serious debate, but one basic premise of that debate is the fact that writing and the role of writing are constantly changing and always have been.

Figure 2-5

Change can freak people out. Think of the way people respond to the written conventions used in text messages. A quick Google search ("texting and grammar") will turn up any number of articles about whether or not texting and all of the abbreviations, missing capital letters and punctuation, and other short-cuts are negatively affecting the way people write and speak. Do the search yourself and read a few articles. If you look for the words that describe what's going on, you'll see that what some people refer to as "evolution" others will refer to as "decline," and some describe these new conventions as "inventive" or "efficient," while others refer to them as "lazy" and "ignorant." Talk with your friends or classmates, and you'll see that these different arguments circulate even among people of the same generation—it's not just old people complaining about "kids these days."

Texting may also provide examples of Kress and van Leeuewen's argument about our increasing reliance on **images** in everyday communication. Consider this exchange between a teenage son and his mother. He sends a picture of his friends walking up to a McDonalds with a map of his current location to let his mom know where he is. She can write "OK but when are you coming home?" and choose from any number of emojis to communicate her perspective on the situation—does she send the worried face? the angry face? or the "I'm cool, just chillin' with my sunglasses on" face?

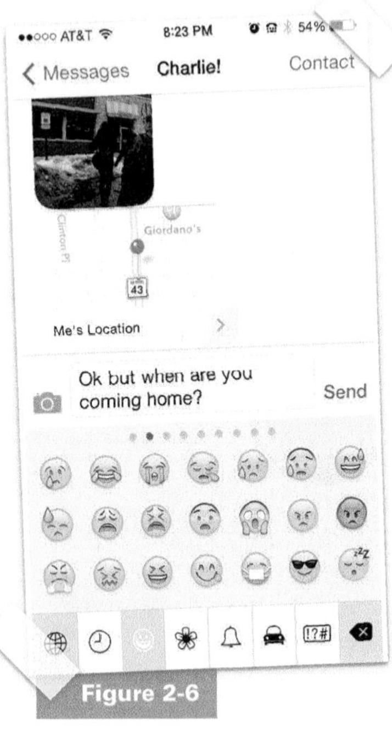

Figure 2-6

Perhaps what we see in this exchange is an example of a more nuanced argument than Kress and van Leeuewen's. John A. Bateman argues that "What we instead find all around us is a far richer range of *combinations* of different ways of making meanings. Visual depictions commonly *include* words and so the visual and the verbal are evidently working together. When this is done well, what results is something *more than* either could achieve alone" (11). Note how the map in the exchange between son and mother would mean nothing without the written names of streets and familiar establishments, or how the written words "OK but when are you coming home?" can mean very different things depending on the emoji the mom chooses.

When you multiply the resources we have available to us when working with alphabetic text alone by the resources we have when we combine it with other modes like **image**, the capacity we have to communicate with other humans is sometimes overwhelming, but always amazing.

Alphabetic text and other concepts

If you consider the range of choices available to you as you work with alphabetic text, you have some sense of the options you have for creating your **ethos** using this mode. Like we demonstrated in the discussion of the Michael Brown headlines and paragraphs, your credibility as an author can be demonstrated—or weakened—depending on which words you choose and what order you put them in. The visual elements of a text can affect your ethos, too. For example, consider the difference between Comic Sans and Times New Roman, and think about the ethos created by too many exclamation points!!!! Proofreading can also demonstrate your care with alphabetic text, and thus affect your ethos: spelling errors or missing punctuation can negatively affect your ethos.

As the texting example illustrates, though, the rules governing spelling and punctuation depend on genre. You might have noticed that the "hypothetical" mom in that example, who may or may not be a writing teacher, could not bring herself to text "Ok but when r u coming home," which would have been perfectly acceptable, maybe even preferable, in this particular genre. When conventions that are appropriate in texting appear in other genres like a school essay or job application letter, however, we may accuse authors of being careless with alphabetic text, which weakens their **ethos**.

The discussion above about the relationship between alphabetic text and **image** indicates that we are not just responsible for these word- and sentence-level decisions, but we must also consider the visual elements of alphabetic text as well, from choosing font type and size to the use of underlining and bolding to the colors of our alphabetic text. And we must pay careful attention to the **arrangement** of the chunks of alphabetic text on the page or screen, and how they are positioned in relation to other modes.

The questions in the next section can guide you through some of the choices you need to make.

Writing with alphabetic text

Although the nature and role of alphabetic text is constantly changing in our society, it is premature to say that alphabetic text is no longer important. In fact, considering how networked communication potentially enables us to reach a far wider and more diverse audience, perhaps our written words are more important than ever. It is also true, though, that each time we go to communicate with others, we must decide whether alphabetic text is the best choice for this rhetorical situation. Then, as you write, and especially after you've written and while you revise, ask yourself questions like:

- Have I chosen the best words in each instance to represent other people, places, things, events, and my own ideas and arguments? Have I ordered the words in such a way that the meaning I've created comes close to what I intend?
- Have I taken care with my alphabetic text by learning the conventions expected of me in this situation and editing and proofreading so that I adhere to these conventions as effectively as possible?
- Have I used the visual elements of alphabetic text—fonts, bolding, paragraphing, and so on—effectively?
- What **genre** is appropriate or effective here, and how is alphabetic text used or not used in this genre?
- What other modes can I combine with my alphabetic text here, not just as decoration, but as resources for changing and multiplying my meaning?
- How should I **arrange** the alphabetic text and other modes on the page or screen, so that readers get the experience I hope they will, and so that it is aesthetically pleasing?
- Have I considered important principles of design (see "Design" by Sean Morey, included in this textbook)?

3

Arrangement

Arrangement refers to the deliberate placement of pieces of a project in time or in space. We arrange ideas in longer **alphabetic texts** and speeches in a particular order so that they make sense and have the desired effect on our reader or listeners. If you've ever outlined an essay, beginning with introduction and ending with conclusion, and thought about what order to make your main points, you were considering arrangement. Arrangement in multimodal texts must take into consideration where pieces go in time *and* space. We deliberately place pieces (chunks of **alphabetic text**, **images**, sounds) so they are viewed or heard first, second, third, or simultaneously, or so that within a visual frame, they are at the left, right, top, bottom, foreground, background, and so on, in relation to other pieces.

History of arrangement

Arrangement is one of the five canons of classical rhetoric: invention (generating ideas), arrangement (organization and order), style (words and grammar), memory (memorization), and delivery (speaking or writing). These were the five categories that instructors of rhetoric taught their students. When they taught arrangement in classical rhetoric, they were thinking primarily about speeches and in what order an orator should make his or her points. Most of the teachers of classical rhetoric agreed, for example, that there should be an introduction at the beginning, when you focus on establishing your **ethos**, and a conclusion at the end, when you make your main point as memorable as possible, often by evoking the relevant emotions in the audience (**pathos**). Cicero added four other sections between the introduction and conclusion: a statement of facts or the background of the issue; a division between ideas; proof or evidence supporting the ideas; refutation, or the countering of other people's ideas. While different teachers taught different rules for arrangement, the general principle remained the same—that we need to organize our speeches in a certain way.

The rules for how to write the five-paragraph essay or a lab report are about arrangement and when you were expected to produce these **genres**, you were experiencing the influence of classical rhetoric even today. In this context, arrangement is similar to organization.

More recently, arrangement has also referred to the visual arrangement of the pieces of a text on a page, and so the concept is also related to design and layout. This understanding of the concept is relatively new for most writers, but word processing and other programs make it increasingly easy for everyone with access to a computer to more deliberately achieve the necessary effects of their visual design. (See "Design" by Sean Morey, included in this textbook, for further discussion of the principles of visual arrangement, especially the section on the Use of Space.)

Using the same term for both the organization of ideas in **alphabetic text** and speech and the placement of visual elements on the page suggests that the practices are profoundly interrelated and that both are important for achieving your goals when communicating.

Arrangement today

The rules for organizing print and speech are usually very specific to the different **genres** you will produce (see the chapter on genre). Here we will focus on arranging elements visually on a page or screen, which can be relevant to a variety of genres and media.

Kress and van Leeuwen write about what they refer to as the "grammar of images" and they identify three different things we should think about as we are arranging or analyzing a visual space, whether it is a multimodal page or a single **image**. The first aspect we should consider is "information value," which means noticing what's at the left, right, top, bottom, center, and margin of a space. The authors suggest that when items are placed side by side (left and right), the elements on the left are usually about what we already know as common sense or self-evident, things we assume as "given," while things on the right are new information or the ideas that we should pay closer attention to or something we may not automatically agree with (*Reading Images* 181). When elements of a page or image are arranged at the top and bottom, they argue, we see "what has been placed at the top is presented as the Ideal, and what has been placed at the bottom is put forward as the Real" (186). By Ideal, they mean general or aspirational ideas, while Real is facts, details, or examples. Finally, when there is an obvious center and margins of a page or image—which they say is relatively uncommon in Western cultures (194)—then what is at the center is the most important, and everything around it is dependent or secondary information. For example, in this old car ad, you see the aspirational statement "Chevrolet. Building a better way to see the U.S.A." at the top of the page, with the image of the handsome couple in a beautiful landscape. At the bottom, we get the Real, the facts about what makes the car so great.

The second aspect of arrangement that we need to think about is salience, or figuring out what is most noticeable in a space. Something might be more noticeable if it's in the foreground, if it's larger, or if it's clearer (201). And finally, the last aspect of arrangement we should pay attention to is framing, whether there are any lines on the page that divide it up, so that there is an inside and outside (*Reading Images* 203).

Figure 3-1

One thing to notice about some of our writing these days is how little choice we have in the arrangement of our texts. Most social media sites such as Facebook, Twitter, Instagram, or Soundcloud, allow you to upload content in the form of **alphabetic text**, **images**, videos, music, links, and so on, but they do not allow you to arrange the content on the page as a whole. The ubiquity of the profile picture in a variety of social media is an interesting example. We might stress over exactly what photo to upload for our profile picture, or use that square to make a statement of some kind, as in the case of the red equal signs during the Supreme Court hearings about gay marriage (see the chapter on kairos). In other words, we take seriously how the profile picture contributes to our ethos.

However, we don't have any control over the placement of the photo relative to the rest of the content—the photo is always on the left. In some respects, this makes sense. As Kress and van Leeuwen point out, the way we "read" arrangement is that what we take as given or self-evident information is on the left, and the new information is on the right. Our physical appearance is a given, but our status update or tweet is new. However, there is more going on here: the profile picture is the same size and shape as the picture on our driver's license, passport, and various ID cards, and its placement relative to the content—to the left—is the same as well. Because we have no choice about where to place the photo, we are complicit in the blurring of our legal, social, and personal selves, and given the financial interests in a site like Facebook, our

IDENTIFICATION
Name: Your Name
Surname: Your Surname
Department: department
Phone: 012 345 67 89
Source: Shutterstock

Figure 3-2

identity has become monetized. When we can't make decisions about arrangement in a case like this, it can be an ideological issue.

When working with sound, **image**, and moving image simultaneously one must be thinking about the **affordances** of the different elements and their orientations in both space and time. For example, Columbia College instructor Katherine Goldstein wrote an essay about her grandfather, using chronology as the organizing principle: her story begins when she's young and ends when she decides to go to graduate school to pursue an MFA in poetry. Her video essay, available on our course website, arranges her spoken narrative by layering her voice and soft music with moving images of ocean waves and still photographs. Her first line, "Even in the winter, my Grandpa Morty always smelled like the ocean," is spoken over a moving image of ocean waves, and the next shot is a still photograph of her grandfather, the same one the video ends with. The juxtaposition of the ocean waves and her grandfather's photo establishes visually the central setting of the narrative, the beach house where her grandfather told her and her cousins stories, and the spoken words tie together the two seemingly disparate entities. Note, too, how she provides a transcript across the top and bottom of the screen throughout the video so that her movie is accessible to people who can't hear, an attention to the **affordances** of the different modes that is admirable.

Arrangement and other concepts

Arrangement matters when you're trying to produce a **genre** that readers have firm expectations about. For example, resumes typically have predictable arrangements, the order in which you provide details about your education, your job experiences, your skills. However, different professions arrange their resumes differently and even have different categories of information, and it's important to learn what arrangement your **field** expects. Moreover, according to a study titled "Keeping an Eye on Recruiter Behavior" (available on our course website), recruiters look at a resume for an average of six seconds, and the visual arrangement of the different pieces of information profoundly affects the success of the resume.

While in classical rhetoric and in many **genres** today, the rules for arrangement can be pretty strict, arrangement is also an opportunity for a lot of creativity. **Remixes** in music and other media are primarily about arrangement. We take pieces of other people's work, add some of our own, and arrange them to communicate an entirely new idea.

A primary consideration when we deliberately arrange our work is the **affordances** and constraints of the different elements. Whether to put the **image** at the top, bottom, left, or right of the page is in part determined by what the **image** can do that the other elements can't. Moreover, the juxtaposition of different elements will create meaning that the elements alone can't achieve. Again, this is where creativity is important.

Considering arrangement in multimodal compositions also means looking at **alphabetic text** differently. Not only do we need to consider the organization of our ideas within the chunks of alphabetic text, but we also need to think about how to arrange the alphabetic text in relation to the other modes, to see the chunks of text as a visual element of our composition. We can change the size and shape of the chunks of text in order to arrange them effectively on the page or screen, and we can place them anywhere we want on the page relative to other modes. (See "Design" by Sean Morey, included in this textbook, for more guidance on typography.)

Writing with arrangement

Arranging written or spoken texts is primarily an issue of genre (see the chapter on **genre**). In multimodal texts, one needs to consider not just the organizing principles appropriate for that given genre, however, but also the visual and audio composition on the page or screen.

Ask yourself questions about your own intentions with the piece and use the space and time available as an opportunity to manifest those intentions:

- What are my options for arrangement within this genre, media, or platform? What are the constraints of this genre, media, or platform, when it comes to arrangement?
- What do I want the reader/viewer to pay the most attention to? You might arrange this item last, chronologically, or to the right, visually. Or you could make it larger or put it in the foreground.
- What is, for me, the general idea or the overarching concept? You could put this at the top of the page visually, and arrange details, etc., below it.
- What happens when I juxtapose these two seemingly disparate ideas or **images**? Does the **juxtaposition** create a new meaning? A dissonance?
- Which mode—alphabetic text, image, sound—carries the greatest burden in terms of communicating my message? How can I arrange the project in order to privilege that mode?

4

Circulation

Circulation refers to what happens to a text once it has been produced. A "text" can be as simple as an email or text message, but a text can also be as complex as a Hollywood movie or graphic novel. One reason it is so important to think about circulation is because it helps us understand how texts get delivered from authors to readers, as well as where it might go, who might see it, and what they might do with it. Sometimes circulation is easy to identify and understand, like sending a postcard or leaving a voicemail. However, circulation is often a little more complicated. Whenever you read, send, post, share, watch, or listen, you are playing your own part in the circulation of texts.

Source: Shutterstock

Figure 4-1

History of circulation

Aristotle suggested that in order to be an effective writer or speaker, a student must become skilled in five different aspects of communication: invention (generating ideas), **arrangement** (organization and order), style (words and grammar), memory (memorization), and delivery (speaking or writing).

Aristotle argued that delivery was just as important to communication as the ideas themselves or the language used to convey them. In ancient Greece, most ideas were communicated orally, through public speeches, debates, or conversations. For Aristotle, the concept of delivery meant giving speeches, participating in debates, or having conversations. Most simply, the concept of delivery has always focused on how an idea is shared from one person to another, between a speaker and audience, or an author and readers. Speech and performance were the dominant modes of communication in the ancient world, and so it followed that discussions of delivery focused on the spoken voice and bodily movement. Only with the development of bound and printed texts like books, newspapers, and posters did the ancient concept of delivery evolve to focus less on speech and more on the written word.

Recording ideas in printed texts was one of the first steps in allowing ideas to circulate in new ways. The first printed texts were created by hand, and making copies of manuscripts required scribes to copy one word at a time into a new manuscript. Because these texts were rare, most manuscripts produced by scribes ended up in the libraries of wealthy individuals or monasteries. Gutenberg's invention of the printing press in 1455 was one of the most important moments in the history of the circulation of the written word. His invention meant that books were more plentiful and less expensive. More people than ever before had access to the world of ideas. As the transition from quill to printing press illustrates, available technologies can affect everything about the circulation of a text: from how it's produced, to how it's consumed, what its material properties are, and who has access to it.

Circulation today

This sort of transition, from one communication medium to another, has become increasingly common as new technologies emerge. The invention of recorded sound and radio radically shifted the way we produced and consumed texts. Certain types of texts were no longer limited by space and time. A symphony performed by an orchestra in London could be experienced by a banker in Cleveland months or years after the actual performance. The same can be said of motion picture cinema and broadcast television. Moreover, the development of radio stations, movie studios, and television networks has always been followed by amateur producers who take advantage of consumer technologies like ham radio, photocopiers, video cameras, or cassette tapes. All of these technological developments have produced new types of texts and new media.

As our writing and media technologies have become more powerful, our texts increasingly seem to take on a life of their own. This idea has never been more true than in our contemporary digital culture of websites, social networks, viral videos, and internet memes. There used to be a clear distinction between producing a text and distributing it. Writing a text and publishing a text were two different activities entirely. The same could be said for recording a song and playing it on the radio or making a movie and showing it in a theater. Writing and sending a letter was a process measured in days, not seconds. Making a movie required a production studio, rather than a smartphone. New technologies continue to emerge at an increasingly faster rate, and the distinction between producing a text and circulating it is slowly disappearing. As a result, writers who have the best understanding of how texts are shared between people, how they circulate within and across social networks, will have the most impact and the biggest presence in the networks most important to them.

Wikipedia is an excellent example of the way that networked and digital technologies have changed the very nature of how certain texts are produced, circulate, and evolve in contemporary culture. For centuries before the World Wide Web enabled and democratized the digital publication and distribution of texts, encyclopedias were one of the most important and respected repositories of knowledge in almost any home or library. Encyclopedias were usually made up of dozens of expensive bound print volumes, each assigned its own letter of the alphabet. Unless a researcher had access to the encyclopedia's most recent edition, the information contained within its covers was likely outdated by some number of years. Even the most recent edition was likely written months or even years earlier, considering the lengthy process of editing and publishing bound books like these. These limitations were taken for granted in an age where print-publication dominated the circulation of texts. But there was no alternative. Acquiring a brand new, updated encyclopedia set every single year was a financial impossibility for most families and libraries.

Wikipedia was designed specifically to respond to these exact limitations and restraints. Although not a perfect solution to the challenges noted above, Wikipedia was accessible to any individual with online access, whether that be at home, school, or a local library. But accessibility is only one of the elements of circulation that Wikipedia addresses. Each of the entries within Wikipedia is constantly evolving. As new knowledge becomes public, as science charges forward, and political events unfold across the globe, Wikipedia is able to accommodate and incorporate those bits of

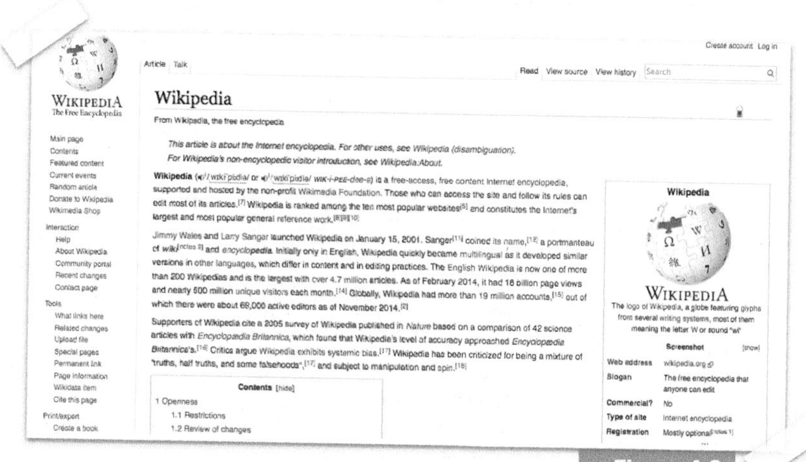

Figure 4-2

knowledge far more quickly and democratically than ever before. With the advent of Web 2.0 technologies, readers of Wikipedia have the option to participate in its existence as writers and collaborators. They can suggest corrections to inaccuracies or add emerging knowledge to the existing entries, and their suggestions become available almost instantly. This interaction, where the boundaries between reader and writer, producer and consumer begin to blur has resulted in one of the most comprehensive and accurate sources of knowledge ever produced.

A fascinating example of just how powerful the idea of circulation can be is the internet phenomenon "Alex from Target." In early November 2014, Twitter user @auscalum tweeted a photo of 16-year-old Alex Lee from Frisco, Texas as he was working in the checkout line of a local Target store. Then Twitter user @_twerkcam retweeted the photo and attached the hashtag "#alexfromtarget." From there, and for reasons that can be endlessly debated, Lee's photo went viral on Twitter and inspired an entire meme phenomenon. By the time his mother picked him up from work, and he finally turned his phone on, he realized that the number of people following him on Twitter had ballooned from 144 to more than 100,000. More significant than how far and fast the original photo and tweet circulated is how internet users modified the originals, **remixing** them, and taking the idea of Alex from Target in directions that neither @auscalum or Lee himself had any control over. Memes like "Betty from Walmart" or "Matt from Red Robin" started popping up, new words were **juxtaposed** with the **image** such as "I fell in love with the way he scans my items slowly then all at once," and Target appropriated the phenomenon and circulated their own version as a spontaneous advertising event.

Figure 4-3

This sort of phenomenon could never have occurred before the advent of digital media. The ability to quickly and easily share photos, make comments on them, and encourage other people to share them is particularly unique in the history of the circulation of texts. The circulation of such a simple text is both inexplicable and indicative of the circulatory power of social media. Authors don't always have control over the ways their texts circulate, but it's important to consider how others might manipulate or share *your* text even before you begin composing. (See the piece by Jenkins et al. in this textbook for more about circulation and spreadability.)

Circulation and other concepts

It's one thing to think about circulation in terms of viral videos, Internet memes, or popular movies and television, but it's just as important (and more practical) to think about circulation in terms of texts being exchanged among a smaller group of people who share a common **field**. For instance, a scholar might write an article for a journal, and he or she could reasonably assume that it would only circulate among his or her fellow scholars interested in that topic. Scholars have a sense of the people who might encounter their texts, so they can make intelligent guesses about their audience's expectations regarding the features of the **genres** they are producing: citation styles, referencing the work of previous scholars, or using certain words that might only be familiar to the people among whom the texts circulate.

Certain types of text afford different types of circulation. It's not likely that you'll see a brilliant meeting memo being shared among Facebook friends, and you likely know better than to include a link to your favorite cat videos as part of your job application materials. If you want something to be shared among friends, you're more likely to produce an **image** with a caption or a video, maybe even a blog post. If you're responding to a request for job application materials, you'll write something meant for one or two specific people, and you won't have to worry about producing a text that could be easily shared outside the company with whom you are applying. When looking at circulation and **affordances**, it's best to think about them as being dependent on each other.

If you want something to circulate to as wide an audience as possible, there are certain choices you can make about the modes and genres you take advantage of to produce your text. If you want to be someone who is well-known and respected for being able to do tricks on your bike, you'll likely put together a demo or highlight video so it can be shared among as many people as possible. On the other hand, if you know that you're only going to have access to email or a text message to communicate your idea, you can guess that it won't circulate much beyond the people you send it to directly. Sometimes circulation will be limited or determined by the affordances of the materials to which you have access. But at other times, you might have a very specific sense of the audience among which you'd like your text to circulate, even if it's just one person, and you'll select your materials accordingly.

For examples referred to in the textbook, additional resources, and further reading, please visit the course website: www.fountainheadpress.com/keyconcepts.

Writing with circulation

With so many texts competing for our attention and our memory, it's important to understand how texts operate in people's everyday lives. Knowing how they might encounter a text, or when it might be most appropriate for them to receive it, will often make the difference between being noticed and being passed over. Some things to consider:

- What sorts of things make a text memorable? Why do I notice or remember certain texts and not others?
- How are texts circulated in my particular **field**? What **genres** circulate most?
- In what sorts of social networks do the people I'm trying to reach participate most? Do people participate more as a consumer, producer, commenter, or sharer in these networks? Do they share things from one network on another? Why?
- What sorts of experiences, good or bad, have I had with the means of publication on the Web that focus primarily on **alphabetic text** (for example Google Docs, blogs, Tumblr, Twitter, wikis, forums, and message)? Which ones do I prefer and do I think my audience will prefer, and what is it about them that attracts me to them?
- What are the **affordances** or constraints of the various methods available to me for circulating my text?

5 Ethos

Ethos refers to who other people think we are, based on what and how we write and speak. One of the ways we can try to persuade people to do or think something is to create a positive ethos. We do this by writing or speaking in such a way that others trust us and think we are a good person. Ethos refers to who *other* people think we are, so the way we construct our ethos will depend on who our audience is in each particular rhetorical situation. Different people value different character traits. Think of the contrast between the way you write and speak with friends, and the way you write and speak when applying for a job.

History of ethos

Ethos is one of the key concepts that comes from ancient Greece. In *On Rhetoric*, Aristotle identified three methods of persuading listeners to think or do something. The first is ethos, about which he says "it makes much difference in regard to persuasion. . .that the speaker seem to be a certain kind of person" (120). The second approach to persuading listeners according to Aristotle is **pathos**, which is when the speaker or writer arouses particular emotions such as pity, anger, or fear that will lead the listeners to do or think something. The third approach is **logos**, which is when we appeal to reason, or the soundness of the argument itself. (You can read more about pathos and logos in the chapter on Additional Key Concepts.)

Aristotle's discussion of ethos in *On Rhetoric* can be a little confusing. Sometimes it seems like he thinks ethos is something we invent in our text; elsewhere in this work, he is clear that ethos refers to one's moral character, and thus refers to something that exists in the person. Other rhetoricians of the time debated whether ethos was something one could just make up depending on what one is trying to achieve at that moment, or whether it had to come from a deeper sense of justice and wisdom within one's character. Isocrates, for example, scolded other rhetoricians for being hypocritical for claiming to be whoever their audience wanted them to be (Isocrates).

One way to understand ethos is that it is both. We have to convince our audience that we are trustworthy, that we have their best interests in mind, and that we know what we're talking about. Perhaps, the best way to accomplish this in our writing and speaking is to actually be trustworthy, generous, and knowledgeable.

Ethos today

Politicians and celebrities rely heavily—in some cases, exclusively—on ethos to persuade people to vote for them or buy their music or merchandise. Consider the candidates who were competing in the primary presidential elections of 2016 and those who were nominated: how did they construct their ethos in order to distinguish themselves from other candidates? What did they say and write, how did they interact with the press and voters, how did they design their website and logos, to persuade people that they should be the next president of the United States?

Perhaps the most interesting case in 2016 is Donald Trump. As this section of *Key Concepts* is being written, in late winter 2016, Trump is running to be the Republican nominee, and therefore trying to distinguish himself from other candidates Marco Rubio, Ted Cruz, Ben Carson, and John Kasich (Jeb Bush has just dropped out of the race). Trump is an extremely divisive candidate. On the one hand, people from across the political spectrum and even across the globe think him to be a dangerous, embarrassing, laughable candidate. Members of the British Parliament considered banning him from the United Kingdom, and during the debate Trump was called "a buffoon" and worse. Karl Rove, a central figure in Republican George W. Bush's administration, called Trump a complete idiot. On the other hand, defying all the predictions, he is considered a serious contender for the Republican nomination, thanks to his enthusiastic base. (Readers of this textbook will know what the writer does not: how Trump's run for office turns out.) Bragging about how loyal his supporters are, Trump said at a campaign event in Iowa, "I could stand in the middle of 5th Avenue and shoot somebody and I wouldn't lose any voters."

While the reasons for Trump's popularity in 2015 and 2016 are far more complicated than we can untangle here, the concept

Figure 5-1

of ethos might help us understand how one person can be so reviled and so admired even by members of the same political party. The way we construct our ethos will depend on who our audience is in each particular rhetorical situation—different people value and believe different things. Again, this is the reason that what you say and how you behave is different when you're in front of your grandparents or an employer than when you're in front of friends: you are constructing a different ethos depending on the audience. According to one analyst, "When his supporters listen to [Trump], they hear the unpolished, impolitic truths that they themselves believe in, things they believe the average American privately agrees with" (Kweku). While other politicians and pundits distrust Trump precisely because of his "unpolished, impolitic truths" about women or Muslims or Mexican immigrants, Trump is constructing an ethos very much in line with the values and beliefs of his main audience: voters.

Most candidates try to appeal to their supporters' values and beliefs, convincing voters that "I am to be trusted, because I believe what you believe." But most candidates also have in mind additional audiences—the media, other politicians in their party, major donors. This is why, typically, candidates in the digital era are very careful about what they say and how, because they know that their every move is scrutinized by the media and **circulated** within moments to millions of Internet users. Trump, however, does not appear to be careful. He's willing to get into a Twitter war with the Pope, and he'll even say things *his own voters* might disagree with, like when he criticized George W. Bush, blaming him for 9/11. In these situations, it's his willingness to say such offensive statements that is contributing to his ethos. One supporter explains that "she craves a president who is fearless, *really* fearless, and that of all the candidates in the race, Trump seems the least bowed, the least cowed" (Bruni). Notice the way this citizen explains her support for Trump not in terms of his policies, but in terms of his ethos.

While classical rhetoricians were mostly concerned with how individual politicians and lawyers persuaded an audience to believe them, today we can use the concept of ethos to think about institutions and brands, too. Recall that our short definition of ethos is "who other people think we are, based on what and how we write and speak." A brand is what customers think of a product, based not just on the product's performance, but on what the company says and does in ads and other PR, and creating a successful brand is the attempt to persuade people to purchase what you're selling.

In a November 2014 article, *Forbes* magazine wrote that "the Apple brand is worth $124.2 billion and almost twice as much as any other brand in Forbes' annual study of the world's most valuable brands" (Badenhausen). For a long time, Apple's brand was wrapped up in Steve Jobs's ethos, and in part because of this, we might describe Apple's brand as smart, polished, confident. However, this ethos gets communicated not just through spokespeople, but also in product design, ad campaigns, brick and mortar stores, and websites. You might visit www.apple.com and consider how the arrangement of the website, the images they choose, the stories they tell, and even details like the sans serif font contribute to the company's ethos.

Figure 5-2

One of Apple's most successful ad campaigns was "I'm a Mac, and I'm a PC" ads? (You can see videos of these ads on the course website.) Those ads are interesting because it took the ethos of the Apple brand and embodied it in the hip, relaxed actor Justin Long, and contrasted it with frumpy, clumsy PC, embodied by John Hodgman. This is the reverse of how many ads work, which is to borrow the ethos of a celebrity and try to associate it with a brand (like Nike did with Michael Jordan). Apple also clearly understood that the audience is crucial when inventing one's ethos, because Apple knew that the particular demographic they were trying to reach would more easily identify with jeans-and-t-shirt-wearing Long, than with the clean-shaven and bespectacled Hodgman.

Ethos and other concepts

Richard Lanham (in the readings at the back of this book) argues that we have to think about not just the stuff we produce—our arguments and stories, or in the case of Apple, the products—but how we might bring positive attention to that stuff. Successful rhetoricians do both in such a way that readers go back and forth between the two. Alphabetic text is particularly important in this respect, because it involves choices about the stuff, or what you put into words, as well as choices about the surface features such as fonts, colors, and **arrangement** on a page or screen.

attention + stuff = ethos

It might be tempting to just "throw a picture in there" to make a page pretty and bring attention to what you're saying. However, inventing a positive ethos requires making deliberate decisions about our use of **image** as well as sound, video, and other modes, and thinking carefully about the **affordances** and constraints of each. And writing in the 21st century requires making these various, complicated decisions not just in each piece we do, but across platforms. If you use social media at all—Twitter, Facebook, Instagram, Tumblr, any of it—your ethos is in constant, possibly eternal, **circulation**. It's important to be mindful of circulation as you construct your ethos on various sites.

This is especially the case when you are applying for jobs. The ethos you want to create in your career will depend on your **field**, and what the values and principles are that govern that field. Is the field hip and fast-paced or more conservative? Does it value intelligence, playfulness, rigor, creativity? Depending on your answers to these questions, you will have to decide how you fit in, how you will communicate those values, and whether you do so across all the pieces of your online presence. This is ethos.

Writing with ethos

Like many of the key concepts in this book, ethos is common sense: we tend to do things instinctively that we think will persuade people to like us or to do or think the things we want them to. However, writing in an online, networked environment multiplies the number of decisions we have to make, so it's important that we don't always rely on instinct. Not only does technology increase the resources (words, image, sound, video, color, and so on) available to us as we communicate, but the Internet makes our ethos far more public than it used to be. Therefore, it's worthwhile to consider questions such as the following:

- Who am I trying to persuade with this piece of communication, and what do they value? Do I share those values, and if so, how do I demonstrate that I share those values?
- Do I know what I'm talking about? Do I actually care about my readers? Am I being honest? And if I answer "no" to any of these questions, how should I proceed and what are my goals?
- Do all of the elements of this piece of communication—font, **images** and other **modes**, **arrangement**, and so on—work together to contribute to the positive ethos I am trying to create?
- How important is careful editing and proofreading for creating a positive ethos with this particular audience? How do issues such as word choice, spelling, punctuation, and format affect my ethos in this text?
- Is my ethos in this piece of communication consistent with the other texts I've produced that are **circulating** online, for example, my social media profiles and updates, my website, my portfolio?

6

Field

A *field* is a group of people, the texts they write, and the things they do, in order to generate and circulate knowledge related to a particular idea or question. The concept of field reminds us that, especially in our public or professional lives, we almost always write and read in the context of other people, previous texts, and particular goals, and success typically requires familiarity with the way our field works. Learning how people in a chosen field communicate with each other is one of the purposes of attending college.

A field is not static. Even an expert in a particular field is never done learning: as new texts and practices emerge, and people move in and out of a field, the nature of that field necessarily changes. Moreover, many fields overlap with each other, as people and texts and ideas move between and among fields. Networked communication today may increase the speed at which a field evolves, facilitate access among fields, and also blur the line between expert and amateur.

History of fields

Even the most rudimentary texts can inaugurate a new field of study. Consider the Neolithic Revolution (900-700 BCE), when humans began cultivating plants and animals for food. This was a complex endeavor that required farmers to remember and convey large quantities of information. So Neolithic farmers invented pictograms (simple writing) that they used to count and measure their products. Then, something astounding happened: as farmers reread and analyzed their own records, they began to see larger patterns of success and failure. During droughts, some crops failed; in rainy seasons, certain plants thrived. When farmers realized that their records held the key to deeper intellectual and practical knowledge, the field of agriculture was born. To identify important texts in our own field, we can begin by considering the simplest records all around us: the notes, logs, and instructions we use to track our own progress and plan our work.

But it would be difficult to make sense of all the ephemeral records without shared methods for systematic inquiry. By 300 BCE, agriculture had spawned so many fields of study that it would have been impossible for one person to become an expert in them all: botany, medicine, astronomy and meteorology, just to name a few. How could these fields coordinate their efforts to turn information into knowledge? Aristotle devoted his life to answering this question. Famously, Aristotle developed a taxonomy (classification system) that outlined how the fields fit together. But he also introduced a system of logic that allowed experts to reason from particular cases to universal principles, thus formally linking practical and academic knowledge together.

Of course, it would be very difficult to study hundreds of years' worth of texts on one's own. In the Medieval to Modern periods, the first institutions of higher education appeared in order to guide novices through the process of acquiring expertise. These early universities and *madrasas* (Islamic colleges) prepared students for three main fields: medicine, theology and law. Because early universities had no meeting place or campus, it would not be an exaggeration to say that the early university was made of texts. These texts included written texts described above, plus a new type of multimodal text we know as the *lecture* in which experts in a field discoursed with other experts and students. These lectures included plenty of back-and-forth interaction (always in Latin). No matter what field we belong to, we can identify the higher education requirements necessary to become an expert—and the interactive texts (like lectures) that guide and facilitate our reading.

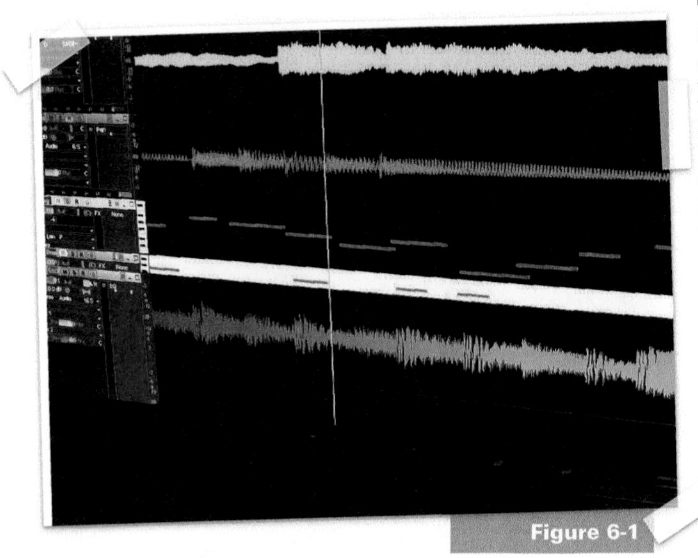

Figure 6-1

Fields today

Digital technology has transformed texts, the ways texts circulate, and therefore the ways members of a field communicate with each other. The field of music recording and production is an interesting example. Anyone with a laptop can record himself or herself singing or playing electric guitar, and after some time messing around with GarageBand, Logic Pro, or another digital audio workstation, they can produce highly sophisticated-sounding music. How does the kid in the basement with a computer become a member of the field of professional digital musicians?

Let's consider the case of a specific 15-year-old kid, Alex, who composes digital music on his family's computer. Alex might listen to a lot of music and do a lot of remixing on his own, but it is the **circulation** of knowledge via specific types of texts that constitutes a **field**. Alex begins to explore the field by sharing songs via SoundCloud. The songs themselves and the comments listeners post on each others' songs are one way that members of the field communicate.

Figure 6-2

The screenshot of the SoundCloud page offers a glimpse of the writing practices Alex has to learn: the vocabulary for describing types of music ("neuro glitch hop"), the use of hashtags to link his page to similar music and artists, and the **ethos** he is creating—he is learning the conventions of this community. He knows he must write to this group of people, this field, differently than he would in school, to his grandparents, even with other circles of friends.

However, even if Alex achieves some success (measured through plays on SoundCloud), he might not have a full grasp of the field yet. In college or through professional experience, he will need to seek out the answers to several questions related to the concept of field: How does one achieve "expert" status in this field? What are the paths toward professionalization (degrees and certificates, job experiences, and so on)? Are there professional organizations where one networks with colleagues? What other fields overlap with music recording and production, and what subfields/specializations are most common? What is the history and what are the current issues in this field?

Moreover, he will have to practice reading and writing the **genres** that members of this field **circulate** and how to construct an **ethos** that is credible in this field when working with other professionals. In fact, this is the most important point about the concept of field: when asked,

Alex will say he makes music, but in fact, even early in his exploration of the field he also writes: comments on others' songs, language promoting his own music, messages to collaborators. This is the case for almost all creative fields—the vast majority of work takes place in written texts. And learning one's field is about learning how members of that field write.

In this example, the concept of field can help us think about the difference between success and failure in one's own profession, but the concept of field also helps us think about and evaluate the expertise of professionals in others' fields. This is especially important when we rely on these other professionals for our own well being. For example, medicine has a long tradition of rigorous higher education; one cannot enter the field without years of study. This education includes reading and spoken interaction to ensure that professionals correctly apply knowledge from texts to the practical problem of human illness.

Now, a new generation of patients enjoys unprecedented access to medical texts online. These texts include expert texts from PubMed, articles on WebMD written for laypeople, and patients' experiences represented on online forums. Most of us have encountered this information through the common practice of Googling our symptoms.

Is this information-sickness the patient's problem, or the doctor's? As early as 1998, the Journal of the American Medical Association reported that spurious online information posed problems for doctors and patients (Jadad and Gagliardi 611-614). Because patients' Web searches have begun to affect their health behavior, Web searching has become an unlikely topic for the field of medicine. Devastating problems have emerged from apparently harmless phenomena. Because an individual's unscientific opinions can circulate widely online, patients are refusing life-saving treatments such as vaccines and chemotherapy. The digital revolution has shaken the core of the field of medicine, requiring doctors to reconsider how medical texts circulate and impact the spoken text of the doctor-patient relationship. Fields change when they go digital.

Fortunately, we can return to the key concept of field to evaluate the mélange of information we find online. Because we know fields are made of texts, we can begin with a commonsense assumption: texts within a field are probably more credible than texts outside it. To determine whether and to what extent a digital text situates itself within an established field of study, we only need to ask three questions:

1. Did the author draw on other texts in the field?
2. Did the author use the field's research methods?
3. Did the author complete higher education in the field?

For any digital text, these questions are easy to remember and answer. For example, many of us have encountered Web videos such as a clip, available on our course website, of Jenny McCarthy decrying the Measles, Mumps and Rubella (MMR) vaccine, which she believes caused her son's autism. Many parents are understandably concerned about McCarthy's controversial claims. But, using the concept of field to evaluate McCarthy's clips allows us to sidestep the controversy; we only need to answer the three simple questions outlined above. Judging from the clip, the answer to each question is clearly "No": McCarthy frankly disregards established science, her research methods are unclear and she has earned no degree in medicine or the related fields. Consequently, we are faced with a simple decision: either discount McCarthy's claims as probably false or instead dismiss the modern field of medicine as an unnecessarily laborious undertaking.

Field and other concepts

The concept of field not only helps us evaluate others' texts. It can also offer a powerful tool for motivating our own writing. Consider the way most high school students are taught to write. At the beginning of their first writing class in college, new college students feel most comfortable expressing personal opinions on topics like abortion and veganism. Then, when we are asked to write a college-level term paper for history or biology class, we suddenly face a type of writers' block known as the blank screen problem. The first time we have to write a paper on a topic we have no personal opinion about (cellular mitosis, for example), it feels impossible to move forward. We stare at the blank computer screen; a blinking cursor stares back.

But the concept of field reassures us that we are not writing alone in a void. Thousands of scholars have produced texts on our subject, and we can stand on the shoulders of these giants to compose our own text: the term paper. In other words, we can solve the blank screen problem by writing with the field. We can do this by using the concept of **kairos** (seizing the opportune moment) to discover new motivations for writing—motivations that arise from an entire field of study instead of just our personal opinion.

How can the concepts of field and kairos solve the blank screen problem? Imagine a college student, Sharon, who is writing her first term paper for American history class. Right now Sharon is staring at the blank screen in a panic; she has no paper topic or plan for writing. Remembering the concept of kairos, she decides to seize the opportune moment to write about something timely. Several films and videos have recently debuted depicting Black history during the antebellum period preceding the Civil War: *Django Unchained*, *12 Years A Slave* and *The Story of Catcher Freeman*, to name a few examples. Sharon knows these depictions are controversial, so she decides to seize the opportune moment (kairos) to research antebellum Black history.

At this point Sharon has identified a paper topic but she has not developed her unique angle. A general paper on antebellum Black history would be uninteresting to historians, who have read much about this topic and may have even served as consultants on movies such as *Django*. To satisfy the history field's exacting standards of kairos, Sharon must contribute a fresh insight to the conversation.

While researching credible sources on her topic, Sharon eventually notices that something is missing. There is much scholarship about nuclear family relationships in antebellum Black America, but little on extended family ties including grandparents and grandchildren (scholars refer to this as a "research gap" or "gap in the knowledge"). From her own experience, Sharon knows that these ties are critical to transmitting the family's history to a new generation. Sharon decides to fill this important research gap by writing her paper about family ties between grandparents and grandchildren in antebellum Black America. What began as a blank page now represents a unique contribution to the field of history, albeit from an undergraduate's perspective. Sharon is ready to write.

Writing with a field

Writing with a field is not an all-or-nothing process. As we progress through higher education, we gradually begin to write less from our individual perspective and more from the perspective of our chosen field of study. Writers at any level can take advantage of the **affordances** that fields offer to writers: a well-defined set of topics to write about, a wealth of expert texts on the topic, and clues to interesting new topics to explore (i.e., the "research gap" described above). We can begin to write with a field by asking ourselves these questions:

- What's the official name of my field? Or: What field is this class about? What are the boundaries of my field?
- What are the central texts that make up my field?
- What current world events or problems involve this field?
- What's missing when I explore scholarly sources in this field? What research would I like to see that is not there?
- What **genres** do experts use to **circulate** ideas within this field?
- What rules do these genres have for writing with **alphabetic text** and **images** and arranging ideas? Am I required to follow these rules when writing for this course?
- When I have learned to write with my field, what new ideas of my own do I hope to circulate?

To return to the blank screen problem, most first-year college students can expect to spend some time feeling mocked by a blinking cursor. As we encounter different fields of study and interact with the texts that constitute them, our ideas begin to push the cursor along—transforming the once-blank screen into a sphere of interest, inquiry and action.

7

Genre

Genre refers to a category or classification of something. Etymologically, the term is related to "gender" and "genus," both of which are significant classification systems. We can talk about various genres of music (dubstep, hip hop, pop, classical, country), of literature (poetry, short fiction, novel), of film (romantic comedy, horror, action), of paintings, video games, dance, and so on. *Genre* actually means a lot of different things to different people. However, in the context of writing and rhetoric, we use genre to talk about oral, written, and multimodal texts and how they function in society. Norman Fairclough argues that "a genre implies not only a particular text type, but also particular processes of producing, distributing, and consuming texts" (*Discourse and Social Change* 126). When we produce the same kind of text over and over to do the same thing over and over, these kinds of texts emerge as genres with recognizable features that readers come to expect.

History of genre

In classical rhetoric, Aristotle focused on three genres, distinguished by their audiences and their occasions. Deliberative rhetoric was used to persuade audiences to do something and typically happened in political settings. Judicial rhetoric happened in courts of law and was used to determine whether or not someone was justly accused. (Deliberative rhetoric was about future events, and judicial rhetoric was about past events.) Epideictic rhetoric occurred during ceremonies like funerals, and was used to praise or blame someone. Distinguishing among these genres was important for Aristotle as he taught students how to produce the kinds of texts their audiences would recognize and admire. But genre studies has persisted throughout intellectual history, especially when new genres emerge and challenge scholars' sense of order.

The work of two important contemporary scholars of genre in rhetoric, John Swales and Carolyn Miller, illustrate how widely divergent theories of genre can be. Swales is concerned with the descriptive enterprise of genre analysis—identifying key textual characteristics of various genres—because these descriptions can easily turn into rules that students can use to master the genres that circulate in higher education. Miller, on the other hand, argues for a view of genre "as a specific, and important, constituent of society, a major aspect of its communicative structure, one of the structures of power that institutions wield" (71). Miller is less concerned with teaching students how to reproduce already established genres, and more concerned with understanding how genres function in society.

There are genre scholars in a variety of fields—film studies, literary studies, musicology—and the theories of genre are numerous. The concept persists as an important object of study, because it helps us to better appreciate the works we create and to better understand ourselves as creators.

Genre today

A genre, for example, "obituary," is most productively studied and understood in terms of the specific features that the texts in that category share. Before you read further, try to list the features of the genre "obituary," or the things you expect to read in an obituary. These features emerge when people have to do the same thing over and over, in this case, notify the community that someone has died. Some features include: the date (and occasionally the cause) of death; the date and place of birth; a positive account of schools attended, careers, and other accomplishments; a brief list of people that the deceased was "preceded in death by"; and the details about funeral arrangements and memorial services. Very often, this text is accompanied by a photograph of the deceased when he or she was young and/or healthy. Knowing the features that readers expect in a particular genre make it easier to write. So, when a loved one dies and you are asked to write the obituary, you don't have make up from scratch what to include in it.

Reddit and Buzz Feed circulated an obituary a while ago that illustrates just how predictable this particular genre is. Walter George Bruhl, Jr. wrote his own obituary because he was familiar with the features of the genre, and because he knew his readers would be familiar with them as well, he was able to make it one of the sweetest, funniest obituaries you'll read. (A link to the Buzz Feed article with the complete obituary is available on our course website.) For example, he writes, "Walt was preceded in death by his tonsils and adenoids in 1936, a spinal disc in 1974, a large piece of his thyroid gland in 1988, and his prostate on March 27th 2000." And where we expect the positive discussion of his schooling, we read "He drifted through the Philadelphia Public School System from 1937 through 1951, graduating, to his mother's great relief, from John Bartram High School in June of 1951." About the details of the service, he wrote, "There will be no viewing since his wife refuses to honor his request to have him standing in the corner of the room with a glass of Jack Daniels in his hand so that he would appear natural to visitors." Because he knew this genre so well, he was able to write it in a way that depends on readers' expectations of the genre, only to subvert those expectations with humor.

Perhaps what is most interesting about the concept of genre in the digital age is how genres change when they move from print into networked, digital environments. For example, most obituaries appear online now, as part of the page of a funeral home's website. These obituaries will still include many of the features described above, but they borrow from other online texts, too: there might be a "Guestbook" where people leave comments for the family, and links to articles about handling grief or funeral home etiquette. And the story of the life of the deceased **juxtaposed** with ads for cell phone plans can be somewhat jarring in this context.

Some genres have not changed much, even though we circulate them electronically rather than on paper. A grocery list is still a list of nouns that is written as a reminder of what is needed while out shopping. Whether this list appears on a scrap of paper or in a notes app on the phone, its general features and function haven't changed. On the other hand, reviews (of restaurants, movies, music) have changed to the extent that they are written by everyone now, instead of solely by professional writers, and they are collected on sites like Rotten Tomatoes or Yelp, instead of circulated in newspapers.

Source: Shutterstock

Figure 7-1

The email is an evolved form of the paper memo that was circulated in offices: we can recognize the features of the To, From, Date, and Subject lines that existed in that earlier genre; when sent from co-worker to co-worker, we see the function of the paper memo; and we talk about our email "inbox," a remnant

Source: Shutterstock

Figure 7-2

of the actual box on desktops that held the paper memos. However, in some ways, an email is no longer a recognizable relative of the memo. We might use emails to communicate with friends or relatives (that was never the case with memos); we can distribute emails to countless people instantaneously; some people use a far more casual, conversational tone in email than they ever would have in traditional memos. Other genres are completely new. Tweets, for example, don't seem to have a parallel in terms of form, function, and **circulation** methods in the world of print.

Blogs are an interesting case, because they seem to be a hybrid genre or maybe even a multi-genre (see Miller and Shepherd). They started out as a kind of diary or ongoing personal narrative that authors shared with their followers. Now, though, companies use blogs to provide up-to-the-minute communication with customers and investors. Politicians use blogs to connect with voters. And individuals use blogs for countless reasons. The accessibility of blogging sites like WordPress, Blogger, or Tumblr means just about anyone with an Internet connection can create a blog for just about any reason: to do academic work; to showcase artwork; to communicate with family; to write about movies, music, politics, or any other topic; to collect articles and images from the web; to launch a media empire.

Well, ok, not everyone can launch a media empire with a blog, but Tavi Gevinson did. She started a fashion blog, Style Rookie, when she was just an awkward 11-year-old student in nearby Oak Park, IL. She is now 18 and the success of Style Rookie has turned her into an actress, an invited guest at premier fashion shows, a close friend of musician Lorde, and the editor-in-chief of a hugely popular website, Rookie, and print books that compile the best of Rookie. (Links to Gevinson's sites are available on the course website.)

Considering the extremely wide variety of how blogs are used, and their multi-layered relationship with other genres (like Gevinson's website and print books), is it fair to even consider "blog" a genre? Do blogs share enough features for us to recognize them as a discrete category? And what about microblogging: is that closer to blogs or to something else entirely? The concept of genre remains useful for navigating the communication landscape today, both as authors and readers, despite the fact—or perhaps *because of* the fact—that genres are emerging and evolving as fast as the technology used to create them.

Genre and other concepts

Genres emerge when people do the same thing over and over, and therefore produce the same kind of text over and over. This happens most obviously in specific **fields**. Experts in the field of biology, for example, wanted to share with other biologists what they learned after doing experiments. After doing experiment after experiment, and writing about their experiments for others over and over, biologists figured out what to include in their report and what order to put that information in. The lab report emerged as a genre. Our **ethos**, then, becomes wrapped up in whether or not we can reproduce the genres that our field circulates. Readers have expectations of what their genres will do and say, and when those expectations are disappointed, the author's ethos suffers.

Sometimes, however, messing with readers' expectations is precisely what we want to do—possibly to catch readers' attention or to disturb the status quo. (This is what George Walter Bruhl, Jr. did with his obituary.) Rearranging a genre or **remixing** a genre with other genres may catch the reader off guard in just the right way. The marriage proposal is a genre: participants expect one partner to get down on (typically) his knee, profess his love, produce a ring, and say "Will you marry me." In the video available on our course website, Isaac Lamb did just that, but only after staging an elaborate song and dance that involved over 60 friends and family members and has since been viewed by over 25 million strangers. The girl had to say yes.

We might consider the **affordances** and constraints of the genres available to us, and decide that the genre that is expected of us just won't accomplish our particular goals. This is when new and hybrid genres emerge.

Writing with genre

As writers learn how to learn about writing, one of the most important skills they can cultivate is to be able to do a genre analysis of the texts that they read and write. When you approach texts to do a genre analysis, here are some of the most important questions to ask:

- What are the genres that my **field** expects?
- What are the most significant features of these texts? (Some of the most obvious features are also the most important.) Consider, for example, the physical features of material, format, layout, sites of **circulation**, relationship between text and **image**. Consider features such as **arrangement**, diction, types and purposes of quotation.
- What is the intended purpose of these texts and what are the expected replies? What might some unintended consequences of these texts be?
- Where does the genre typically appear? How and when is it written and read and used? What are the typical methods of delivery and **circulation**?
- What topics or issues does this genre typically address?
- What are the **affordances** and constraints of this genre?

8

Image

Image refers to a visual representation of someone or something in material form. We readily recognize images in the form of paintings and photographs, or in three-dimensional forms like statues and sculptures, or as visual displays on screens and monitors. But the word, "image," also refers to immaterial functions of mind and consciousness. We visualize things to ourselves in our thoughts and our dreams and our memories. These mental images are much more difficult for us to share, but no less real (or are they?). Images also come to us in the form of words. Verbal images are pictures in our minds that result from the descriptive powers of language, whether written or spoken. In another sense, even the printed word is a kind of image, particular marks on a page to which we can pay visual attention.

History of image

The word, "image," is complex and tricky, because it refers to the visible and the invisible, the physical and the mental, the material and the spiritual. We can trace the word's ambiguity to its earliest usages in ancient Hebrew where it conveyed both a material and immaterial presence, a concrete object in the physical world and a spiritual essence or ideal. Indeed, early Jewish commentators insist that the original authentic meaning of the Hebrew *tselem*—like the Greek *eikon* and the Latin *imago* (ancient words that we translate as "image")—is not "picture," but rather spiritual "likeness," as in Genesis 1:26, "And God said, 'Let us make man in our image, after our likeness" (Mitchell, 31-36). There can be no possibility of mistaking man for a picture of God, so goes the predominant interpretive strain of the Judeo-Christian tradition, but rather man possesses certain spiritual attributes that derive from and reflect God's glory. But even in the Old Testament, image (*tselem*) is an equivocal term, because it also refers to idols, those false material objects that the Lord commands Moses and the children of Israel to destroy when they cross from Jordan into the land of Caanan (Numbers 33:52).

Of course, as material forms in space and time, images enter human history long before words. Many many thousands of years ago, the substances of plants and animals, even the blood of human beings, were used to make pictures, representation by visual signs—marks, scratches, shapes, lines, colors—depicting human perception, aspiration, fear, hunger, and so on. We really know very little about the genesis of the earliest cave paintings. The art historian, E.H. Gombrich, suggests that perhaps it was the recognition of resemblances that prompted the first cave drawings, some rock or boulder suggesting a specific animal or object, which were then worked through artistic means into an even greater likeness. Whatever the origins, ancient cultures developed increasingly complex symbolic systems of pictorial signs that eventually evolved into writing. Scholars tell us that the first writing in **alphabetic text,** completely independent of pictorial elements, does not appear until sometime in the middle of the second (or maybe third) millennium B.C.

Image today

If the word "image" is paradoxical (for example in the Old Testament examples discussed above), images are just as ambiguous and equivocal when we're referring to visual objects. Think of how strange an ability it is to recognize a material image as image: we see it, we name it, and at the same time we know that it's not really there! In an ancient Greek legend, birds flew to peck the grapes from the picture by the famous painter, Zeuxis, because they were not seeing an image of grapes, but rather the grapes themselves. Human beings too are capable of being fooled by the illusory tricks and powerful magic of images. The legend goes on to describe how Zeuxis's rival, the painter, Parrhasius, tried to pull back the curtain from the same painting, only then to realize the curtain was itself a part of the picture. "What is that?" someone asks, looking at the still life of grapes and curtain. "That is an image," we reply. "You mean that canvas full of colors and lines? Or do you mean those grapes and that curtain?" (Mitchell 17)

Figure 8-1

Perhaps no one has explored this paradox of the image as provocatively as the Belgian surrealist painter, Rene Magritte, especially in his two pipe paintings, "La trahison des images" ["The Treachery of Images"] (1929), and the much later "Les Deux Mystéres" ["The Two Mysteries"] (1966). The first is a simple image of a pipe, and underneath it the sentence, "Ceci n'est pas une pipe." [This is not a pipe.] Fair enough. We know that's not a pipe; it's a picture of a pipe. But realist pictures rarely announce their own status as representations. In everyday conversation, if asked to identify that painting we are very likely to say indeed, "That is a pipe." In a very straightforward yet provocative way, Magritte's image explores the confusion between pictures and things. This confusion accounts for so much of the power that images possess.

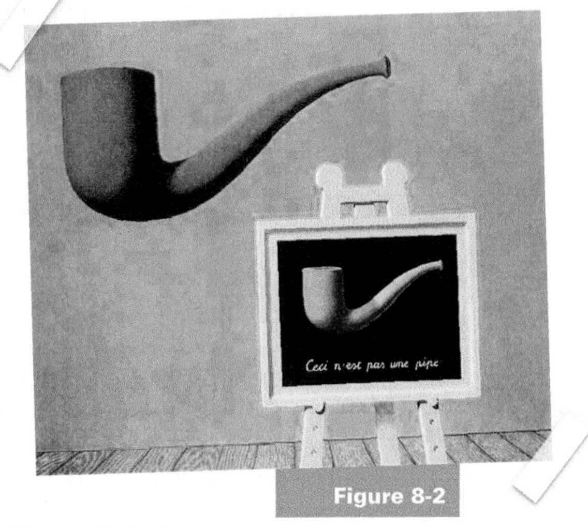

Figure 8-2

The second painting radically extends the ambiguities of the first. Like the earlier painting, it too is an image about images. But it is far more difficult to describe what is represented here. To help get us started, let's look at a brief passage from a famous essay on the painting by the French philosopher, Michel Foucault. "There are two pipes," he begins simply.

> Or rather must we not say, two drawings of the same pipe? Or yet a pipe and the drawing of that pipe, ... Or two drawings, one representing a pipe and the other not, ... Or yet again, a drawing representing not a pipe at all but another drawing, itself representing a pipe so well that I must ask myself: To what does the sentence written in the painting relate? ... perhaps the sentence refers ... to the disproportionate, floating, ideal pipe--simple notion or fantasy of a pipe. Then we should have to read, "Do not look overhead for a true pipe. That is a pipe dream. It is the drawing within the painting, firmly and rigorously outlined, that must be accepted as a manifest truth." (16-17)

As Foucault's analysis demonstrates, the serious contemplation of images can lead to a sort of vertigo. If we really think about how images work, there is a feeling of endlessly spinning about, which many modern theorists and commentators have identified as the predominant characteristic of contemporary life. The overwhelming abundance of cultural images has made it increasingly difficult for us to distinguish between image and reality.

Today, images are everywhere! So much so, we might say, that in the 21st century the **affordances** of image are overdetermined, so pervasive an element in our everyday life that we tend to think of and through them as a matter of course, without necessarily understanding both their power and their limitations. We make constant use of images to help us achieve all sorts of goals, desires, and rhetorical ends: to access and understand the past, both our own and the larger cultural societal groups of which we are a part; to elicit desire and get people to buy goods and commodities; to express feelings and identity; to distract and enthrall; above all, to record and to provide evidence—*"yes, sir, you did indeed go through the red light—here are the pictures to prove it."*

"A society becomes 'modern' when one of its chief activities is producing and consuming images," writes Susan Sontag in her 1987 book, *On Photography*, and throughout the second half of the twentieth-century cultural theorists have consistently described our modern age in visual terms. They refer to it as the society of the spectacle, the society of simulations, the age of surveillance, and so on. The intimate relation between the modern and the visual goes at least as far back as the nineteenth century, an era that produced an explosion of visual technologies, culminating in the invention of the camera. From its very beginnings, photography was wildly popular, producing images of "reality" of a kind never seen before, and on an increasingly vast scale, a great democratization of the ability to produce images, for private as well as public use. Of course, today, with the advent of social media and myriad cloud-sharing applications, the ability to produce, to **circulate**, and to consume images are activities the majority of us take for granted and perform with great facility in astonishingly large numbers.

Magritte's seemingly simple statement, "Ceci n'est pas une pipe," painted almost 100 years ago, seems ever more significant. Photoshop and other sophisticated photo-editing software help alert us to the artifice of the image: framed, focused, even retouched. But images, digital and otherwise, mediate so much of our experience that we may still find it difficult to see beyond them. The more we understand how images work, the better we can use them to our advantage, and guard against them when they are trying to take advantage of us.

Image and other concepts

The relation between image and word, or between the arts of painting and poetry, has long been a central and much contested issue in discussions of art and philosophy. While there is a long tradition of identifying resemblances between the two arts, the relation between visual and verbal signs becomes increasingly understood in terms of a contest or rivalry. The expression, "A picture is worth a thousand words," is a commonplace example, an assertion of the power of images and their ability to express things that words cannot. On the other hand, many commentators have come down on the side of tell, not show. **Alphabetic text**, they say, is more powerful than images for a picture needs words to indicate its story. Otherwise it is but a frozen narrative illustrating any number of possibilities. Sontag, for instance, in her book, *Regarding the Pain of Others,* points out that in the Balkan wars of the 1990s, the same photographs of children killed in the shelling of a village were passed around in both Serb and Croat propaganda briefings, only their captions were altered. Words, she argues, are more powerful than pictures in mobilizing opposition to war, for pictures are mute, without context, utterly susceptible to appropriation.

Of course, the real question is not which sign, visual or verbal, is better in any absolute sense, but rather, what are the peculiar **affordances**, in any given situation, of using images or words or some combination of the two. Typically, we regard images and painting as best suited to represent the visible world, words and poetry the invisible world of thoughts and ideas. We associate images with space and immediacy; pictures are static and represent the "here and now." We associate words with time and development; narratives are in motion and represent the "beyond" and "beneath." That is not to say that images cannot represent time and action, words not represent space and stasis. But it may not come as easily to them.

Writing with image

More often than not, we encounter words, images, and other **modes** (sound, video, etc.) together. Television, cinema, websites, illustrated books, comic books, photographs with captions, museum objects and labels—the visual and the verbal are involved in many different kinds of relationships. The interesting question is to determine, in each specific instance, the impact that one has on the other, and to decide for ourselves how we can best bring them together to suit our own purposes. You might ask yourself questions like these to determine when and how to use images:

- What are the **affordances** and constraints of images in this situation?
- Have I chosen the best images in each instance to represent other people, places, things, events, and my own ideas and arguments?
- How do these images affect my **ethos**?
- How are images used or not used in this **genre**?
- What other modes can I combine with my images here as resources for changing and multiplying my meaning?
- How should I **arrange** the images and other modes on the page or screen, so that readers get the experience I hope they will, and so that it is aesthetically pleasing?
- Is my use and **circulation** of images legal and ethical? Have I considered issues surrounding intellectual property and copyright? Is my manipulation of images deceptive?

Storyboard Exercise:

- Using the 9 storyboard panels, compose a love story in either image only or image + text.
- Once finished, translate that illustrated story into spoken words. Working with a partner, use your storyboard as notes to tell the story out loud.
- Next, partners should write ***each other's*** stories without referring to the pictures.
- Finally, look at your partner's storyboard and adjust your written version of her story to reflect the content and **ethos** of the pictures.
- Exchange written stories and discuss the **affordances** and effectiveness of each version.

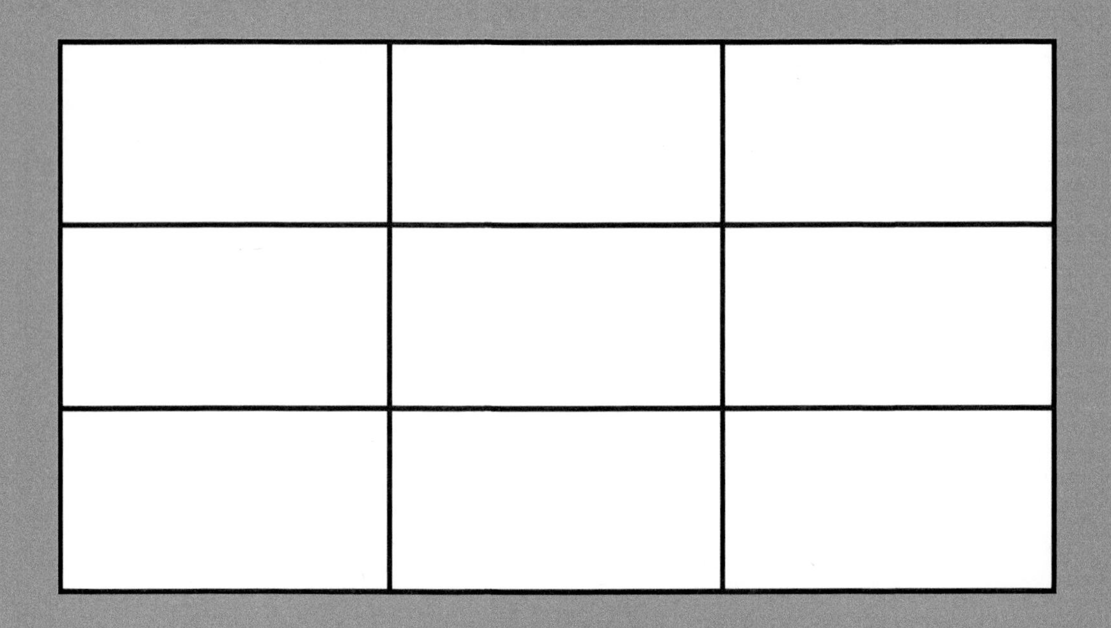

9 Kairos

Kairos refers to a qualitative sense of time, an intangible sense of opportunity. In ancient Greek, kairos simply means "time," but it doesn't mean the same thing we understand by time. For ancient Greeks, there were two different understandings of time. The first, chronos, is similar to what we mean by time: quantitative, linear time (it's where we get the word "chronological"). The second word for "time" in ancient Greek is kairos. A moment is kairotic when something happens that couldn't happen at any other time or place. As writers, we might recognize a kairotic moment and seize the opportunity to put our ideas out there, or we might try to create a kairotic moment by generating a sense of urgency and significance in our audience about an issue or topic.

History of kairos

Kairos was a minor god for the Greeks, the god of opportunity, the youngest son of Zeus. He is often depicted as having wings on his feet to represent fleeting time, but his most distinguishing physical characteristic is a long piece of hair on his forehead that represents the need to grab opportunity as he is racing toward you. If you let him get by, you've lost your chance, because notice how his head is shaved in the back. Kairos as a theoretical concept was absolutely central to classical Greek rhetoric, philosophy, and education. In ancient Greece, it carried a variety of meanings, including among others, "symmetry," "propriety," "decorum," "wise moderation" (Sipiora 1).

Source: Shutterstock

Figure 9-1

For both Plato and Aristotle, kairos was very important. Plato and Aristotle gave their students lots of rules and principles about writing and performing different kinds of texts. However, rhetoricians knew that, especially when you were speaking in front of a live audience as most ancient Greeks were, no matter how carefully you followed all the rules, you also had to pay close attention to the particular circumstances of that moment—what exactly you were trying to accomplish, what people were talking about that day, the general mood of the audience, and anything else that might affect listeners' attitudes toward the speaker's topic and argument. Considering all those other forces that would affect the speech is considering kairos.

Judeo-Christians borrowed the Greek concept of kairos to talk about the ways that God intervened at particular opportune moments (kairos) in human history (chronos) (Smith 54). The English phrase "a time to" in the oft-quoted passage in Ecclesiastes—"For everything there is a season, and a time for every purpose under heaven: a time to be born and a time to die. . ."—is a translation of the Greek term kairos.

Kairos today

An athlete probably already understands what "kairos" means, even if he or she doesn't use the word. You might think of "kairos" as timing your move just right to achieve the results you want—throwing the pass at just the right time, stealing a base, making the final sprint, putting up a block just when the opponent shoots. A quarterback doesn't just count seconds when he gets ready to pass (that's time as "chronos"); he also thinks about what he knows about this particular defense's tactics and whether his receiver is where he needs to be, he thinks about how the weather affects play in this stadium, and he thinks about how he feels that day and how the game has gone so far. When all of these circumstances are lined up, the quarterback seizes the opportunity to score. That's kairos.

Writing in the 21st century requires that we all think more carefully about kairos now. Consider, for example, the writing we do via social media. Tweets and status updates are typically about events happening in the moment, and a writer with a sense of kairos is more likely to be "liked" or re-tweeted, because he or she has hit on something that responds successfully to what others are thinking and doing at the time. We might think of Google trends (a link is available on our course website) as an up-to-the-minute snapshot of topics that are particularly kairotic. Web sites like BuzzFeed (a link is available on our course website) determine the placement of their articles by the number of clicks: the articles with the most clicks get moved to the top of the page, which suggests that they are figuring out how to make money off of kairos.

In fact, many of the best current examples of kairos come from marketing. A company like Apple, for example, times—in the sense of kairos, not chronos—the release of their newest models or products to maximize profit, and they do a lot of work to create a kairotic moment by building up the hype among customers before the release.

Source: Shutterstock
YOU CAN STILL DUNK IN THE DARK

Figure 9-2

Television ads during Super Bowls are as much a part of the game as the play, and given how expensive it is for companies to advertise during the game, and how much attention the ads are given in media the next day, you know that the marketing teams work all year on those spots. However, during the Super Bowl played in February 2013, when a 30-second spot on TV cost around four million dollars, arguably the best ad of the game was developed in a matter of minutes and was entirely free. During the third quarter, power went out, and play stopped for almost 35 minutes. Oreo tweeted an ad with just a picture of a cookie and the line "You can still dunk in the dark." There is almost no analysis of this ad that doesn't use the word opportunity—the company seized the opportunity to get their brand out there. It was clearly a kairotic moment.

Unlike all of the television ads that night, this one took advantage of the particular circumstances of the situation. The marketing company working for Oreo knew that, without play on the television screen, the Super Bowl audience would turn to their other screens and have their full attention on social media. They identified the right **circulation** methods, the right **genre**, and the best **image** to fit the moment. That's kairos. Carolyn Miller explains kairos this way, and it seems relevant here: "The challenge is to invent, within a set of unfolding and unprecedented circumstances, an action (rhetorical or otherwise) that will be understood as uniquely meaningful within those circumstances" (xiii).

(It's also interesting to think about how the company responsible for the ad, 360i, continues to take advantage of the hype surrounding their brilliant kairotic moment. Check out the ad about the ad on their website.)

But kairos isn't just about making money. Another example comes from the politics surrounding gay marriage. Popular opinion of gay marriage changed drastically in the last decade or so. Many commentators suggest that the 2015 Supreme Court ruling that made gay marriage legal in all 50 states would not have been possible if citizens had not been so vocal about their support for gay marriage. One of the most significant moments of popular expression of support for gay marriage happened in 2013, when the Supreme Court was hearing two previous cases about marriage equality.

On March 26, 2013, when the Supreme Court was hearing the cases, Facebook reported a 120% increase over the previous week in the

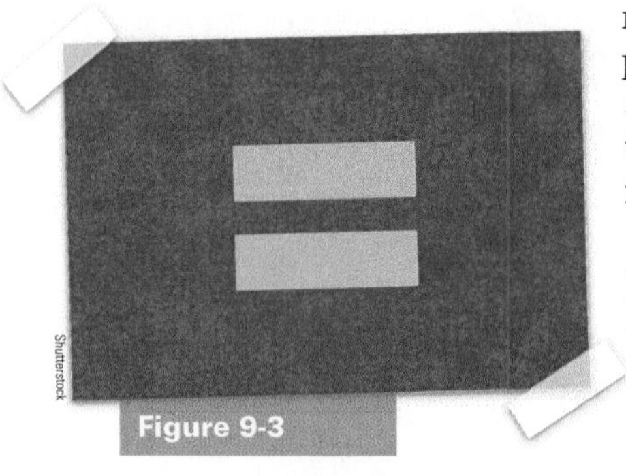
Shutterstock

Figure 9-3

number of people who changed their profile picture (Bakshy). While Facebook did not analyze what people changed their profiles to, the assumption is that the main explanation for the sharp increase is the Human Rights Campaign urging people to change profile pictures to the red equal sign to demonstrate support for marriage equality. (The ways that people took that image, shared it, and in some cases changed it up to make it their own, are examples of **circulation** and **remixing**.)

The Human Rights Campaign recognized a kairotic moment: they knew that support for gay marriage was growing, that there was a specific event that provided an opportunity, and that social media like Facebook provided **circulation** methods among the demographics most likely to support marriage equality. They then composed an **image** that took advantage of the variety of forces--social, political, technological--that converged to make their efforts successful. A similar Facebook phenomenon happened during the hours following the 2015 Supreme Court decision, when many enthusiastic supporters added the rainbow filter to their profile picture. In both instances, it's difficult to tell whether people were creating or responding to a particular kairotic moment, but these examples illustrate the increasing speed with which we must consider kairos, as well as the power of doing so.

Figure 9-4

Kairos and other concepts

Kairos is about timing our communication—whether it's in words or some other media—so that we can accomplish what we want to accomplish. We need the word kairos, because we can't time this kind of thing by looking at a clock. We have to time it by thinking about all the other circumstances that will affect what happens to our ideas once we put them out there. As the examples above indicate, we not only have to be ready (the marketing team for Oreo was watching the Super Bowl at work so they were ready for just such an occasion), but we also have to be aware of how we intend for our ideas to circulate, how our ideas might get **remixed** (consider how the red equal sign was remixed throughout Facebook), and the **affordances** and constraints of various media and technology.

There isn't a set of "10 easy steps" to circulate our ideas in the **field** we're trying to reach. It should be obvious why this is the case: what people are talking about, their mood, even their physical location are constantly changing. In some respects, this makes kairos really difficult to learn. But we need to think about kairos in terms of what is possible *right now*. What can we do right now that will take advantage of everything we know about our **field**? Part of the answer will lie in the **genres** we choose to use, the way we construct our **ethos**, how we arrange our text. Part of the answer will lie in **circulation** methods—is Facebook, Twitter, Instagram, or just standing on the street corner the best way to circulate our ideas? And part of the answer will lie in pure chance. Still, it's important to remember that kairos isn't the same thing as chance; kairos is recognizing when it's best to take a chance and making your own luck.

For examples referred to in the textbook, additional resources, and further reading, please visit the course website: www.fountainheadpress.com/keyconcepts.

Writing with kairos

Think again about the quarterback getting ready to pass: a good quarterback knows how to seize the opportunity to score when all the circumstances are just right, and a better quarterback can create some of those circumstances by dodging a tackle or making a last-minute play change. Even the best quarterback cannot control all the circumstances that matter: the speed of his opponents, the weather, how well his receivers slept the night before, the noise of the crowd, and so on.

The same is true of writers: much of what matters when we write in the 21st century is beyond our control. The concept of spreadability, which Henry Jenkins, Sam Ford, and Joshua Green, discuss in the essay included in this textbook, is about how much an audience's decisions about whether to share content matters. Authors can try to create content that is spreadable (like the red equal sign) and put that content in places where others will find it, but the audience's decisions—like much of kairos—is ultimately beyond their control.

Nevertheless, when we write, we can be attuned to the relevant circumstances by asking a series of questions:

- What are the historical circumstances, both locally and more broadly, that have given rise to this issue? How does my topic respond to these circumstances?
- What are other people saying about my topic right now? Why do people care about this right now?
- Where are people talking about this topic (on Twitter, in mainstream media, in informal conversations, in academic journals)?
- When people talk about this issue, what else are they talking about? What are the most current examples or points of debate? And what aren't they saying?
- What **genres** and media are best suited to the **circulation** methods that will most likely generate the attention I want?

10

Remix

Remix is the manipulation and rearrangement of "original" materials, modes, genres, and stories into something new. Remix refers to both a product and a process; it is a noun and a verb. We listen, watch, and create remixes all the time. It involves sampling beats, citing familiar themes, and incorporating allusions to other texts and stories in our work. We remix when we retell a narrative in a new setting or historical period, create fan fiction, generate memes, or use well-known formats to create new multimodal platforms for delivering content to audiences. Remixing requires knowledge of existing historical and cultural materials, modes, and genres, along with their **affordances**, so that we can create and circulate particular messages to our targeted audiences.

History of remix

Artists and other creators have always remixed materials as part of their creative process, starting when the earliest tales were passed orally from poet to poet and were eventually written down in **alphabetic text**; with each telling, new elements and details were added in or taken out as the stories were customized and circulated for different audiences.

Source: Shutterstock

Figure 10-1

Linda Hutcheon suggests that an adaptation or remix is: "[a]n acknowledged transposition of a recognizable other work or works, [a] creative *and* an interpretive act of appropriation/salvaging, [and] [a]n extended intertextual engagement with the adapted work" (8).

Scholars have long debated what the best term is to describe this process and product of adaptation; they have used imitation, alteration, offshoot, parody, revision, mash-up, spin-off, appropriatios, hybridization, and remix. Each of these terms stresses a particular element of the remix process and the connection between the original source text and the remixed product.

While all of these terms apply to using established texts and modes to create new works, remix, which has alliances with musical recording and sampling, explicitly stresses how one or more texts can be cut up, reordered, inserted, **juxtaposed**, and **arranged** in new ways.a

Terms for Various Types of Remix	What It Does	Can You Complete the Chart With Some Examples?
citation	quotes or paraphrases other texts in the new text	
imitation	sticks as close to the original as possible	
parody	stresses the comical and humorous aspects of the new text	
alteration and revision	revises the original in a new way that stresses particular aspects or changes only some parts of the situation (such as updating the language or turning a sad ending into a happy one)	
offshoot and spin-off	focuses on a selected element of the original (such as creating a new story for a minor character)	
mash-up and hybridization	joins together more than one text or mode	
appropriation	implies the forceful takeover of another's ideas or work to make it our own, and often raises ethical issues around authorship or ownership of materials	
adaptation	revises the original to make it work for a new purpose or setting or time period	

Remix today

Engaging in remix requires knowing and paying attention to how other artists have remixed and adapted their own texts so that we can learn how to use remix in our own creative and critical works, whether those are **alphabetic texts**, digital artifacts, image-creation, or any number of multimodal formats. Daniel Fischlin and Mark Fortier argue, "[t]he task of a careful reader is to see exactly how an adaptation functions in any particular situation, and what effects it has or may have on the literary politics of author and canon, as well as on larger social and political questions" (7). Remix, as a concept, allows writers and artists to look at **genres**, forms, texts, and stories and to analyze those elements, their **affordances**, and figure out what is most useful to them in their goal of creating new texts and meanings in their own work. When we learn these processes we are prepared to seize our own **kairotic** moment to get our own messages out to our particular audience or **field**.

Part of the popularity of remixing is in the pleasure of recognizing similarities, differences, connections, and variations between the old and new material. Also, when we remix canonical materials such as Shakespeare's works we participate in long-standing artistic discourses or **fields** of practice that Shakespeare, himself, was involved in. For example, Shakespeare draws from Ovid's *Metamorphosis* (8 AD), an early Roman alphabetic retelling of over 250 oral myths, to create two of his most famous plays: *Romeo and Juliet* and *A Midsummer Night's Dream*. Both plays were remixed from Ovid's story of "Pyramus and Thisbe"—a story of two young lovers separated by a wall who decide to run away to be together and end up killing themselves after Pyramus mistakenly thinks that Thisbe has been eaten by a lion. Shakespeare remixed Ovid's story into the core plot of *Romeo and Juliet* by setting the tale in Verona and fleshing out the narrative to include witty dialogue, a fancy ball, sword fights using the latest weaponry, and contemporary drug references, to update the story and address the cultural interests of his early modern English audiences.

At the same time he remixed Ovid's story more directly, almost sampling it, as a comical subplot to the fairies' and lovers' antics as a play within a play in *A Midsummer Night's Dream*. In it, Bottom and his crew of laughable mechanicals perform the story of "Pyramus and Thisbe" as part of the marriage entertainments at the end the play. By studying how Shakespeare made his own remixes we can see how he used the **affordances** of his **genre** (the public theatre—a new and cutting-edge mode of delivery in the 1590s) to address the needs of his multi-class and multi-gendered audience who went to the theatre regularly and wanted a wide variety of narratives that were pleasurable due to their familiarity and difference from the known source tale. And, by making two different remixes of the same source material, Shakespeare engaged in the exact same process as any artist that makes a club, radio, dance, techno or video version of a song, thereby increasing **circulation** of the song by rearranging the music according to the **affordances** of the specific sub-genres, and, in the process, making money by diversifying his audience.

The last several decades have seen a shift in textuality from print-based alphabetic texts to online digital texts. Video sharing sites such as YouTube have assumed a dominant presence on the Web and our culture at large. At the same time, tools for recording and editing digital materials such as audio and video have become accessible to large numbers of people. For a while now, it has been well within the reach of anyone with a web browser and a little bit of editing knowledge to download online music or video and remix them into new texts.

In keeping with the Shakespeare thread we've been following, an excellent example of "remix," or in this case a "mashup," can be found in the "Ten Things I Hate About Commandments" YouTube video, available on our website. In 1999, Touchstone Pictures released *Ten Things I Hate About You*, a loose film adaptation of Shakespeare's comedy, *The Taming of the Shrew*. However, instead of having the action set in historic Verona, this modern reimagining transplants a similar story set in a modern day Seattle high school. In this regard, the film is certainly a remix.

Then, the trailer for the movie became an element for remix as well. In 2006, YouTube user Vayaboboo produced an original mashup video combining the Shakespeare remake's trailer with the trailer for one of the most famous films of all time, *The Ten Commandments*. Apparently recognizing some connection between the two films, Vayaboboo recut both trailers and combined them into a new trailer titled "Ten Things I Hate About Commandments." The resulting remix has amassed more than three million views, equaling the number of views of the two original trailers combined.

Clearly, the mashup touches on something either insightful or entertaining by juxtaposing the two wildly different trailers. Depending on how one makes sense of this remix, it might be understood as poking fun at how seriously *The Ten Commandments* takes itself, or one might interpret it as some sort of condemnation of the decline of modern cinema. Either way, there's no denying that **juxtaposing** two, seemingly unrelated trailers has resulted in the expression of ideas that neither of the original texts intended.

Remix thus encourages writers and other creators to engage in cultural-historical discourses or **fields** and to realize that literary, creative, and professional "geniuses" (Shakespeare or our favorite bloggers) cobbled together materials to repackage them. They used the means available and/or created new modes and means, if necessary, to take advantage of their specific **kairotic** moment and achieve their creative and critical goals. Furthermore, by studying remix and learning a few skills, we realize that we can all make our own adaptive remix, which is a very empowering process to engage in.

Discussing remix and adaptation, and the multitude of terms that can be used for the process and product, requires writers to address issues and questions of: audience, time, transmission, reception, what constitutes an "original," futurity, the lives of texts beyond authors, the role of editors and other secondary creators and selectors on the framing and presentation of meaning—all this before discussing any specific social-cultural messages *in* the remixed works, themselves. In addition, anyone engaged in remixing works has to be aware of copyright and the limits of fair use so that they give credit to anyone's work they are adapting and do not unintentionally plagiarize.

Remix and other concepts

Remixing is central to the writing process, whether one is creating **alphabetic text**, **images**, or other multimodal projects. We remix when we draft and revise our own written work to emphasize **ethos**, logos, or pathos, or when we alter and rearrange it to suit new modes and **genres** that allow **circulation** to different audiences and **fields**. When we remix our work for new audiences we may have to change our language and style, include more images, sound, video, think about different **arrangements** and **juxtapositions** of content on the page or screen, etc. Adaptation and remix involves knowing how texts circulate and spread via media and culture—diachronically and synchronically. It is a very holistic process.

Remix requires us to think about the **genre** that we want to engage in. Is it a critical or scholarly genre that expects formal **alphabetic texts** that present arguments based on research? Are we being asked to engage in a creative **field** that has many sub-genres that we need to know the differences between such as web design or personal alphabetic narratives? Who are our audiences and how will the material circulate? For instance, web designers need to know the differences between blogs, wikis, commercial pages, new sites, content creation pages, and how advertisements and hyperlinks affect the presentation, **circulation**, and **ethos** of the page. For each of these genres we need to think about the requirements, expectations, and **affordances** of the mode if we want to successfully participate in that field of discourse related to that genre. We also need to know these same things if we want to remix the genre and create new modes of engagement.

Ethos is also very important to consider when engaging in remix. What we choose to remix and how we go about adapting it say a lot about us, as creators. Whether we adapt a canonical text, such as one of Shakespeare's plays, or decide to remix the latest Grumpy Cat meme says something about what is important to each of us. Even when we are assigned a particular set of core texts to think about and adapt, we are still responsible for the messages that we choose to create and circulate to our audiences. When we remix we participate in a long history of adaptation and we create new spaces for cultural politics and can give voice to individuals and issues that have been ignored or silenced by the mainstream media. We can use **images**, sound, and **alphabetic text** to remix familiar tales, along with our own writing, to raise awareness of political and social issues. Remixing allows us to take a stand in a way that can be very powerful and attractive to whatever **field** of discourse we engage in.

Writing with remix

When we analyze someone else's remix or create our own, we need to think about the critical and creative choices involved, what **affordances** led to or help us make the remix, how it is or will be **circulated**, and what socio-cultural and historical issues are or will be addressed through the remixing of the text or mode. When we remix others' texts and creative works we need to pay special attention to copyright and fair use to make sure that we don't unintentionally plagiarize their works.

We need to ask ourselves the following questions when we remix:

- What core texts or modes do I want to remix?
- What specific socio-cultural issue would I re-imagine and how do I define that issue? Why is that issue important to incorporate in my remix?
- Who is my audience and how will my remix **circulate** to them?
- What messages do I want to get out to my audience and why is that message important?
- How am I going to make my remix, and, most importantly, ***why*** would I re-create the text or mode in the specific way that I would?
- What medium, **genre**, or multimodal form will I choose for my remix? What are the **affordances** of each that will allow me to create my remix as I want it?
- Have I made sure to cite my sources and pay attention to issues of copyright and fair use?

Remix allows for endless opportunities to be creative and innovative, while building on the inventiveness of the past. Each of our creative and critical choices is important when we remix, so we should always think about our reasons for why we make those choices and what other options we could have picked.

11

Additional Key Concepts

In this chapter, we offer four additional key concepts that some students and instructors may find useful. As with all of our key concepts, they are not meant to be learned in isolation, but to be practiced and applied in relation to all of the others.

Juxtaposition

Juxtaposition is the positioning of items next to each other in time or space to create a particular effect or meaning. The effect or meaning of the items side by side is different than either item could accomplish alone. At the same time, each item individually takes on new meanings. Juxtaposition can refer to elements within a single **mode** (words or phrases juxtaposed in a sentence) or different modes next to each other (somber music playing over a seemingly happy scene in a video).

One way to understand the power of juxtaposition is when it fails. (The Internet loves juxtaposition failures—try a Google image search for "juxtaposition fail.") A juxtaposition failure might be a bright "Back to School Supplies!" sign next to a rack of condoms, or a billboard advertising a gun show right above a billboard advertising caskets. You might also feel the effects of unintentional juxtaposition in your Facebook or Twitter feed, when one person

Figure 11-1

you follow posts a trivial comment ("I love Spaghettios!"), and the next person to appear in the feed posts news of a personal tragedy ("News from the hospital isn't good. Dad may not make it through the night.")

These examples are of unintentional juxtaposition, but they illustrate how juxtaposition works. The store running a back-to-school sale is typically appealing to parents purchasing supplies for their (young, innocent) children who are looking forward to a year of art projects and math tests. Next to a rack of condoms, though, school becomes a place for hook-ups, and children are not young and innocent, and they are not looking forward to art projects. Likewise, thinking of condoms as "supplies" brings connotations to sex that typically are not there. Juxtaposition changes the meaning of each item—the words on the sign and the rack of condoms—and together they create a humorous effect that neither would have alone.

As you approach the **arrangement** of a piece you're working on, you can deliberately juxtapose items for humorous or dramatic effect. An image could take on new meanings next to something you've written, and together the **alphabetic text** and **image** could have an effect that neither would alone. Or juxtaposing two adjectives in a surprising way could enrich a narrative. Or play around with the ways that different types of music create different emotional effects (**pathos**) when juxtaposed with images in a video you've created. You might also use juxtaposition while you're drafting a piece, as a way to generate ideas. For example, if you were assigned to write an essay about Chicago, you might make a list of the best things about the city next to a list of the worst things about the city. The juxtaposition of those lists could yield interesting connections and help you come up with ideas that one list alone could not.

Logos

Logos is an appeal to reason. In *On Rhetoric*, Aristotle identified three methods of persuading listeners to think or do something: ethos, pathos, and logos. **Ethos**, which you can read more about in Chapter 5, is when the author uses his or her own character to persuade an audience ("you can trust me!"). **Pathos**, covered elsewhere in this chapter on Additional Key Concepts, is when the author evokes an emotion to persuade the audience ("if you don't do what I suggest, terrible things will happen! Be afraid!"). The third approach is **logos**, which is when we appeal to the soundness of the argument itself. In any communicative situation, we might use all three.

Ancient rhetoricians argued that the job of the rhetor was to look for methods of persuasion within the language itself. These methods of persuasion can take several shapes, such as the syllogism or enthymeme, and they can involve inductive or deductive reasoning. Other strategies we traditionally associate with logos include cause-

and-effect and either/or reasoning, analogies, examples, and anecdotes, in addition to the deployment of facts or statistics that support one's position. But as both readers and writers, we must be thoughtful, critical thinkers when approaching any of these methods of persuasion.

For example, just because A happened and then B happened, it does not mean that A caused B to happen. The argument that vaccines cause autism illustrates the importance of carefully approaching arguments that appear logical. Diagnoses of autism have increased in recent decades, so some people have looked for an environmental cause that would explain this increase. Because children who had been diagnosed had also received common childhood vaccines, people—most notably, actress Jenny McCarthy—have argued that A (vaccines) caused B (autism). The scientific and medical community has repeatedly demonstrated through carefully designed studies that this is not the case, and that the increase of diagnoses might actually be explained by more knowledge about and awareness of autism. More persuaded by Jenny McCarthy and the anti-vaccine movement, however, some parents have avoided having their children vaccinated, leaving their children and those around their children vulnerable to preventable illnesses and death.

This same example also illustrates the relationship between **ethos**, **pathos**, and **logos**. We must think carefully about the ethos of the authors we trust for serious arguments like this: actress Jenny McCarthy who openly admits that Google is the source of her evidence, or the Center for Disease Control and the scientists and doctors who have done peer-reviewed research? And pathetic appeals like the scare tactics used by the anti-vaccine movement are also worth pausing over. They make parents afraid that their children will develop autism, and this fear alone is reason enough to avoid vaccines. This use of pathos assumes two things that we should question: that a person with autism is something to be afraid of or sad about, and that autism is worse than the possibility that a child could develop and spread a life-threatening disease like polio.

Modes

Modes are the material resources we have available to us as we make decisions about how best to communicate with other people. We discuss two modes in this textbook at length: **alphabetic text** and **image**. Additional modes include moving image, spoken word, music, gesture, and 3D objects. We think of these as material resources, because each mode is made up of stuff that exists in the material world—ink or pixels in the shape of letters in the case of alphabetic text, for example, or sound waves in the case of music, or our bodies in the case of gestures. The **affordances** and constraints of these different material properties should be considered when choosing which is the best mode for a specific purpose. A fairly straightforward example is when you are communicating with an audience that may include deaf people. Using a mode that relies on sound waves will be far less effective than a mode that relies on visual stimuli.

Likewise, we might consider what Gunther Kress refers to as different modes' specific orientations to the world: some modes are temporally oriented, some are spatially oriented, and some are a combination (Multimodality 154). For example, sound is temporally oriented; it happens in time. We hear one sound after another and meaning depends on the order in which we hear the sounds; therefore, the producer of the sound is primarily responsible for the organization of the meaning. (Think of the significance of the order of words in speech or notes in music.) **Alphabetic text** is what Kress refers to as a "border category" in terms of temporal or spatial orientation (Multimodality 81). Alphabetic text is written on the page or screen so that it moves from left to right and it occurs in lines, so in these respects it uses spatial logics for meaning to occur. However, writing also shares with speech the fact that we need to put our words and phrases in a particular order for them to make sense.

How a mode works also depends on the social context. Modes mean different things at different points in history. We might argue that the mode of **image** is undergoing a shift right now. As Scott McCloud argues in the piece included in this textbook, in literature, we have associated pictures with children's fiction. Put another way, images in a book have meant something like "this story is for young people." However, just in the decade since McCloud published that piece, the graphic novel has achieved far more recognition as a way of dealing with serious and adult themes in both fiction and non-fiction. Modes can also mean different things in different cultures. If you've traveled outside the U.S., you may have learned that what we accomplish with swear words, other cultures accomplish with gesture.

Though we sometimes intuitively choose the mode that will work best for a given communicative task, thinking about the **affordances** and constraints of different modes in this way will help us make the best choices. Moreover, while each mode brings its own affordances and constraints in different rhetorical situations, even more complicated and exciting is the potential for multimodality. Multimodality simply refers to communication that includes more than one mode. This textbook includes images and alphabetic text, and so is multimodal, for example. The potential in digital, networked texts for productive combinations of modes is limitless. When a website can include words, images, videos, music, audio files of speech, and so on, and when we have available to us a limitless number of texts to draw on and **remix** in our own work, authors must consider what each mode contributes and how the modes can best be **arranged** to work together.

Pathos

Pathos is an appeal to emotion. (Pathos is the root word of "pathetic.") In *On Rhetoric*, Aristotle identified three methods of persuading listeners to think or do something: ethos, pathos, and logos. **Ethos**, which you can read more about in the chapter in this textbook, is when the author uses his or her own character to persuade an audience. **Logos**, which is covered elsewhere in this chapter on Additional Key Concepts, is the appeal to the soundness of the argument itself. Pathos is when a writer tries to make the audience feel a certain way so that they do or believe what the writer wants them to. In any communicative situation, we might use all three.

An organization that is trying to raise money for people in need might focus on pathos in persuading people to donate. Through words and images, they could try to make their audience feel sad for the people, or they might try to make the audience feel guilty about ignoring the individuals' situation, or they could arouse a sense of patriotism: "We're a nation that helps each other!" The different emotions may be more or less effective in achieving the goal, depending on who the audience is.

As you approach a situation in which you are called on to produce and circulate a text, you need to consider what types of emotion are appropriate in this situation. It's worth noting that in some situations, audiences might resent or dismiss a text that seems to be trying to manipulate their emotions, or one that seems to be trying to cover up a lack of substance with excessive or inappropriate emotions.

Likewise, as you approach a situation in which you are called on to consume a text, it's worth paying attention to how the text affects your emotions. Savvy advertisers and politicians are particularly adept at foregrounding emotion over reason, pathos over logos. You might study a range of ads and try to articulate what emotions they inspire: is it desire to be a certain type of person? Fear that without a product, you will be unpopular or unhealthy? Humor and happiness that the product promises? Or look at the campaign slogans of candidates running for president and figure out which of them rely on ethos, which rely on logos, and which rely on pathos.

There is simply no tried and true method for determining how pathos works in every situation. Especially in networked, digital texts, we have available to us a wide range of resources—from sad images to happy music to bittersweet metaphors—that can help us evoke a variety of emotions in our readers. The **affordances** of different **modes** may lend themselves to evoking different emotions in a particular rhetorical situation.

Readings

Economists of Attention

By Richard A. Lanham

> In the *spontaneous* unfoldings of history, the imaginative expression of a trend precedes its conceptual-critical counterpart.
>
> Kenneth Burke

Our recently ended twentieth century overflows with monuments to artistic outrageousness. Never have so many artists flung so many paint pots and puzzles in the face of so many publics: urinals turned upside down and exhibited as art, Rube Goldberg machines that do abstract drawings, canvases that are all white or all black, paintings of Campbell's soup cans, sculptures of the boxes the soup came in, trenches dug in the desert where nobody can see them, the Pont Neuf in Paris wrapped up in gold cloth for a few days and then unwrapped again. One strand of this outrageousness isn't outrageous at all, once we see the lesson it teaches: During the twentieth century, art was undergoing the same reversal from stuff to attention described in chapter 1. Art's center of gravity henceforth would lie not in objects that artists create but in the attention that the beholder brings to them. Some examples.

In 1917, the French artist Marcel Duchamp got together with two friends, the painter Joseph Stella and the connoisseur Walter Arensberg, to play a joke on the Independents' art exhibition. They bought from the J. L. Mott Iron Works a urinal on which Duchamp, after turning it upside down, painted the nom de plume R. Mutt. They then sent it into the show under Mutt's name, with the $6 registration fee. Since, under the rules of the show, any artist could submit any piece of work, it had to be shown. But the committee refused to show it. Nevertheless, none has engendered more comment than this *Fountain*. In 1989, an entire museum show and book were built around it. The usual explanation of the joke has been that it illustrated the premise of the show: art was what an artist decided it was. This ipse dixit definition of art, though, however much it may elevate the artistic ego to godlike stature, doesn't help much unless you take it a step further. Art is whatever the artist wishes to call to our attention. Art is an act of attention the artist wishes to invoke in the beholder.

Duchamp had developed this theme a few years earlier with his "Readymades." The first, apparently, was a bicycle wheel mounted on a kitchen stool. You could spin it around when you felt like it. Early "interactivity." Later came a kitchen bottle rack, less user interactive but equally stimulating to serious interpretation. You could say, for example, that there was a great deal of beauty hidden in a bicycle wheel, but so long as it was attached to the bicycle, its utility obscured its beauty. Likewise with the bottle rack. From such efforts descended the long list of "found objects" littering the museums of the last century. The lesson was simple and, once learned, tedious. Art is not stuff made out of stuff taken from the earth's crust. Art is the attention that makes that stuff meaningful. The more commonplace and physical the objects teaching the lesson, the more they taught the final insignificance of physical objects.

But Duchamp himself repudiated this interpretation. He said he did not think his Readymades had any hidden beauties to reveal. Furthermore, as he said on more than one occasion, he despised the high seriousness the beholder brought to art. Art, he thought, was a worse religion even than God. He made his feelings clear when he annotated a postcard of the Mona Lisa by drawing a mustache on it. Art not only was a way of paying attention to the physical world, it was a pompous and overblown one as well. His oeuvre since then, indeed over his lifetime, is slender. Yet his recent biographer Calvin Tomkins argues that he is the most important artist of the twentieth century. How could this be?

Duchamp said that he wanted to deflate the seriousness of art. He wanted to make a game out of it, a game with the beholder. We might, thus, consider his career as fabricating a series of attention games with the art-loving public. Consider the famous urinal. It illustrated the premise of the Independents' Exhibition and so constituted a serious statement. It mocked the premise of the Independents' Exhibition ("See, art is a real pisser, isn't it?") and so mocked the serious statement, and the conception of the artistic ego that the exhibition stood for. The art historians and interpreters have fallen into this ironic bear trap every time they've walked over it.

Inquiry of all sorts has to be serious. That is its organizing premise. But if you subtract the object of that seriousness by putting a urinal in its place, that seriousness is turned into a game. To understand it, you must then write a serious treatise on games and play, wondering all the while what you are about. The critic, like a bull bemused by the toreador's flashing cape, starts pawing the ground, angry and confused. Such confusion has made Duchamp famous. The urinal proved to be an extraordinarily efficient generator of fame because other people—the critics and historians—did all of Duchamp's work for him.

Likewise with the Readymades. Duchamp said he made the first one, the bicycle wheel, just because it was fun to spin the wheel around. But when you exhibit it, when you put it into an attention field called "art," it becomes a catalyst. You must look at it differently. Yes, we should indeed pay more attention to the utilitarian world, savor its beauty as beauty. But when you find yourself gazing at it worshipfully, Duchamp turns around and says, "It's just a bicycle wheel, you silly jerk." The final result is to make us oscillate back and forth between the physical world, stuff, and how we think about stuff. It makes us look at our own patterns of attention and the varieties of "seriousness" we construct atop them.

That oscillation constitutes a serious lesson about seriousness. But it does not constitute great art, if we think of art as composed of stuff shaped into beauty, as forming part of a goods economy. In this industrial framework, Duchamp is the charlatan some have taken him for. But if you are willing to put him into an attention economy rather than a goods economy, let him work in attention, not in stuff, then things look different. Duchamp, as few before him, knew how to catalyze human attention in the most economical way possible. The disproportion between his oeuvre, the physical stuff he left behind, and his reputation can be explained in no other way. If we are looking for economists of attention, he provides a good place to start, an excellent lesson in efficiency.

When we consider the twentieth century from this point of view, we are reminded that futurists not only ushered us out of it but into it as well. These first futurists were led, and often financed, by Filippo Tommaso Marinetti, a wealthy Italian intellectual who wanted to catapult Italy into the future, or at least into the sophisticated present of Paris, where Marinetti lived in spirit and often in the flesh. He announced his utopian vision in an advertisement, a "Futurist Manifesto," that appeared on the front page of the Parisian journal *Le Figuro* on 20 February 1909. Marinetto would have made a stupendous ad man in our time but, more remarkably, he already was one in his own, before blitz ad campaigns had been invented. He was, above all, an economist of attention. "Italian Futurism was the first cultural movement of the twentieth century to aim directly and deliberately at a mass audience." He ran his intellectual campaign at the beginning of the century exactly as spin doctors would conduct political campaigns at its end. To reach this audience, Marinetti generated a torrent of manifestos and position statements. And, like an Internet company trying to buy "eyeballs" by giving away its product, he gave his products away to purchase attention: "It is believed that two thirds of the books, magazines and broadsheets that the futurists published were distributed free of charge as 'propaganda' material."

The platform of this campaign for Italian cultural leadership, the famous "Manifesto," might have come right out of the sixties. Here's a sample: "It is from Italy that we are launching throughout the world this manifesto, charged with overwhelming incendiary violence. We are founding *Futurism* here today because we want to free this land from its foul gangrene of professors, archaeologists, guides and antiquarians. For too long Italy has been a market-place for second-hand dealers. We mean to free her from the innumerable museums that cover here like so many graveyards." Get rid of everyone over thirty, especially those gangrenous professors. Forget the past. Fearlessly mount the *Star Trek* holodeck. Marinetti's friendship with Mussolini and his association with Italian Fascism and its glorification of war have brought futurism into well-deserved discredit. But in a later manifesto, from 1913, he points to a less horrific future, one that Marshall McLuhan was to describe later at greater length: "Futurism is grounded in the complete renewal of human sensibility brought about by the great discoveries of science. People today make use of the telegraph, the telephone, the phonograph, the train, the bicycle, the motorcycle, the automobile, the ocean liner, the dirigible, the aeroplane, the cinema, the great newspaper (synthesis of a day in the world's life) without realizing that these various forms of communication, transformation, and information have a decisive effect on their psyches." Later on he speaks of an earth shrunk by speed and of the global awareness thus engendered. Like futurists today, Marinetti had no use for the past but rather tried to glimpse the operating system of the global village to come: "The earth shrunk by speed. New sense of the world. To be precise: one after the other, man gained the sense of his home, of the district where he lived, of his region, and finally of his continent. Today he is aware of the whole world. He hardly needs to know what his ancestors did, but he has a constant need to know what his contemporaries are doing all over the world."

We're not so far here, in the preceding, from the Internet-based paradise of perfect information prophesied by digital seers like George Gilder. And not far, either, from Peter Drucker's conviction that information is the new property, the new stuff. Marinetti's cultural campaign, in fact, makes sense only if we assume that such a world already exists. Assume that, in an information economy, the real scarce commodity will always be human attention and that attracting that attention will be the necessary precondition of social change. And the real source of wealth. Marinetti's conviction that attention was the vital stuff ran so deep that it went without saying. Everything he did implied it.

Look at how this worked out on a small scale, in his declaration of war on conventional typography. One favorite battleground of this war was the journal *Lacerba*, a revolutionary Italian journal published between 1913 and 1915. A page from it can be seen in figure 1.

Why would anyone want to construct such a ransom-note pastiche? The usual explanation—conventional typography symbolizes bourgeois convention, which the avant garde exists to épater—works well enough here. That's what the journal was all about, after all, and what Marinetti certainly yearned to do. He called it "spitting on the altar of art." But might there be another lesson lurking here? Who, or what, is actually getting spat upon?

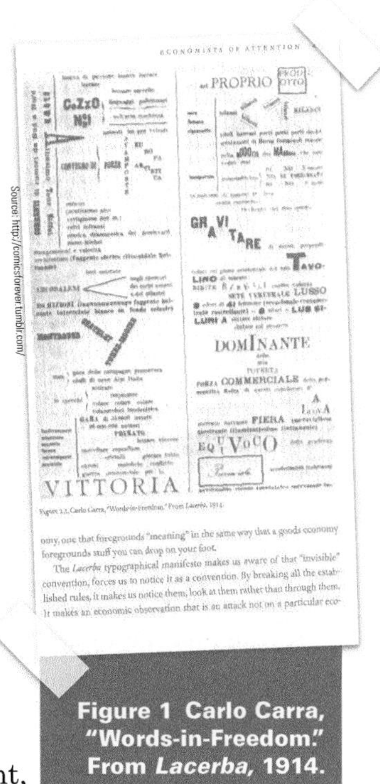
ECONOMISTS OF ATTENTION

PROPRIO
GRAVITARE
LUSSO
DOMINANTE
COMMERCIALE
FIERA
EQUIVOCO
VITTORIA

Figure 1.1. Carlo Carra, "Words-in-Freedom." From *Lacerba*, 1914.

omy, one that foregrounds "meaning" in the same way that a goods economy foregrounds stuff you can drop on your foot.

The *Lacerba* typographical manifesto makes us aware of that "invisible" convention, forces us to notice it as a convention. By breaking all the established rules, it makes us notice them, look at them rather than through them. It makes an economic observation that is an attack not on a particular eco-

Source: http://comicsforever.tumblr.com/

Figure 1 Carlo Carra, "Words-in-Freedom." From *Lacerba*, 1914.

It helps if you don't know Italian and look only at the visual pattern. Conventional printed typography aims to create a particular economy of attention, but, since this economy is so ubiquitous, the basic reality of reading, we have long ago ceased to notice it. Print wants us to concentrate on the content, to enhance and protect conceptual thoughts. It does this by filtering out all the signals that might interfere with such thinking. By nature a silent medium and, for people of my generation at least, best read in a silent environment, print filters out any auditory signal. It also filters out color, prints only black on white. By choosing a single font and a single size, it filters out visual distraction as well. Typographical design aims not to be seen or more accurately, since true invisibility is hard to read, to seem not to be seen, not to be noticed. We don't notice the verbal surface at all, plunge without typographical self-consciousness right into the meaning.

Print, that is, constructs a particular economy of attention, an economy of sensory detail. It economizes on most of the things we use to orient ourselves in the world we've evolved in—three-dimensional spatial signals, sounds, colors, movement—in order to spend all our attention on abstract thinking. The "abstraction" can be abstruse philosophy, but it can also be a particolored landscape description. Doesn't matter. They both work within the same economy, one that foregrounds "meaning" in the same way that a goods economy foregrounds stuff you can drop on your foot.

The *Lacerba* typographical manifesto makes us aware of that "invisible" convention, forces us to notice it as a convention. By breaking all the established rules, it makes us notice them, look at them rather than through them. It makes an economic observation that is an attack not on a particular economic class but on a particular economy of attention. It aims to make us economists of expression.

In conventional typographical text, meaning is created through syntactical and grammatical relationships. In figure 1, "meaning," such as it is, is created by visual relationships that pun on the meaning of the words. One example: on the right side, halfway down, "Gravitare" (to gravitate, tend toward) "of perpendicular masses onto the horizontal plane of my little table." But little table gets a big bold font and an even bigger *T*, which is a letter and a table at the same time. We read the words for meaning—we can't help doing that—but we are made to "read" them for shape as well, and in an uneasy combination. The print economy of attention has been destabilized. It is still there, but it toggles back and forth with a new one.

Marinetti's spiritual successor was Andy Warhol. Warhol the commercial artist, Warhol the painter, Warhol the filmmaker, Warhol the writer, Warhol the collector, Warhol the philosopher, and, superlatively and climactically, Warhol the celebrity: all these roles float on a sea of commentary, nowadays mostly hagiographical. Let's try, as a perspective by incongruity, to describe Andy Warhol as an economist, an economist of attention. And perhaps the perspective would not in fact seem so incongruous to him. Here's what he said about the relation of art to business: "Business art is the step that comes after Art. I started as a commercial artist, and I want to finish as a business artist. . . . Being good in business is the most fascinating kind of art . . . making money is art and working is art and good business is the best art."

Warhol was an avid collector of stuff. His last house was so stuffed with his collected stuff, from cookie jars to diamonds, that there was no room left for the people. He would have been delighted, had he been able to attend Sotheby's auction of it all after his death, to see it knocked down for nearly $27 million dollars, far more than the pre-auction estimates. And to see his silk-screen painting of *Marilyn Monroe Twenty Times* (the actress's face, taken from a publicity photo, silk-screened onto canvas twenty times) fetch nearly $4 million. He did not share the conventional liberal intellectual's distaste for stuff and the advertising of stuff. It was his life's work to illustrate the paradoxical relationship of stuff and attention.

Warhol used to ask his friends what he should paint. One friend suggested that he should paint what he liked best in the world. So he began to paint money. This wasn't what he truly liked best in the world, however. That was attention. But you couldn't paint attention, at least not directly. So he went about it indirectly.

He began, in 1960, to paint pictures of Campbell's soup cans. Never has a single source of inspiration been so commercially exploited. People usually remember him as the painter of a can of tomato soup but he developed the product far beyond this simple notion. His soup cans "had legs." He painted pictures of the different kinds of soup—vegetable beef, beef noodle, black bean—in single portraits and in a group of two hundred that seemed, at least, to run through all the flavors. He painted them half-opened, crushed, in the act of being opened, with torn labels, without a label (you know it is a soup can because the caption tells you so), stuffed with money, and so on. Most were photorealistic in technique but a few were sketches. He then made exact models in wood of the boxes that the soup cans came in, along with the now-famous Brillo and Heinz ketchup boxes. These boxes then made wonderful gallery shows, stacked in various new and exciting ways. How's that for brand name exploitation?

When he began, the New York galleries would not show him. You can't blame them. The great pop explosion of the 1960s, the style that took the attention economy as its central subject, had not yet occurred, and nobody knew what to make of this new genre of mass-produced commercial still life. And so it was left to the Ferus Gallery in Los Angeles to mount the first Campbell soup can show in 1962. Let that show stand for many to follow. What happened there? Like Duchamp with his urinal, Warhol put a banal object in an alien attention structure. An art gallery, public or private, is a place to which we come with a definite set of expectations. Duchamp mocked these expectations; like Marinetti, he was spitting on the altar of art. Not young Andy. No disrespect intended either for the soup or the public who looked at it. No meaning, in fact, at all. What you saw was what you got. He never pretended otherwise.

The surface, he said, was all there was. He sung not of the soup but the can it came in. Obviously no art critic could be content with this dead-end candor. Those soup cans had to mean *something*. You could repeat the mantra of "art for art's sake" but no critic can actually accept this as truth because it leaves the critic no function. There had to be *some* reason why the soup cans were put into an art gallery, why we were asked to admire their beauty, even take one home and hang it over the mantelpiece. There had to be *some* soup in the can. And so all the interpretive machinery, professional and amateur, went into action. The soup cans represented the detritus of consumerist capitalism, its vacuous tastelessness, etc. Or the tastelessness of modern mass-prepared foods. Or they represented the signage with which we are surrounded these days, no less fitting a subject for a still life than a dish of pears was for Renoir. Or, since the paintings were all the same, they represented the sterility of mass production. Or they allegorized the bankruptcy of the masterpiece tradition in Western art, a tradition based on skill of hand and beauty of form. Or, quite to the contrary, because formal decisions were required to transform the soup can labels to canvas, they represented an exquisite case of ever-so-slight formal transformations that elicited the beauty implicit in the Campbell's label, lent it a tailor-made beauty the store-bought can did not possess.

It took time for this flood of commentary to flow downstream. Meanwhile, when the show was still up in the Ferus Gallery, another gallery close by put some real soup cans on display, suggesting that you could get the real McCoy for much less. Nice comparison. What did the exhibit do that a local grocery store could not? It created a powerful yet economical attention trap. A maximum of commentary was created by a minimum of effort. Subject? Off the shelf. Basic design? Off the shelf.

Technique? Ditto. Replication? Silk screen, off the shelf too. Thought, allegory, philosophy, iconography, meaning? Nothing in that line required at all. Drafting ability: *de minimis*. The meaning, since this was an attention trap, would be supplied by all the interpreters waiting out there to make sense of such artifacts. For them, the more puzzling or outrageous the artifact, the better. Altogether, a dynamite niche product at a bargain basement cost.

But hasn't it always been so? No. Attention traps had been tried before—Rabelais set them for his humanist explicators all the time—but they could come into their own only when there was a powerful and established Interpretive Bureaucracy of Attention Economists waiting there to be used. The Interpretive Bureaucracy was what made pop art such a success. Made it possible, in fact. The right cultural judo expert could make use of all that established power to get talked about, to get famous. And if asked about the meaning of it all, as Warhol repeatedly was, he could make up the meanings expected (I was raised on Campbell's soup. I had it for lunch every day. I love it.). Or he could shrug and say that there wasn't any meaning. What you saw was what you got. The surface *was* the meaning. Once the Interpretive Bureaucracy got started, it didn't matter. With the bureaucracy's relentless seriousness, it could philosophize surface as well as depth. And so what if Andy did say one thing one day and contradict himself the next? More grist for the mill. That's how an attention artist works.

So there was a way to paint "attention." You had only to add the right enzyme to a preexistent mixture. Then that enzyme—and a soup can would do as well as anything else—could represent the subsequent interpretive conversation. It would, as time passed, embody a complex attention structure, an entire cultural moment in the same way that, say, Barbie dolls do.

Once the attention-trap formula was worked out, it was easy to apply it elsewhere, to the celebrity portraits, for example. The day after the Ferus Gallery closed, Marilyn Monroe died. David Bourdon describes what happened next: "Within a few days of Monroe's death, Warhol purchased a 1950s publicity photograph of her and, after cropping it below her chin, had it converted without any alteration into a silkscreen. The silkscreen enabled him to imprint her portrait hundreds of times onto various canvases. He screened her face one time only on small, individual canvases, and repeated it—twice, four times, six times, twenty times—on larger canvasses, positioning the heads in rows to create an allover pattern."

Marilyn was already a cultural icon, and her death ensured that the golden hair would never gray. Here was an attention trap already made, waiting to be exploited. Its power could, in a simple judo throw, be harnessed for mass production. Some of the silk screenings were out of register, blurring the image, but that only individuated the various iterations. Again, it was such an economical, such a profitable and efficient, way to paint attention. A 1950s publicity shot, silk-screen technology, and you were ready for mass production. Vary the size, the number of iterations, the color, actually induce the off-register blurring, all these were the signs of real artistic creation and cried out for interpretation. The next step? Obvious. Extend the franchise to other celebrities. Get them into a contest to have their faces replicated.

Thus was attention converted into money by instantiating the attention in physical objects, stuff. The ingeniousness of the solution should not blind us to the difficulty of the problem. The Internet dot-coms have not yet solved it, and this indeed may be what shortened their life. Information, digital or otherwise, is not like stuff. You can eat your cake, let somebody else eat it too, and you both still have it. Books are a great way to bring information down to earth in a salable product. Warhol found a way to bring a certain category of information—somebody else's celebrity, maybe even celebrity itself—down to earth in salable products. And no one sued him for copyright infringement, or unauthorized use of personal image, or trademark violation. All these starlets lined up to be violated. An amazing business coup.

The celebrity portraits, like the celebrities themselves, drew their power from *Homo sapiens*' fondness for the centripetal gaze. We love looking at movie stars, sports stars, royalty. We simply cannot get enough of it. Louis XIV based the plan of Versailles on this centripetal gaze (all the alleyways radiated out from the king's bedroom) and palace plans ever since have striven for the same visible ego enhancement.

The centripetal gaze, the flow of energy from the margins of a society to its center of attention, creates by its nature the winner-take-all society. To be one of the winners who took all, Andy knew, he had to create a public personality that would function as an attention trap as efficient as his artwork. As he himself said of his endless party-going and art-going: "But then, we weren't just *at* the art exhibit—we *were* the art exhibit, we were the art incarnate and the sixties were really about people, not about what they did." Such self-dramatization is as familiar as Douglas MacArthur's corncob pipe or General Patton's ivory-handled six-shooters. Andy's social self stood out from the crowd, however. The celebrity press is built on trying to find out about the private selves of the social selves, the celebs' scintillating inner lives. Andy preempted this effort. He had, he kept saying, no central self, no private self to peer into. As with the soup cans, he was pure *wysiwyg* (what you see is what you get). He aimed to impersonate a purely social, two-dimensional self with no central interiority other than the ambition to be rich and famous.

A more resonant incarnation of his time would be hard to contrive. And, apparently, he didn't need to contrive it. He was naturally shallow, selfish, and unreflective, a person who would let his kind old mom take care of him for much of his life and then not bother to go to her funeral. Like Henry VIII, he was a genius at playing off the members of his entourage (and what a gallery of grotesques the Warhol entourage comprised) against one another. True enough. But he was unusual, truly unusual, in not pretending otherwise. Each time when asked about his early life, he sketched a new one. He even sent an impersonator on a college lecture tour for him, explaining when the imposture was exposed that the impersonator was much better at saying the kinds of things college audiences expected to hear. The customer is never wrong! The colleges asked for their money back or a visit by the real Warhol. When the real Warhol did come and was asked if he was the real Warhol, he answered no. He was a creature of the surface and happy to be so. "If you want to know all about Andy Warhol, just look at the surface of my paintings and films and me, and there I am. There's nothing behind it." The question of a "real" Andy, like the question of meaning in his painting, simply didn't arise. In a pure economics of attention, one of his college-attuned impostors might have replied for him, such questions simply make no sense.

In Andy Warhol, then, our perpetual hunger for sincerity was finally given a rest. If you looked only at the surface, and if the surface was all there was, you did not need to peer beneath it. He was all package. That's why he knew a genuine celebrity like Judy Garland when he met her: "To meet a person like Judy [Garland] whose real was so unreal was a thrilling thing. She could turn everything on and off in a second; she was the greatest actress you could imagine every minute of her life." But what was such candor but another attention trap? The more he confessed that he had no central self, except hunger for the centripetal gaze, the more the celebrity-interpreting bureaucracy would try to pry out, or synthesize, a central self. There had to be one, just as there had to be soup in the can. Otherwise they would be out of a job. So also with the celebrity writers who perpetually searched for the "real Marilyn" or the "real Princess Diana."

Warhol once remarked, "That's what so many people never understood about us. They expected us to take the things we believed in seriously, which we never did—we weren't intellectuals." He was not lying but he was not telling the truth either. He did take the economics of attention seriously. That seriousness, however, differed from the kind the "intellectuals" operated under. They were always looking through the self-conscious surface of things to find the meaning hidden there. He was always looking at the surface instead.

We can see, too, that he understood the paradox of stuff. The stuff you dig out of the earth's crust becomes, in an information economy, less important than the information that informs it, what you think about the stuff. Yet the more you ponder that information, the more you understand about that stuff, the more real the stuff becomes. To put it in terms of the art world Andy lived in, the more you see that style matters more than substance, the more you see the vital role, the vitality, of substance. So, like Andy, you pursue your twin hungers: for the spotlight and for collecting stuff, knowing that each needs the other to make it real.

Let's summarize the rules of attention-economy art as Andy practiced them:

- Build attention traps. Create value by manipulating the ruling attention structures. Judo, not brute force, gets the best results. Duchamp did this for a joke. Do it for a business.
- Understand the logic of the centripetal gaze and how to profit from it.
- Draw your inspiration from your audience not your muse. And keep in touch with that audience. The customer is always right. No Olympian artistic ego need apply.
- Turn the "masterpiece psychology" of conventional art upside down:
  - Mass production not skilled handwork
  - Mass audience not connoisseurship
  - Trendiness not timelessness
  - Repetition not rarity
- Objects do matter. Don't leave the world of stuff behind while you float off in cyberspace. Conceptual art gets you nowhere. Create stuff you can sell.
- Live in the present. That's where the value is added. Don't build your house in eternity. "My work has no future at all. I know that. A few years. Of course my things will mean nothing."

Now for a different kind of attention economist. Once upon a time, long ago, in the early 1970s, there dwelt in New York an artist named Christo Javacheff. Born in Bulgaria, he came of age in the perpetually avant-garde artistic atmosphere of Paris. From his Paris beginnings in the early sixties, Christo was a wrapper. He wrapped magazines, flowers, mailing boxes, and on occasion and temporarily, naked young women. Later he scaled up and wrapped a portion of the Great Barrier Reef, the Pont Neuf in Paris, and the Berlin Reichstag.

We can look at a 1966 project, *Wrapped Boxes*, as representing the early small-scale wrapping. A design class he taught at Macalester College in St. Paul, Minnesota, wrapping a hundred boxes in plain kraft paper and tied them with ordinary string. These were then mailed out to members of the Walker Art Center's Contemporary Arts Group. Twenty of the members fell into the attention trap and opened the boxes. Inside was a note from Christo: "The package you destroyed was wrapped according to my instructions in a limited edition of a hundred copies for members of Walker Art Center's Contemporary Arts Group. It was issued to commemorate my '14130 Cubic Feet Empaquetage 1966' at the Minneapolis School of Art, a project co-sponsored by the Contemporary Arts Group."

What had these unwitting desecrators (unacquainted with the game? simply curious? determined to find the "soup"?) desecrated? Not a beautifully wrapped parcel in, say, the Japanese manner but only a tidily wrapped ordinary one. No aesthetic offense. They had destroyed not a thing of beauty but Christo's economics lesson and, in the process, they taught it to themselves. The lesson could not have been simpler. Wrappings matter. You should pay attention to them. They are more important than the content. And, in extreme cases, such as this exemplary one, they may be the content. If, in your zeal to get at the content, you destroy the container, you've missed the fundamental reversal of our time, the reversal between stuff and what we think about stuff. The wrapping is the attitude surrounding the contents, the spirit in which it has been sent or given. If all you can think of is the stuff contained, if you keep looking for the soup in the can, you'll overlook where the real value lies. You've failed to see that style and substance have traded places.

Nowadays, when a product's design has become a powerful, often the dominant, attribute of the product; when brands and brand recognition are acknowledged as attention assets often worth far more than the physical assets of a company (the last I knew, the Coca-Cola brand was reckoned to be worth $70 billion plus); when the publicity campaign for a book is designed before the book is finished, or in some cases before it is written, we may well claim to have learned this lesson. Thirty-five years ago, much less so. We were so accustomed to looking through the package to the contents that it took an auctioneer's sealed box trick like Christo's to make us pause and look at it and, thus, finally to restore the balance between inner and outer, to think of "stuff" as a complex toggling between the physical object and what we think of it.

Christo is often, for lack of a better pigeonhole, called an "earth artist." But the term is more properly applied to artists like Michael Heizer and Robert Smithson who move around a lot of earth, dig gigantic holes in the desert, or build spirals in the Great Salt Lake. Christo himself liked to talk about "public art," and for good reasons. But it is clear from the simple example of his *Wrapped Boxes*, and true I think throughout his career, that the material he worked in, as against the material he worked with, was human attention. He has always been an "attention artist."

His large-scale wrappings, of which we may take the Pont Neuf project as exemplary, teach a lesson that is both less extreme and more inclusive than the one we've examined. The main difference is not, as we might think, in the scale of the enterprise, vast as that difference is. The difference is that the outsized wrappings—the Great Barrier Reef, the Surrounded Islands in Miami, the Pont Neuf—were all beautiful. In the case of the Pont Neuf, with its golden fabric, breathtakingly so. The Macalester boxes taught their lesson entirely within an economics of attention. It was purely didactic, a classroom lesson. The wrapping was not beautiful and did not need to be. The box contained only the note explaining the attention trap that had been fallen into. The Pont Neuf lesson is altogether more complex. There is content, for a start, the best-known bridge in Paris. Real stuff. Substance. And the wrapping was extraordinarily beautiful, as the many photographs of it document. By way of contrast, once you learned the lesson of the Macalester boxes, that game was over. There was no aftereffect, no resonance, no point in looking at it any more. As with Duchamp's R. Mutt urinal, and its immense artistic progeny, once you get the point, learn the lesson, the experience evaporates. But the large-scale Christo wrappings still inhabit the traditional "masterpiece" conception of art where beauty matters. There is more to them than the didacticism.

All this is by way of introduction to the Christo project that illustrates most richly how he shapes attention: the *Running Fence*, which stood in Marin and Sonoma Counties in northern California for two weeks in September of 1976. In 1973, Christo and Jeanne-Claude—his wife and chief executive officer—scouted sites for the fence in California and Oregon, settled on the Marin-Sonoma site for the twenty-four-mile long fence, formed the Running Fence Corporation to create and dismantle it, and ordered the 165,000 yards of eighteen-foot nylon that would constitute its twenty-four-mile wide sail. Carrying the 2,100 eighteen-foot by sixty-eight-foot sail panels would be 2,050 twenty-one-foot steel poles, 312,000 steel hooks, and ninety miles of steel cable. The project employed twenty vehicles, some of them specially designed. From April to September 1976, sixty employees installed the steel poles, and then at the end of August and the beginning of September 360 employees were hired to install the fence. Some stayed on after the fence was built to direct traffic and then, two weeks later, disassemble it. All of them had to be trained and fed, managed, transported, and paid. It was an immense civil engineering project. It was an even more immense social engineering project. The fence was to run through fifty-five parcels of private land. It required easement agreements from each. It also required building permits, removal bonds, seventeen public hearings, several court sessions, an Environmental Impact Report, the input of fifteen governmental agencies, and the services of nine lawyers.

It cost $3 million. Christo and his wife, as in all their projects, paid for it themselves.

It stood for two weeks.

What did they have in mind in constructing this extraordinary temporary monument? What economic lessons, in the framework of our discussion here, did they propose to teach?

Easiest to start where the fence ended—beauty. The fence was extraordinarily beautiful. I was not privileged to see it in person but I have always found the many photographs of it haunting. It created a generous beauty, one that moved outward to transform everything around it. Its extraordinary ribbon of sails made us see the invisible. As Christo said when he looked at it: "See how it describes the wind." We could, with the fence, look at the wind rather than through it—and, as the film by David Maysles et al. illustrates, hear the wind as well. Perhaps most magical of all its transformations was how it (let me phrase it as a pun) caught the light. It allowed the viewer to see what the light looked like by refracting it back in a million ways. It allowed the beholder to see what before was only seen through. It measured where the sun was and what density the air had at that particular time and place. It created new ways to pay attention to the world. It calibrated our attention.

We perceive the world around us according to different scales: the regular 3D world we walk around in; the minute world of the microscope; the unimaginable light-year measurements of astronomy. By its very nature a scale of perception is not something we can see. We look through it, not at it. It is our means of perceiving the world. To view *Running Fence*, its participants had to become self-conscious about spatial scale. The sheer size of it required a view 24,000 feet up to see it entire. Walking alongside it meant seeing an altogether different object. And an infinite number of focal lengths in between created an equal number of *Running Fences*. Its participants were able to see, to look *at*, how they paid attention to the world, how they saw. And it calibrated timescale as well. No monument lasts forever, as Ozymandias taught us in another famous lesson. But to restrict deliberately the life of an immense and expensive piece of sculpture to fourteen days is to make us see timescale as well. You can't hold in your mind's eye the life of the Parthenon. But two weeks? Anyone can do it. You are allowed to see the scale of time, look at it as you pass through it.

Beauty, however, was not Christo's avowed central purpose. Instead, it was to work, as in the small-scale wrappings, in human attention. This work of art, as he said repeatedly, was composed of the human behavior that was required to create it, not only the building of the fence but also the hearings, lawsuits, rulings, reports, meetings, and pleadings that were necessitated by the project. To create the fence he needed a myriad of permissions and to obtain those permissions he needed to persuade a myriad of people to grant them. The fence was created as an attention structure that dramatized how persuasion works in human society. It was not only a thing of beauty that did not last forever, it was, as well, a model of how persuasion works in human society, which is to say a model of rhetoric, which should last, if not forever, at least as long as such things can last. He persuaded people of what? What rhetoric has always persuaded people of: to share a beautiful attention structure. To cherish eloquence.

Vital to the fence's artistic integrity, Christo felt, was continuing it right down into the sea. The fence was to end in a long, downward-sweeping plunge from cliff to sea; full height at the top of the cliff, it would taper off to nothing as it married the sea. Certainly the dramatic photographs of this section show the climactic visual drama this plunge created. They also show why Christo was willing to risk a climactic bureaucratic drama by building it without the Coastal Commission's approval. After he had decided to do this, he offered to release the contractor from responsibility to protect him from legal action. If someone went to jail, it would be Christo himself. The primary construction contractor was A&H Builders, Inc., of Broomfield, Colorado, and its president was Theodore Dougherty. Dougherty declined to hide behind Christo's coattails. He then remarked, "The amazing thing is how one man, with his idea, can get so many people so involved."

That involvement, as Christo frequently pointed out, was why he built the fence, why he pursued all his projects. His business as an artist was to create attention structures, structures that would teach particular lessons. The fence has always been considered, and has been richly annotated, as a work of avant-garde art. Let's consider it, instead, as a series of lessons.

Suppose you wanted to teach a civics lesson. Suppose you wanted people to become aware of how they form collective purposes, how they resolve their differences to complete grand endeavors. Suppose you wanted to teach them how leaders, entrepreneurs, worked in this drama of social purpose. Suppose you wanted to show how ideas get built in a highly regulated society. How would you do it? Well, I can give the conventional answer by telling you what I would do. I'm a school teacher, and I would invent a nifty course and try to persuade people to take it. With what success, however engagingly I might teach it, who could predict? I have, in fact, spent a substantial part of a long career trying to do precisely this, to do what Christo was trying to do with the *Running Fence*: teach about rhetoric, usually defined as the "art of persuasion" but in our framework as "the economics of attention." Rhetoric has, since Plato first calumniated the Sophists, been synonymous with the art of deception. In democracies, we always call the methods by which we come to common purpose "politics" and scorn them, as if there were some other way to decide business in a democracy. Nowadays, we've come to call it "spin." The flipside of this definition is the art of cooperation. That is the fundamental lesson Christo sought to teach. How to create social cooperation from the bottom up. How to persuade people to reflect on the social machinery of persuasion and thus to understand its necessity. To redeem the "rhetoric" in daily life.

Dictating from the top down is much easier. That is the conventional direction of the magisterial artistic ego. In our time, you get a government grant to make a large sculpture and then you place it where a builder needs one to fulfill a government mandate. If your sculpture interferes with what people see or where people walk, tough. Philistines must be made to recognize the primacy of artistic purpose. Let them walk around it every day and learn this vital lesson of humility before art. (I am instancing here the lesson taught by Richard Serra's *Tilted Arc*, in Jacob Javits Plaza in New York.) Christo went about the job differently. If attention is the prime economic asset, as Christo's creative universe assumes, how do you raise this new species of money? How do you provide the attention financing? How do you "get so many people involved"? You start with a grand idea, dramatic in the making, beautiful in the execution. This is what beauty is for in an economics of attention, not to be gazed on for its own sake but to focus social purpose.

(It may work the same way in other species too, but that is another story.) Such a focus does not mean that the beauty need be of the "Seven Brave Tractor Drivers" socialist sort. Far from it. The more absolute it is, the less connected it is with social purpose, the better it works in leading social purpose.

Then you take your grand idea and you persuade people to share its grandeur. You do this in all those hearings and applications. This plunges you deeply into the paradox of stuff. You are trying to build something—the stuff is vital—but the attention structure the stuff creates, both in the making and the standing, is what finally matters. You create, as persuasion must, a participative drama. It must include, if it is to have dramatic vitality, a vociferous opposition. This was supplied by the local artists. They hated this foreigner coming in and hogging all the attention and redefining art in a way that left them clerks of a forgotten mood. And so they organized the opposition. But this was the part they were cast for in Christo's drama anyway, and the madder they got, the better they played their parts. When Christo pointed their roles out to them, they got madder still.

Participatory drama of this sort does what drama always does: it makes us see ourselves acting. It makes us look at our behavior rather than through it. But here, no proscenium arch, no theater, no suspension of disbelief. Christo always stressed that he, and his art, "lived the real life." No artistic isolation. His enterprise was as real as that of the sheep ranchers through whose land his fence must pass. *Running Fence* was far more like a startup company (was in literal fact a startup company) than like the Mona Lisa or the self-satisfied little joke Duchamp played on her by giving her a mustache.

Christo kept his enterprise in the real world by his method of financing it. He neither sought nor accepted outside support. The project was entirely self-financed. The financing constitutes a vital and original part of the story. When the project was fully conceived, a number of museums were offered a chance to share in its sponsorship. They would receive, in return, credit as coproducers. In token whereof, they would also receive, as a stock certificate issued in a corporation that made attention, sketches of the fence signed by Christo. Something you could collect, put on the wall, buy and sell. And something that, as when you back the right stock, would increase in value. It was joint-venture capitalism, but in a new breed of enterprise and with a new breed of capital: attention. The money was derivative—a theme often heard in venture-capital halls today: Money isn't the problem—it is finding good ideas to back.

To this new kind of joint-stock company he added a medieval means of finance, the sale of relics. The two big Christo books I own, the *Running Fence* one and the Pont Neuf one, both contain relics, actual pieces of the fence's silver and the Pont Neuf's golden cloth. In addition, these books and many others like them are photographic reliquaries for the photos taken of the projects, both by the public and by professional photographers. Each creates relics. And relics, as the medieval Church knew so well, walk off the shelf. The spirit can be made flesh with a big markup to the maker. The paradox of stuff in a well-documented theological manifestation.

The local artists accused Christo of seeking only profit and notoriety, not creating "art for art's sake." It was an accusation that, as we've seen, would have fit Andy Warhol perfectly, but it was perfectly wrong for Christo. Both Christo and Jeanne-Claude stressed that a central part of their project was the financial risk, and this risk they assumed themselves. They put all their assets into the project. All the money they raised by their distinctive fundraising techniques was plowed back into the company. They bet their company and stood behind it in their private persons. The financial risk was real and ever-present. The fence nearly did not get built. It was one cliffhanging hearing after another. If they had not been willing to go ahead and build the last segment without Coastal Commission approval, and assume the legal risk for that, the project would have lacked its artistic climax. Risk stood at the center of the project. And the risk conferred genuine daring on those who assumed it. This bravery was not lost on the ranchers through whose property the fence had to run. It was the artists who never understood.

I once had occasion to talk about the *Running Fence* to a group of distinguished media moguls, a group that included their then-favorite prophet, George Gilder. The two gospels that Gilder has preached from the beginning have been the power and the importance of the individual entrepreneur and the new rules of the information paradigm for wealth. In my naïveté, I thought he might find my remarks interesting and see how they agreed with his thinking. I was right about the interesting but wrong about the agreement. Christo was, according to Gilder's outraged postlecture comment, part of a postmodern plot of anarchistic God knows what, etcetera, etcetera. He responded the way the local artists did to the project. He was still thinking in their box, he who prides himself in having escaped all boxes whatsoever. Why, I wondered, the knee-jerk response from such an informed commentator on the present scene? He bought, I think, the interpretation that the art critics had handed out, the avant-garde artist doing one of those strange things: digging holes in the desert, piling up bricks on the gallery floor, painting paintings that did nothing but reflect the light of the room that hung them. The fundamentally economic focus of *Running Fence*, and Christo's work in general, had simply not occurred to him, and he did not expect to find a friend for entrepreneurship in the artistic community. Yet no greater monument to business entrepreneurship has ever been erected. I wonder how many of the many courses in entrepreneurship that have sprouted up like mushrooms include *Running Fence* in their case studies?

No wonder Gilder couldn't understand what Christo was about. The artistic community has always stressed the need for separation, for protection, and above all, for governmental and philanthropic financing. The artist is a top-down Platonic lawgiver and the society should have enough sense to understand this and to pay generously for the ex cathedra pronouncements, and the works of art, however insulting they might be to their audience, created by such a system. Artists are the priests, after all, in the religion of art.

Christo's modus operandi stood opposite to this. He raised the money by his own labors, by reinventing the joint-stock corporation on a medieval attention model. He took the risk. Courted the risk because risk was part of the lesson he wanted to teach. It was to its core a lesson in entrepreneurship. Here was a development team, Christo and Jeanne-Claude, who bet the company on every new project they undertook. How's that for lessons in entrepreneurship? This commitment was part of the persuasive argument Christo offered to the community whose support he needed. This was a private enterprise, a startup business, and this guy might well fail and was willing to take the rap if he did. He didn't take the pulpit and preach the gospel of art. Instead, he said, "Look, this is what I want to do and how I propose to do it. I don't ask for any money from you, or from your state humanities council, or your National Endowment for the Arts either. The financial system is one of the systems I'm trying to teach you how to work. My economics lesson won't work if I suspend the ordinary rules."

Because he sought to teach a lesson in pure attention entrepreneurship, he subtracted the conventional purpose from the project: permanence and profit. The corporation created to create the project was self-liquidating. It spent the money it raised to raise the fence. And the fence would be taken down after two weeks. Two powerful objections were dealt with thereby, the two knee-jerk objections of the local artists, in fact. The local artists argued that Christo was an Andy Warhol, motivated by ego and profit. No ego involvement in a project that was going to disappear in two weeks. And no profit either. The lesson was pure: How do you bring an idea to fruition in an economics of attention?

One of the amazing things about the public response was its understanding of the temporality of the fence, the deliberate choice to put it into time rather than trying to stand it outside time, constitute a "timeless" masterpiece. As one supporter of the fence said at one of the many hearings: "My husband is a farmer and I am a housewife. Some of the meals I prepare aren't much. But sometimes I go to a lot of work to prepare a meal that I think is 'art.' It is a masterpiece. And what happens to it? It gets eaten up."

One opponent of the fence, objecting to Christo's redefinition of art as an attention structure rather than a physical object meant to endure through the ages, pointed out that by such a definition "every land developer is an artist and every land development is a work of art." Lesson learned, or at least half-learned. Christo made land development into a work of art by subtracting the practical purpose and the lasting physical entity. The lasting monument, the Environmental Impact Report pointed out, was not going to be environmental damage but the changed thinking and feeling of the community that debated the project at such length. Land development was, and is, a big issue in places like Sonoma and Marin Counties. The *Running Fence* offered a different way to pay attention to that development. We return thus to the paradox of stuff in a society that transfers its center of gravity from stuff to information. The stuff becomes more important, not less, than before. What changes is the relationship between stuff and what we think about stuff. What is learned is how to move from the one to the other, hold both in mind at once. This ability was Christo's target in *Running Fence*. Talking about an artist's intention has been forbidden in aesthetic circles for a long time, and more recently, the very idea of a creating artist has been dismissed as a Romantic delusion. But economists, so far as I know, are still permitted to have intentions and purposes. They are still permitted to teach lessons about human behavior, and Christo teaches an unmistakable one here.

It is instructive to compare these two economists we've just considered, Andy Warhol and Christo Javacheff. Christo insists on living "the real life," as he puts it. His projects are built at real risk. Andy admired Judy Garland because "her real was so unreal" and wanted (at least according to one anecdote told at his funeral) to be reincarnated as a ring on Elizabeth Taylor's finger. Christo is a planner, a builder, a responsible bill payer; he knows what he wants to do and why. Andy was a drifter, schemer, and opportunist who asked his friends to suggest subjects for his painting so he wouldn't lose touch with current trends. Christo is deadly serious about his artistic entrepreneurship and what it intends to teach. Warhol kept insisting that he was not serious about anything except making money and being famous. They embodied two antithetical conceptions of self and society. Christo has a clear central self and lives, and wants to live, in "the real world." Andy said, and nothing in his life contradicts it, that he was entirely a creature of the social surface, that what you saw was what there was, and that his ideal society was the hyperventilated self-consciousness of the New York art scene.

And yet both of them made their art from the same substance: attention. Not stuff but what we think about stuff. They were both rhetoricians, economists of attention. Rhetoric has always, in its long history, seemed to divide into two parties: those who created attention structures to form and strengthen social purposes and those who sought only to serve themselves. The division was reenacted in this pair of attention economists.

Artists are supposed to be, as our epigraph from Kenneth Burke reminds us, prophets of things to come. To an uncanny degree, the artists we've been considering here, and a great many more, have done just that for an information society. From Marinetti onward, they have singled out attention as the central asset in a new economy and tried to "paint" it. They have, in the process, sketched out a new expressive field, a new means of cultural notation, one that has moved, with little change, from artistic prophecy to reality on the digital screen. That electronic expressive field finds its home no longer in the printing house but in the computer graphics studio, and to it we now turn.

Show and Tell

By Scott McCloud

IT'S THIS THING AND IF YOU PULL IT, IT GOES LIKE THIS.
KUNK!
THE HEAD FLIPS BACK.
...?
YEAH.
AND... AND THEN YOU CAN DO THIS AND IT GOES UP AND YOU FLIP THIS.
I DID IT WRONG. WAIT.
LOOK, IT'S A AIRPLANE NOW!
THANK YOU, TOMMY.
WE ALL STARTED OUT LIKE THIS, DIDN'T WE? USING WORDS AND IMAGES INTERCHANGEABLY. IT DIDN'T REALLY MATTER WHICH WE USED, SO LONG AS IT WORKED.
PSST! HEY, TOMMY!
HEE! HEE!
IT'S CONSIDERED NORMAL IN THIS SOCIETY FOR CHILDREN TO COMBINE WORDS AND PICTURES, SO LONG AS THEY GROW OUT OF IT.
Tommy

TRADITIONAL THINKING HAS LONG HELD THAT TRULY GREAT WORKS OF ART AND LITERATURE ARE ONLY POSSIBLE WHEN THE TWO ARE KEPT AT ARM'S LENGTH.
THE GRAPES OF WRATH
HOLY BIBLE
GREAT EXPECTATIONS
THE THEBAN PLAYS
WAR AND PEACE TOLSTOY
LOOK HOMEWARD ANGEL
TO KILL A MOCKINGBIRD HARPER LEE
WORDS AND PICTURES TOGETHER ARE CONSIDERED, AT BEST, A DIVERSION FOR THE MASSES, AT WORST A PRODUCT OF CRASS COMMERCIALISM.
Greetings from
Kool Aid
Small Dog Biscuits
BATMAN
ARE YOU HUNGRY TONIGHT? Recipes for the King
HOME ALONE
PEANUT BUTTER CRUNCH
QUAKER OATS
NEWS
AS CHILDREN, OUR FIRST BOOKS HAD PICTURES GALORE AND VERY FEW WORDS BECAUSE THAT WAS "EASIER."
THEN, AS WE GREW, WE WERE EXPECTED TO GRADUATE TO BOOKS WITH MUCH MORE TEXT AND ONLY OCCASIONAL PICTURES--
--AND FINALLY TO ARRIVE AT "REAL" BOOKS-- THOSE WITH NO PICTURES AT ALL.
OR PERHAPS, AS IS SADLY THE CASE THESE DAYS, TO NO BOOKS AT ALL.
WALLY

MEANWHILE, WORDS AND MOVING PICTURES HAVE HALF THE WORLD IN THRALL TO THEIR CHARMS, BUT MUST STRUGGLE TO MAKE THEIR POTENTIAL UNDERSTOOD.
WORDS AND PICTURES ARE AS POPULAR AS EVER, BUT THIS WIDESPREAD FEELING THAT THE COMBINATION IS SOMEHOW BASE OR SIMPLISTIC HAS BECOME A SELF-FULFILLING PROPHECY.
HEY KIDS! COMICS
VOGUE
THE ROOTS OF THIS ATTITUDE RUN PRETTY DEEP.
AS NEAR AS WE CAN TELL, PICTURES PREDATE THE WRITTEN WORD BY A LARGE MARGIN. HERE ARE SOME BIG HITS FROM THE GOLDEN AGE OF CAVE PAINTING, ABOUT 15,000 YEARS AGO.
SOME OF THIS ART SHOWS CONSIDERABLE ATTENTION TO DETAIL, VERY MUCH CONCERNED WITH PICTORIAL REPRESENTATION.
BUT OTHERS WERE VERY ICONIC, ACTING AS SYMBOLS RATHER THAN PICTURES-- MORE LIKE A PRIMITIVE LANGUAGE!

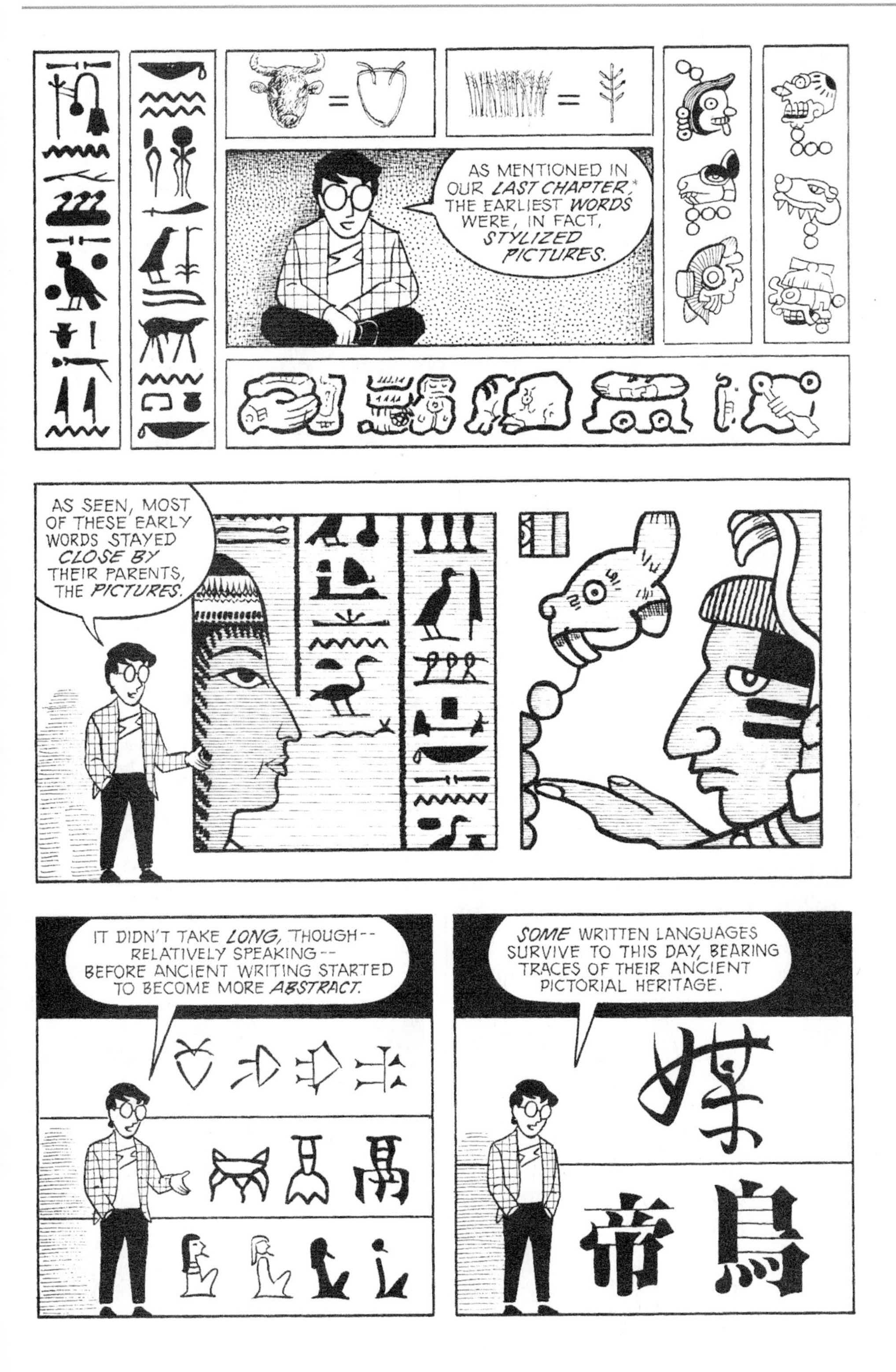
AS MENTIONED IN OUR LAST CHAPTER,* THE EARLIEST WORDS WERE, IN FACT, STYLIZED PICTURES.
AS SEEN, MOST OF THESE EARLY WORDS STAYED CLOSE BY THEIR PARENTS, THE PICTURES.
IT DIDN'T TAKE LONG, THOUGH-- RELATIVELY SPEAKING-- BEFORE ANCIENT WRITING STARTED TO BECOME MORE ABSTRACT.
SOME WRITTEN LANGUAGES SURVIVE TO THIS DAY, BEARING TRACES OF THEIR ANCIENT PICTORIAL HERITAGE.
帝 鳥

BUT, IN TIME, MOST MODERN WRITING WOULD COME TO REPRESENT SOUND ONLY AND LOSE ANY LINGERING RESEMBLANCE TO THE VISIBLE WORLD.
re's N...e! Order Today and receive FREE G
WITH THE INVENTION OF PRINTING, THE WRITTEN WORD TOOK A GREAT LEAP FORWARD--
--AND ALL OF HUMANITY WITH IT.
BUT WHERE HAD THE PICTURES ALL GONE?
WORDS AND PICTURES DID STILL COEXIST AT THIS STAGE IN WESTERN CIVILIZATION.*
BUT THOSE INSTANCES WERE BECOMING THE EXCEPTION, NOT THE RULE.
143
*IN ILLUMINATED MANUSCRIPTS, FOR EXAMPLE.

FACSIMILE DETAILS OF PORTRAITS BY DURER (1519) REMBRANDT (1660) DAVID (1788) AND INGRES (1810-15).

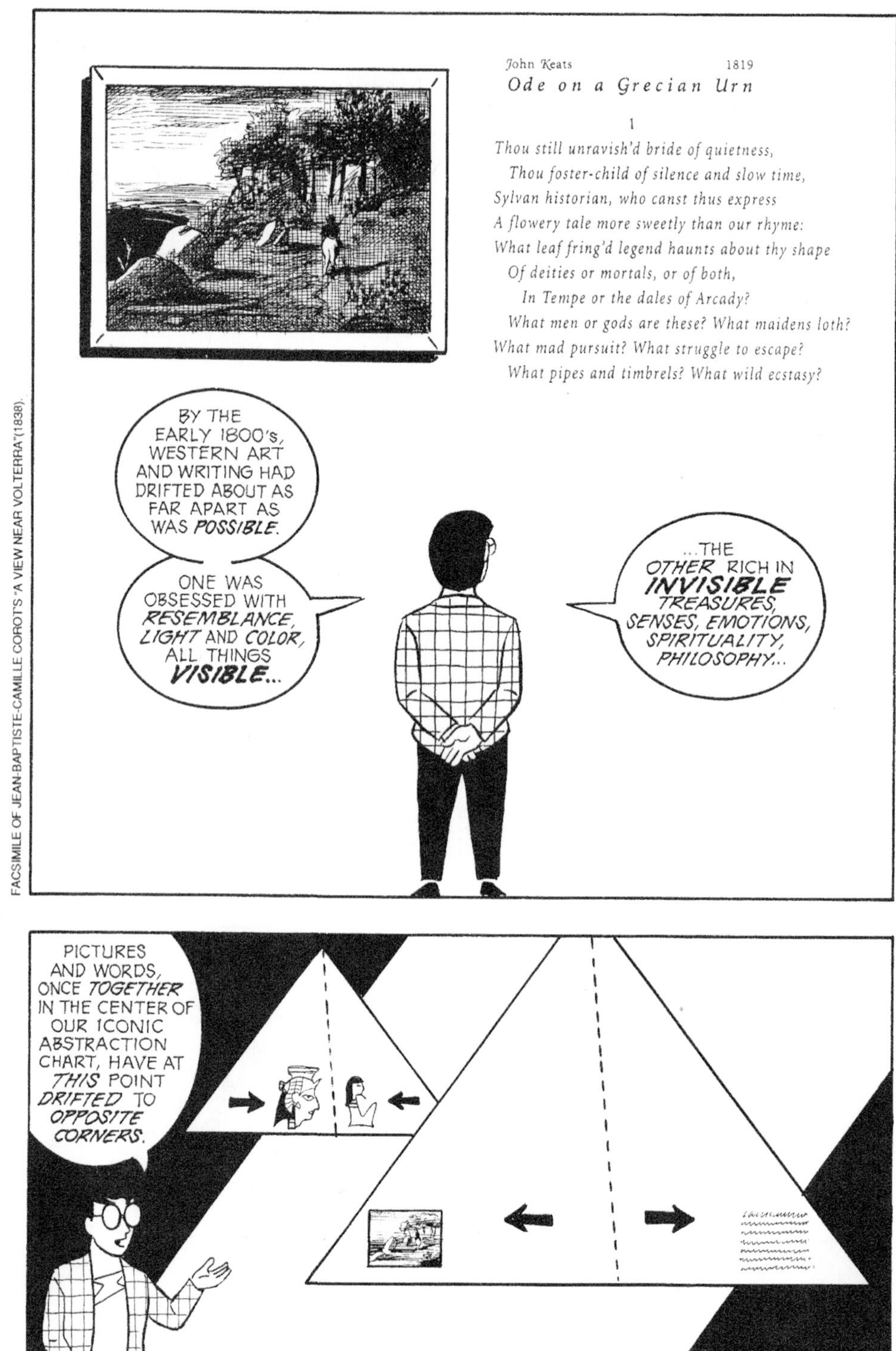

FACSIMILE OF JEAN-BAPTISTE-CAMILLE COROT'S "A VIEW NEAR VOLTERRA" (1838).

FIRST STANZA OF KEATS' POEM.

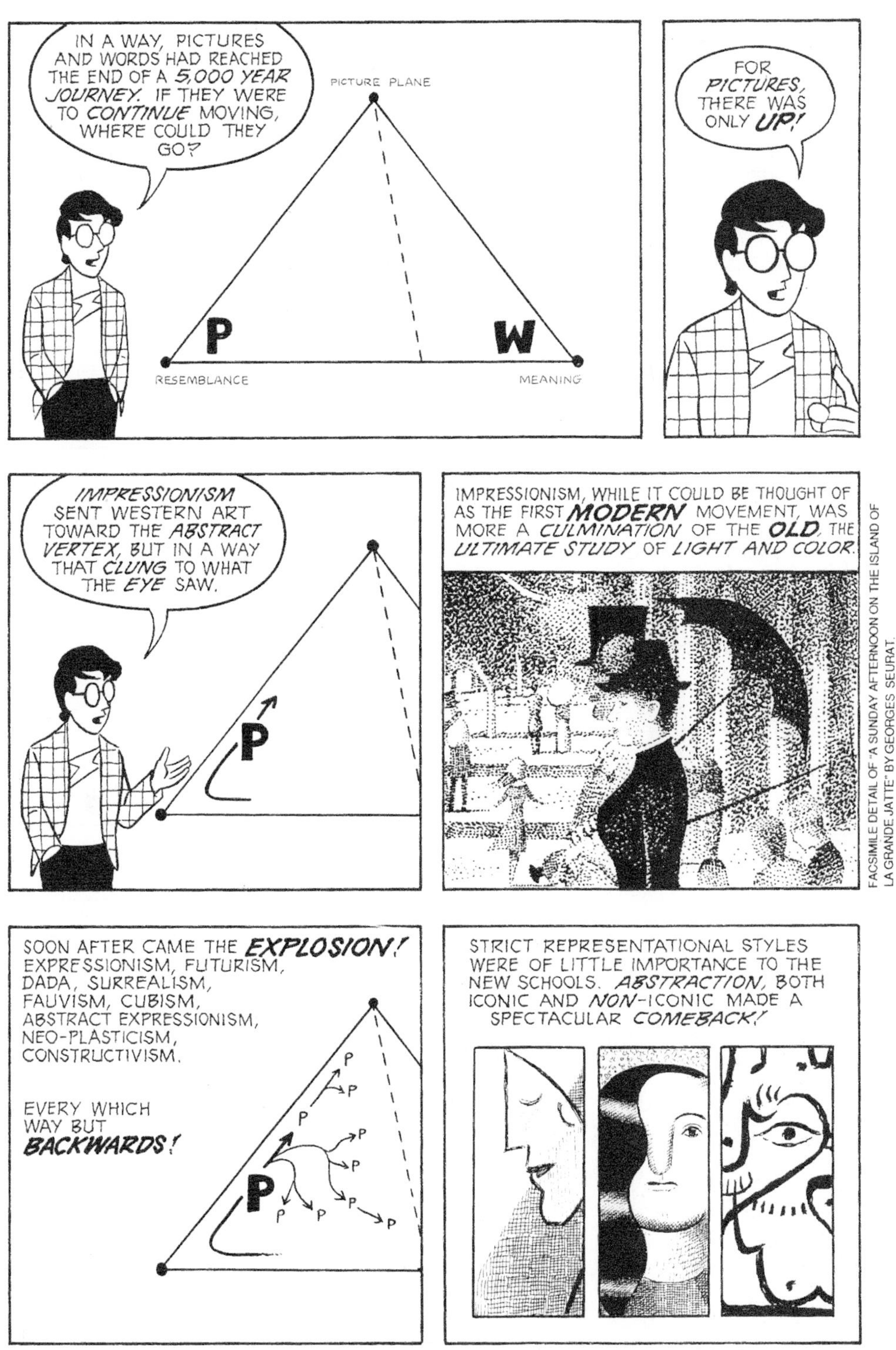

IN A WAY, PICTURES AND WORDS HAD REACHED THE END OF A 5,000 YEAR JOURNEY. IF THEY WERE TO CONTINUE MOVING, WHERE COULD THEY GO?
PICTURE PLANE
P
W
RESEMBLANCE
MEANING
FOR PICTURES, THERE WAS ONLY UP!
IMPRESSIONISM SENT WESTERN ART TOWARD THE ABSTRACT VERTEX, BUT IN A WAY THAT CLUNG TO WHAT THE EYE SAW.
P
IMPRESSIONISM, WHILE IT COULD BE THOUGHT OF AS THE FIRST MODERN MOVEMENT, WAS MORE A CULMINATION OF THE OLD, THE ULTIMATE STUDY OF LIGHT AND COLOR.
SOON AFTER CAME THE EXPLOSION! EXPRESSIONISM, FUTURISM, DADA, SURREALISM, FAUVISM, CUBISM, ABSTRACT EXPRESSIONISM, NEO-PLASTICISM, CONSTRUCTIVISM.
EVERY WHICH WAY BUT BACKWARDS!
P
STRICT REPRESENTATIONAL STYLES WERE OF LITTLE IMPORTANCE TO THE NEW SCHOOLS. ABSTRACTION, BOTH ICONIC AND NON-ICONIC MADE A SPECTACULAR COMEBACK!

FACSIMILE DETAIL OF "A SUNDAY AFTERNOON ON THE ISLAND OF LA GRANDE JATTE" BY GEORGES SEURAT.

FACSIMILE DETAILS OF PORTRAITS BY PICASSO, LEGER AND KLEE.

46

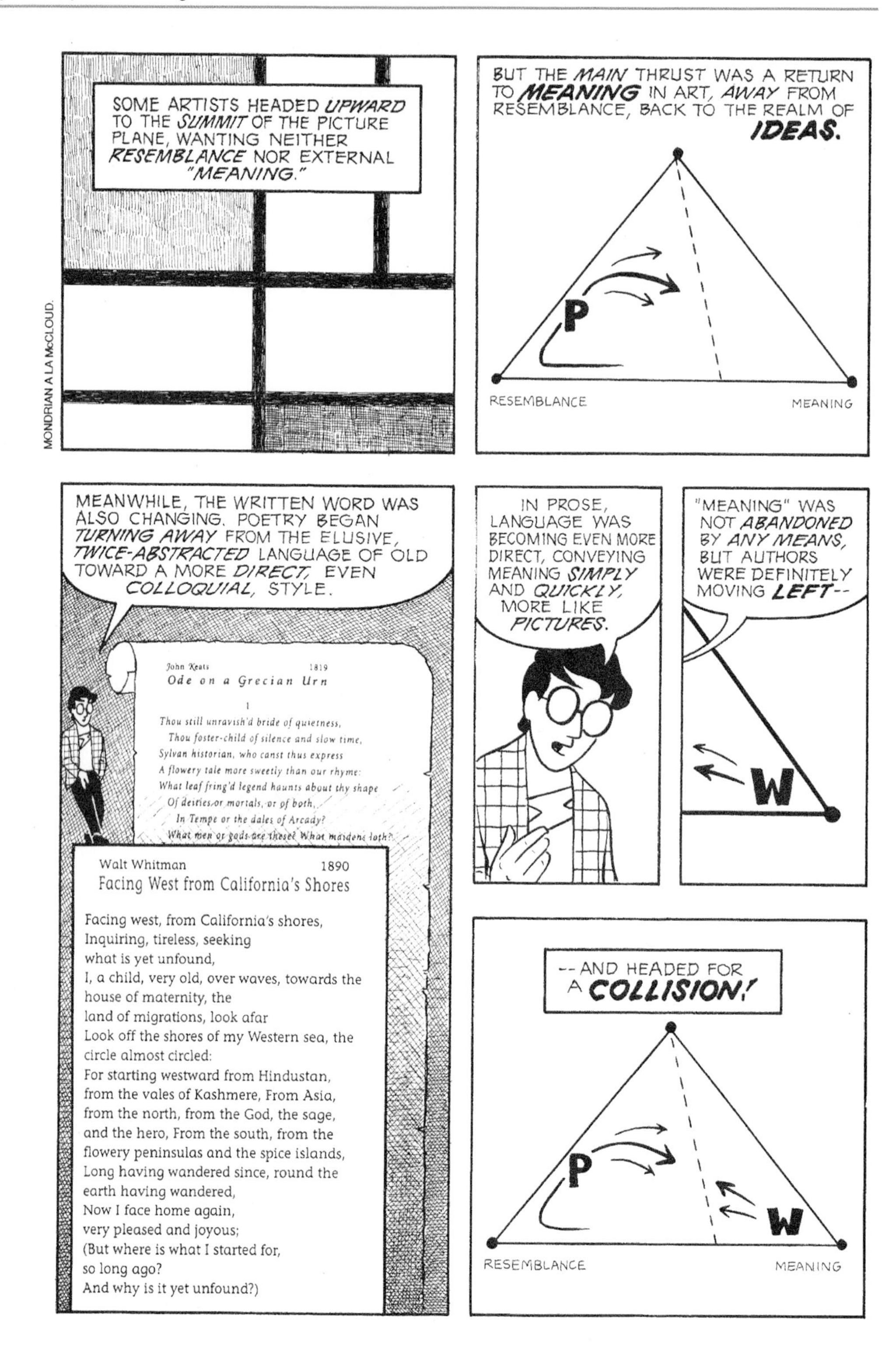
SOME ARTISTS HEADED UPWARD TO THE SUMMIT OF THE PICTURE PLANE, WANTING NEITHER RESEMBLANCE NOR EXTERNAL "MEANING."
MONDRIAN A LA McCLOUD.
BUT THE MAIN THRUST WAS A RETURN TO MEANING IN ART, AWAY FROM RESEMBLANCE, BACK TO THE REALM OF IDEAS.
P
RESEMBLANCE
MEANING
MEANWHILE, THE WRITTEN WORD WAS ALSO CHANGING. POETRY BEGAN TURNING AWAY FROM THE ELUSIVE, TWICE-ABSTRACTED LANGUAGE OF OLD TOWARD A MORE DIRECT, EVEN COLLOQUIAL, STYLE.
John Keats 1819
Ode on a Grecian Urn
I
Thou still unravish'd bride of quietness,
Thou foster-child of silence and slow time,
Sylvan historian, who canst thus express
A flowery tale more sweetly than our rhyme:
What leaf-fring'd legend haunts about thy shape
Of deities or mortals, or of both,
In Tempe or the dales of Arcady?
What men or gods are these? What maidens loth?
Walt Whitman 1890
Facing West from California's Shores
Facing west, from California's shores,
Inquiring, tireless, seeking
what is yet unfound,
I, a child, very old, over waves, towards the
house of maternity, the
land of migrations, look afar
Look off the shores of my Western sea, the
circle almost circled:
For starting westward from Hindustan,
from the vales of Kashmere, From Asia,
from the north, from the God, the sage,
and the hero, From the south, from the
flowery peninsulas and the spice islands,
Long having wandered since, round the
earth having wandered,
Now I face home again,
very pleased and joyous;
(But where is what I started for,
so long ago?
And why is it yet unfound?)
IN PROSE, LANGUAGE WAS BECOMING EVEN MORE DIRECT, CONVEYING MEANING SIMPLY AND QUICKLY, MORE LIKE PICTURES.
"MEANING" WAS NOT ABANDONED BY ANY MEANS, BUT AUTHORS WERE DEFINITELY MOVING LEFT--
W
--AND HEADED FOR A COLLISION!
P
W
RESEMBLANCE
MEANING

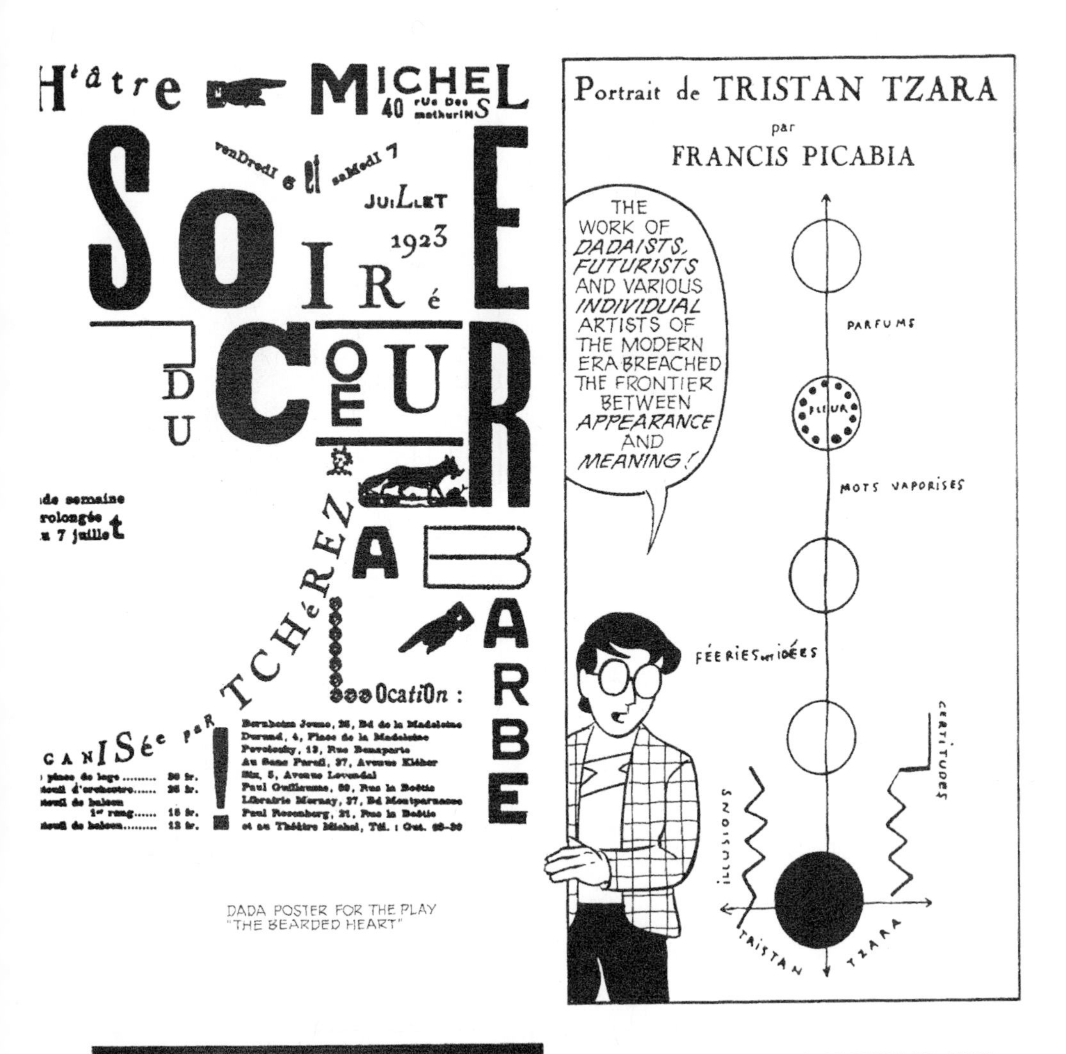

DADA POSTER FOR THE PLAY "THE BEARDED HEART"

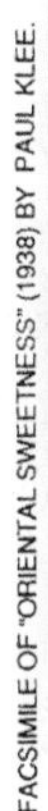

FACSIMILE OF "ORIENTAL SWEETNESS" (1938) BY PAUL KLEE.

WHILE SOME ARTISTS ADDRESSED THE IRONIES OF WORDS AND PICTURES *HEAD-ON!*

AND IN POPULAR CULTURE THE TWO FORMS COLLIDED AGAIN AND AGAIN WITHOUT ANY PRETENSES OF "HIGH" ART.
NOWHERE IS THIS COLLISION MORE THOROUGHLY EXPLORED THAN THE MODERN COMIC. AND IT'S NOT A RECENT OBSESSION.
LET'S GO BACK TO THE EARLY 1800's BEFORE ANY OF THIS HAPPENED, WHEN WORDS AND PICTURES HAD DRIFTED AS FAR APART AS POSSIBLE.
UP TO THAT POINT, EUROPEAN BROADSHEETS HAD OFFERED REMINDERS OF WHAT WORDS AND PICTURES COULD DO WHEN COMBINED.
BUT AGAIN IT WAS RODOLPHE TÖPFFER WHO FORESAW THEIR INTERDEPENDENCY AND BROUGHT THE FAMILY BACK TOGETHER AT LAST.
M. CRÉPIN ADVERTISES FOR A TUTOR, AND MANY APPLY FOR THE JOB.
TRANSLATION BY E. WIESE.

I'M SURE THAT THESE IDEAS WERE THE FURTHEST THING FROM TÖPFFER'S MIND WHEN HE PUT PEN TO PAPER--
--BUT THE FACT THAT THE MODERN COMIC WAS BORN JUST AS ART AND WRITING WERE PREPARING TO CHANGE DIRECTION IS AT LEAST INTRIGUING.
AND PERHAPS THIS COMMON THREAD OF UNIFICATION DID GROW OUT OF A SHARED INSTINCT OF THE DAY...
...AN INSTINCT WHICH SAID THAT WE HAD REACHED THE END OF A LONG JOURNEY AND THAT IT WAS TIME AT LAST TO HEAD FOR HOME.

UNFORTUNATELY FOR COMICS, NO SOONER HAD THE FINE ARTS REDISCOVERED THE LINK BETWEEN WORDS AND PICTURES--
--THAN MODERN ART ITSELF BECAME VIRTUALLY INCOMPREHENSIBLE TO THE AVERAGE VIEWER!
WHAT THE HECK IS THAT?!
IT'S A HOAX, I TELL YA! MY TWO-YEAR-OLD DAUGHTER CAN PAINT BETTER THAN THAT!
DO PEOPLE REALLY PAY MONEY FOR THIS??
COOL
IN FACT, THE GENERAL PUBLIC'S PERCEPTIONS OF "GREAT" ART AND "GREAT" WRITING HASN'T CHANGED MUCH IN 150 YEARS.* ANY ARTIST WISHING TO DO GREAT WORK IN A MEDIUM USING WORDS AND PICTURES WILL HAVE TO CONTEND WITH THIS ATTITUDE.
IN OTHERS AND IN THEMSELVES...
...BECAUSE, DEEP DOWN INSIDE, MANY COMICS CREATORS STILL MEASURE ART AND WRITING BY DIFFERENT STANDARDS AND ACT ON THE FAITH THAT "GREAT" ART AND "GREAT" WRITING WILL COMBINE HARMONIOUSLY BY VIRTUE OF QUALITY ALONE.
FACE
TWO EYES, ONE NOSE, ONE MOUTH.
Thy youth's proud livery, so gaz'd on now...
* NOT AS MUCH AS WE LIKE TO THINK IT HAS, ANYWAY.

THE ART FORM OF COMICS IS MANY CENTURIES OLD, BUT IT'S PERCEIVED AS A RECENT INVENTION AND SUFFERS THE CURSE OF ALL NEW MEDIA,
THE CURSE OF BEING JUDGED BY THE STANDARDS OF THE OLD.
EVER SINCE THE INVENTION OF THE WRITTEN WORD, NEW MEDIA HAVE BEEN MISUNDERSTOOD.
CAREFUL, JACOB! IF YOU KEEP DOING THIS, YOU'LL STOP USING YOUR MEMORY!
EACH NEW MEDIUM BEGINS ITS LIFE BY IMITATING ITS PREDECESSORS. MANY EARLY MOVIES WERE LIKE FILMED STAGE PLAYS, MUCH EARLY TELEVISION WAS LIKE RADIO WITH PICTURES OR REDUCED MOVIES.
FAR TOO MANY COMICS CREATORS HAVE NO HIGHER GOAL THAN TO MATCH THE ACHIEVEMENTS OF OTHER MEDIA, AND VIEW ANY CHANCE TO WORK IN OTHER MEDIA AS A STEP UP.
AND AGAIN, AS LONG AS WE VIEW COMICS AS A GENRE OF WRITING OR A STYLE OF GRAPHIC ART THIS ATTITUDE MAY NEVER DISAPPEAR.

WORDS AND PICTURES IN COMBINATION MAY NOT BE MY *DEFINITION* OF COMICS, BUT THE COMBINATION HAS HAD *TREMENDOUS INFLUENCE* ON ITS *GROWTH*.
A HUGE RANGE OF HUMAN EXPERIENCES CAN BE *PORTRAYED* IN COMICS THROUGH EITHER WORDS OR PICTURES.
AS A RESULT--AND DESPITE ITS MANY *OTHER* POTENTIAL USES -- COMICS HAVE BECOME *FIRMLY IDENTIFIED* WITH THE ART OF *STORYTELLING*.
AND *INDEED*, WORDS AND PICTURES HAVE *GREAT* POWERS TO TELL STORIES WHEN CREATORS FULLY EXPLOIT THEM *BOTH*.
DADA
HORROR
SURREALISM
BLANK VERSE
HISTORICAL FICTION
EPIC POETRY
FOLK TALES
SEQUENTIAL ART
SOCIAL ALLEGORY
EROTICA
MYSTERY
ADAPTATIONS
RELIGIOUS TOPICS
STREAM OF CONSCIOUSNESS
SATIRE
AND SO FAR, WE'VE ONLY SEEN THE *TIP OF THE ICEBERG!*
AS CHILDREN, WE "SHOW AND TELL" *INTERCHANGEABLY*, WORDS AND IMAGES COMBINING TO TRANSMIT A *CONNECTED SERIES OF IDEAS*.
IT'S GOT ONE OF *THESE* THINGS.
THE DIFFERENT WAYS IN WHICH WORDS AND PICTURES CAN *COMBINE* IN COMICS IS VIRTUALLY *UNLIMITED*.
BUT LET'S TRY TO BREAK IT DOWN INTO SOME DISTINCT *CATEGORIES*.

FIRST, WE HAVE THE WORD SPECIFIC COMBINATIONS, WHERE PICTURES ILLUSTRATE, BUT DON'T SIGNIFICANTLY ADD TO A LARGELY COMPLETE TEXT.
WE STUMBLED BACK TO THE APARTMENT SHORTLY BEFORE DAWN, VOMITING EVERY 20 YARDS.
JUDY GAVE ME HER KEYS AND SMILED.
THE UNITED STATES CONSTITUTION WAS ADOPTED BY THE SECOND CONTINENTAL CONGRESS IN 1787 AND PUT INTO EFFECT IN 1789.
THEN THERE ARE PICTURE SPECIFIC COMBINATIONS WHERE WORDS DO LITTLE MORE THAN ADD A SOUNDTRACK TO A VISUALLY TOLD SEQUENCE.
HE DID IT!
MMM...
MMM...
AND, OF COURSE, DUO-SPECIFIC PANELS IN WHICH BOTH WORDS AND PICTURES SEND ESSENTIALLY THE SAME MESSAGE.
GRIM-FACED, GEORGE LIFTED HIS LOLLYPOP.
BUT THE CAPTAIN'S MIGHTY BLOW MISSES ITS INTENDED TARGET!
BLAST! HE DODGED MY PUNCH AND I STRUCK THIS BRICK WALL!
I FEEL SO SAD!
...THOUGHT AMY.

ANOTHER TYPE IS THE **ADDITIVE** COMBINATION WHERE WORDS *AMPLIFY* OR *ELABORATE* ON AN IMAGE OR *VICE VERSA*.
MY HEAD FEELS LIKE A *SMASHED PUMPKIN!*
HOW D'YA LIKE MY *NEW THREADS*, BABE?
IS THIS THE SAME *JUPITER* OF MY YOUTH?
IN **PARALLEL** COMBINATIONS, WORDS AND PICTURES SEEM TO FOLLOW VERY DIFFERENT COURSES--WITHOUT *INTERSECTING*.
"TALKED TO *BILL* YET?"
"*SALLY* DID. *WHY?*"
"THE *TEST RESULTS* CAME BACK. ALL *NEGATIVE*."
"*REALLY?* THAT'S *GREAT!*"
WELL...
PEPPER.
CEREAL.
MILK.
BUTTER.
LIGHT BULBS.
STILL ANOTHER OPTION IS THE **MONTAGE** WHERE WORDS ARE TREATED AS INTEGRAL *PARTS* OF THE PICTURE.
CASH
FLOW
LINE
HAPPY!
154

PERHAPS THE MOST COMMON TYPE OF WORD/PICTURE COMBINATION IS THE INTER-DEPENDENT, WHERE WORDS AND PICTURES GO HAND IN HAND TO CONVEY AN IDEA THAT NEITHER COULD CONVEY ALONE.
MEANWHILE...
DID ANYONE SEE YOU?
THIS IS ALL I NEED TO STOP HIM!
I ASK YOU, DOES THIS GUY LOOK LIKE A C.E.O. TO YOU??
"AND JUST GUESS WHO DROVE UP IN BOB'S TRUCK AN HOUR LATER!"
HEY, MARGE!
OH, MY GOD!
HE'S LYING.
UH-HUH.
"AFTER COLLEGE, I PURSUED A CAREER IN HIGH FINANCE."
HURRY UP, WILLYA?!
INTERDEPENDENT COMBINATIONS AREN'T ALWAYS AN EQUAL BALANCE THOUGH AND MAY FALL ANYWHERE ON A SCALE BETWEEN TYPES ONE AND TWO.
GENERALLY SPEAKING, THE MORE IS SAID WITH WORDS, THE MORE THE PICTURES CAN BE FREED TO GO EXPLORING AND VICE VERSA.
P
W
P
W
W
P

IN COMICS AT ITS BEST, WORDS AND PICTURES ARE LIKE PARTNERS IN A DANCE AND EACH ONE TAKES TURNS LEADING.
WHEN BOTH PARTNERS TRY TO LEAD, THE COMPETITION CAN SUBVERT THE OVERALL GOALS...
YOW!
...THOUGH A LITTLE PLAYFUL COMPETITION CAN SOMETIMES PRODUCE ENJOYABLE RESULTS.
BUT WHEN THESE PARTNERS EACH KNOW THEIR ROLES--
--AND SUPPORT EACH OTHER'S STRENGTHS--
--COMICS CAN MATCH ANY OF THE ART FORMS IT DRAWS SO MUCH OF ITS STRENGTH FROM.

WHEN PICTURES CARRY THE WEIGHT OF CLARITY IN A SCENE, THEY FREE WORDS TO EXPLORE A WIDER AREA.
P
W
LET'S SAY I SHOW YOU A WOMAN WALKING ACROSS THE STREET IN THE RAIN, BUYING A PINT OF ICE CREAM AND EATING IT IN HER APARTMENT--
--ALL IN PICTURES.
GLÜGENN SPLATZEN ICE CREAM
CHOCOLATE CHOCOLATE CHIP

WHEN A SCENE SHOWS YOU ALL YOU "NEED" TO KNOW, LIKE THIS ONE, THE LATITUDE FOR SCRIPTING GROWS ENORMOUSLY.
I MAY BE ALONE LIKE THIS FOR A VERY LONG TIME.
IT COULD BECOME AN INTERNAL MONOLOGUE.
(INTERDEPENDENT)
PERHAPS SOMETHING WILDLY INCONGRUOUS
"MISSION CONTROL, MISSION CONTROL, DO YOU READ ME?"
(PARALLEL)

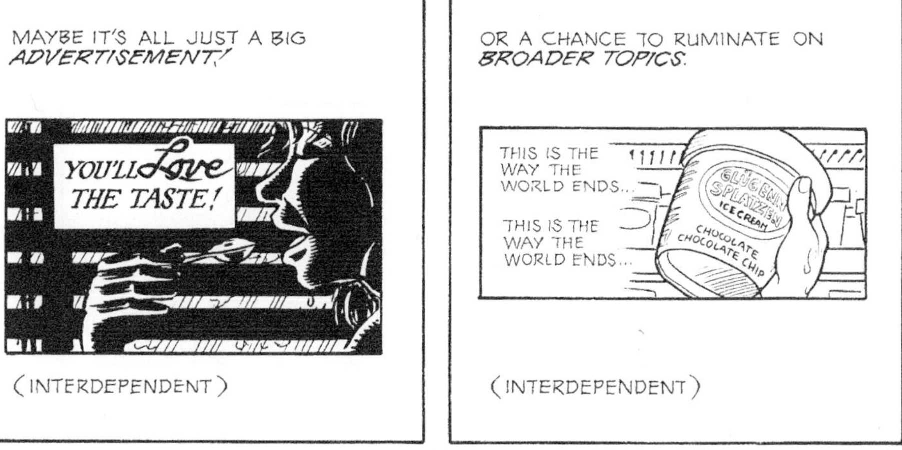
MAYBE IT'S ALL JUST A BIG ADVERTISEMENT!
YOU'LL Love THE TASTE!
(INTERDEPENDENT)
OR A CHANCE TO RUMINATE ON BROADER TOPICS.
THIS IS THE WAY THE WORLD ENDS...
THIS IS THE WAY THE WORLD ENDS...
GLÜGENN SPLATZEN ICE CREAM
CHOCOLATE CHOCOLATE CHIP
(INTERDEPENDENT)

I CROSSED THE STREET TO THE CONVENIENCE STORE. THE RAIN SOAKED INTO MY BOOTS.

I FOUND THE LAST PINT OF CHOCOLATE CHOCOLATE CHIP IN THE FREEZER.

THE CLERK TRIED TO PICK ME UP. I SAID *NO THANKS*. HE GAVE ME THIS CREEPY LOOK...

I WENT BACK TO THE APARTMENT--

--AND FINISHED IT ALL IN AN HOUR.

ALONE AT LAST.

I CROSSED THE STREET TO THE CONVENIENCE STORE. THE RAIN SOAKED INTO MY BOOTS.
I FOUND THE LAST PINT OF CHOCOLATE CHOCOLATE CHIP IN THE FREEZER.
THE CLERK TRIED TO PICK ME UP. I SAID NO THANKS. HE GAVE ME THIS CREEPY LOOK...
I WENT BACK TO THE APARTMENT--
--AND FINISHED IT ALL IN AN HOUR.
ALONE AT LAST.
NOW, ONE COULD JUST COMBINE THE PICTURES FROM PAGE 157 WITH THE WORDS FROM PAGE 159 --
--BUT WHAT ARE SOME OTHER OPTIONS?
I CROSSED THE STREET TO THE CONVENIENCE STORE. THE RAIN SOAKED INTO MY BOOTS.
IF THE ARTIST WANTS TO, HE/SHE CAN NOW SHOW ONLY FRAGMENTS OF A SCENE.
(WORD SPECIFIC)
OR MOVE TOWARD GREATER LEVELS OF ABSTRACTION OR EXPRESSION.
THE CLERK TRIED TO PICK ME UP. I SAID. NO THANKS. HE GAVE ME THIS CREEPY LOOK...
(AMPLIFICATION)
PERHAPS THE ARTIST CAN GIVE US SOME IMPORTANT EMOTIONAL INFORMATION.
I WENT BACK TO THE APARTMENT--
(INTERDEPENDENT)
OR SHIFT AHEAD OR BACKWARDS IN TIME.
--AND FINISHED IT ALL IN AN HOUR.
ALONE AT LAST.
(WORD SPECIFIC)

THE PICTURE PLANE
P
W
RESEMBLANCE
MEANING
HOWEVER MUCH WE MAY *CHART* THESE THINGS, THEY'RE ALL *ULTIMATELY* BEST LEFT TO THE CREATOR'S *INSTINCTS*.
THE MIXING OF WORDS AND PICTURES IS MORE *ALCHEMY* THAN SCIENCE.
SOME OF THE SECRETS OF THOSE *FIRST* ALCHEMISTS MAY HAVE BEEN LOST IN THE ANCIENT PAST.
BUT WE HAVE SOME POWERFUL MAGIC RIGHT HERE IN THE *20TH CENTURY, TOO!*
THE RICHNESS OF MODERN LANGUAGE IS AN *IRREPLACEABLE COMMODITY!*
PUBLIC LIBRARY OF
THIS IS AN *EXCITING TIME* TO BE MAKING COMICS, AND IN MANY WAYS I FEEL VERY *LUCKY* TO HAVE BEEN BORN WHEN I WAS.
STILL, I DO FEEL A CERTAIN *VAGUE LONGING* FOR THAT TIME OVER *50 CENTURIES AGO*--
--WHEN TO TELL WAS TO *SHOW*--
--AND TO SHOW WAS TO *TELL*.

Why Media Spreads

By Henry Jenkins, Sam Ford, and Joshua Green

This book is about the multiple ways that content circulates today, from top down to bottom up, from grassroots to commercial. As we explore circulation, we see the way value and meaning are created in the multiple economies that constitute the emerging media landscape. Our message is simple and direct: if it doesn't spread, it's dead.

We don't mean the kinds of circulation that have historically concerned publishers—that is, how many readers pick up this morning's edition of the *New York Times* or the *Wall Street Journal*. Any publication can cite its "circulation," especially since the rates paid for advertising are calculated based on those numbers. Like the "impressions" that online publishers tout, such circulation is concerned with making audience members into receptacles for mass-produced and mass-distributed content: as eyeballs in front of a screen (in television terms), butts in seats (in film or sports terms), or whatever other body parts media companies and brands hope to grab next. But those definitions of "circulation" are really talking about distribution, where the movement of media content is largely—or totally—controlled by the commercial interests producing and selling it. These logics of distribution best apply in a broadcast media world, where a small number of producers—Random House or CBS or Warner Brothers—create discrete and finished products for mass audiences.

Instead, *Spreadable Media* examines an emerging hybrid model of circulation, where a mix of top-down and bottom-up forces determine how material is shared across and among cultures in far more participatory (and messier) ways. The decisions that each of us makes about whether to pass along media texts—about whether to tweet the latest gaffe from a presidential candidate, forward a Nieman Marcus [sic] cookie recipe email, or share video of a shoplifting seagull—are reshaping the media landscape itself.

This shift from distribution to circulation signals a movement toward a more participatory model of culture, one which sees the public not as simply consumers of preconstructed messages but as people who are shaping, sharing, reframing, and remixing media content in ways which might not have been previously imagined. And they are doing so not as isolated individuals but within larger communities and networks, which allow them to spread content well beyond their immediate geographic proximity. Henry Jenkins (1992) coined the term "participatory culture" to describe the cultural production and social interactions of fan communities, initially seeking a way to differentiate the activities of fans from other forms of spectatorship. As the concept has evolved, it now refers to a range of different groups deploying media production and distribution to serve their collective interests, as various scholars have linked considerations of fandom into a broader discourse about participation in and through media. Previous work on participatory culture stressed acts of reception and production by media audiences; this book extends that logic to consider the roles that networked communities play in shaping how media circulates. Audiences are making their presence felt by actively shaping media flows, and producers, brand managers, customer service professionals, and corporate communicators are waking up to the commercial need to actively listen and respond to them.

While many content creators are struggling with the growing prominence of such grassroots audience practices, an array of online communication tools have arisen to facilitate informal and instantaneous sharing. These platforms offer new capacities for people to pass along media artifacts—and, in the process, to seek models to generate revenue through the activities of their users. However, while new tools have proliferated the means by which people can circulate material, word-of-mouth recommendations and the sharing of media content are impulses that have long driven how people interact with each other. Perhaps nothing is more human than sharing stories, whether by fire or by "cloud" (so to speak). We must all be careful not to suppose that a more participatory means of circulation can be explained solely (or even primarily) by this rise of technological infrastructure, even as these new technologies play a key role in enabling the shifts this book describes.

Spreadable Media focuses on the social logics and cultural practices that have enabled and popularized these new platforms, logics that explain *why* sharing has become such common practice, not just *how*. Our approach doesn't presume that new platforms liberate people from old constraints but rather suggests that the affordances of digital media provide a catalyst for reconceptualizing other aspects of culture, requiring the rethinking of social relations, the reimagining of cultural and political participation, the revision of economic expectations, and the reconfiguration of legal structures.

Throughout this book, we use terms such as "spread," "spreadable," or "spreadability" to describe these increasingly pervasive forms of media circulation. "Spreadability" refers to the potential—both technical and cultural—for audiences to share content for their own purposes, sometimes with the permission of rights holders, sometimes against their wishes. As we have been working on this book, some critics have challenged the term "spreadable," suggesting it sounds more appropriate for describing cream cheese or peanut butter. (The term originated in relation to "stickiness," as we will soon explain.) However, think of "spreadability" as a placeholder, perhaps like a stub in Wikipedia; it is something we can shape a conversation around. Our goal is not to create a new buzzword. Instead, we want to challenge readers to think through the metaphors we all use when talking about how content moves across the cultural landscape—to resist terminology that might distort how we understand these trends and to continue seeking terms that more accurately describe the complexity of how we all engage with media texts.

Our focus on terminology is more than mere semantics. We believe that language matters deeply and that the metaphors we all use to describe the patterns we see shape how we understand our world. We become blind to some phenomena and biased toward others. By discussing "spreadable media," we aim to facilitate a more nuanced account of how and why things spread and to encourage our readers to adopt and help build a more holistic and sustainable model for understanding how digital culture operates.

Sticky Content, Spreadable Practices

"Spreadability" refers to the technical resources that make it easier to circulate some kinds of content than others, the economic structures that support or restrict circulation, the attributes of a media text that might appeal to a community's motivation for sharing material, and the social networks that link people through the exchange of meaningful bytes.

Our use of "spreadability" is perhaps most effective as a corrective to the ways in which the concept of "stickiness" has developed over time to measure success in online commerce. A term that has emerged through marketing discourse and which was popularized by its use in Malcolm Gladwell's *The Tipping Point* (2000) and elsewhere, "stickiness" broadly refers to the need to create content that attracts audience attention and engagement. Gladwell proposes, "There is a simple way to package information that, under the right circumstances, can make it irresistible.

All you have to do is find it" (2000, 132). Gladwell uses "stickiness" to describe the aspects of media texts which engender deep audience engagement and might motivate them to share what they learned with others. In short, to Gladwell, sticky content is material that people want to spread.

As online business models have been built, the use of "stickiness" in the business setting refers to centralizing the audience's presence in a particular online location to generate advertising revenue or sales. This notion of stickiness closely resembles the "impressions" model that has shaped the measurement of audiences for broadcast content. In broadcast media, impressions are measured by how many people see a particular piece of media, whereas stickiness refers to the mechanisms motivating people to seek out and spend time at a particular site. Applied to the design of a website, companies hope to achieve stickiness by placing material in an easily measured location and assessing how many people view it, how many times it is viewed, and how long visitors view it.

Under the stickiness model, companies gain economic value by offering merchandise through some kind of e-commerce catalog, charging for access to information (through some kind of subscription or service fee), or selling the eyeballs of site visitors to some outside party, most often advertisers. Such advertising deals are sold by juxtaposing advertising messages on a page alongside content, and advertising rates are based on the number of impressions a page generates or the number of clicks an ad receives. This conception of stickiness focuses on monitoring and generating specific site data on the actions of each site visitor.

This mindset has also come to define the way companies understand the popularity of content online. Online publications look at which articles are viewed the most and which hold people's attention the longest. Media companies assess which videos are viewed the most and longest. Nonprofits and corporate websites alike define success online based on web traffic. Audiences themselves often think about the popularity of content in terms of views at a particular destination. In short, even beyond the instances when advertising deals are being brokered, this narrow definition of "stickiness" has provided the logic by which success has come to be understood.

Stickiness capitalizes on the easiest way companies have found to conduct business online—rather than the ways audiences want to and do experience material online. It privileges putting content in one place and making audiences come to it so they can be counted. Such "destination viewing" often conflicts with both the dynamic browsing experience of individual Internet users and, more importantly, with the circulation of content through the social connections of audience members.

What we mean by "spreadability" will become clearer by contrasting it with this stickiness model. We compare the terms here not to indicate that web traffic shouldn't matter or to suggest that spreadability is the "opposite" of stickiness, but rather to demonstrate the limits of models too closely focused on stickiness.

The Migrations of Individuals versus the Flow of Ideas – Like other impressions-based constructs, stickiness models focus on counting isolated audience members. Spreadability recognizes the importance of the social connections among individuals, connections increasingly made visible (and amplified) by social media platforms. This approach may still include quantitative measures of how frequently and broadly content travels, but it makes important actively listening to the way media texts are taken up by audiences and circulate through audience interactions.

Centralized versus Dispersed Material – Because deep quantitative audience measurement is at the center of stickiness, online destinations can become a virtual "roach motel." For instance, at an extreme, some sites disable the Back button, making it difficult for users to escape once they have stumbled on the site, without closing their browser. The key to stickiness is putting material in a centralized location, drawing people to it, and keeping them there indefinitely in ways that best benefit the site's analytics. (The process is not that unlike a corral; audiences are pushed along predefined routes matching a publisher's measurement needs and are then poked and prodded for analytics data.) Spreadability emphasizes producing content in easy-to-share formats, such as the embed codes that YouTube provides, which make it easier to spread videos across the Internet, and encouraging access points to that content in a variety of places.

Unified versus Diversified Experiences – A sticky mentality requires brands to create a centralized experience which can best serve the purposes of multiple audiences simultaneously, offering limited and controlled ways for individuals to "personalize" content within a site's format. A spreadable mentality focuses on creating media texts that various audiences may circulate for different purposes, inviting people to shape the context of the material as they share it within their social circles.

Prestructured Interactivity versus Open-Ended Participation – Sticky sites often incorporate games, quizzes, and polls to attract and hold the interests of individuals. The participatory logic of spreadability leads to audiences using content in unanticipated ways as they retrofit material to the contours of their particular community. Such activities are difficult for creators to control and even more difficult to quantify.

Attracting and Holding Attention versus Motivating and Facilitating Sharing – Since sticky business models are built on demographic data, audiences are often constructed as a collection of passive individuals. Spreadability, by contrast, values the activities of audience members to help generate interest in particular brands or franchises.

Scarce and Finite Channels versus Myriad Temporary (and Localized) Networks – Stickiness retains the broadcast mentality of one-to-many communication, with authorized official channels competing against one another for the audience's attention. The spreadability paradigm assumes that anything worth hearing will circulate through any and all available channels, potentially moving audiences from peripheral awareness to active engagement.

Sales Force Marketing to Individuals versus Grassroots Intermediaries Advocating and Evangelizing – By "grassroots intermediaries," we mean unofficial parties who shape the flow of messages through their community and who may become strong advocates for brands or franchises. Grassroots intermediaries may often serve the needs of content creators, demonstrating how audiences become part of the logic of the marketplace and challenging what "grassroots" means, as such activities often coexist or even coincide with corporate agendas. They are not, however, employed or regulated by content creators and also may act counter to corporate goals.

Separate and Distinct Roles versus Collaboration across Roles – In a stickiness model, it's clear who the "producer," the "marketer," and the "audience" is. Each performs a separate and distinct purpose. In a spreadable model, there is not only an increased collaboration across these roles but, in some cases, a blurring of the distinctions between these roles.

•

While stickiness may provide the prevailing logic for the creation of online business models, any content or destination that has gained relevance with audiences online has done so through processes of spreadability, whether authorized or not. From the word-of-mouth spread of recommendations about a brand to the passing along of media content that might ultimately drive interest (and traffic) back to a particular destination, success in the stickiness model has always ultimately depended on audience activity that happens away from the site—in other words, from spreadability.

However, in our focus on spreadability, we are not arguing against the creation of online destinations; we recognize that creators and audiences alike benefit from a central base for their brand or content, whether to serve a business model or simply to have an easy-to-find location. After all, mass-media channels are still valuable resources for getting information out and sharing content of great common interest because they have such widespread reach.

Instead, the "distribution" reach of sticky destinations and the "circulation" reach of spreadable media should coexist, a relationship aptly illustrated by a 2010 experiment by advertising agency Hill Holliday. The firm created an online microsite called Jerzify Yourself that allowed visitors to remake their image in the style of the stars of popular MTV television show *Jersey Shore*. Hill Holliday created the site as part of a project researching the ways word spread about content. The site generated substantial word of mouth, and was featured in a variety of articles and blog posts. Beyond just researching the audiences of those blogs (their immediate "reach" or "distribution potential"), Hill Holliday also used a URL-tracing mechanism to see what additional traffic came from the ongoing spread of those stories and posts.

The experiment created a unique URL for Jerzify Yourself for every site that linked back to the page. Ilya Vedrashko (2010a) reports that five of the top six sites in terms of driving direct traffic to Jerzify Yourself created almost as much traffic through reshares, as people who first discovered the site through that article/mention passed the link on to their networks. One site's coverage generated twice as many eventual visits through ongoing recirculation of the link as it did via direct click-throughs from the original story. Writes Vedrashko, "Counting only the direct clicks from any site is likely to underestimate the site's total value. [. . .] Content that's designed to be spreadable can nearly double the referred traffic through re-shares." Meanwhile, some sites were more "spreadful" than others. In particular, Vedrashko notes that the site which sent the most direct traffic to Jerzify Yourself actually led to the least amount of resharing.

Despite changes in communication and culture, stickiness still matters. Returning to Gladwell's use of the term, stickiness acts as a measure of how interested an audience member is in a media text. Any creator—whether media company, fan, academic, or activist—produces material in the hope of attracting audience interest. (Perhaps peanut butter isn't such a bad way to represent spreadable media after all: content remains sticky even as it is spread.)

What Susan Boyle Can Teach about Spreadability

What happens when many people make active decisions to put content in motion by passing along an image, song, or video clip to friends and family members or to larger social networks? As this question suggests, much of what is being exchanged at the current moment is entertainment, as fan communities have been among the first to embrace the practices of spreadability. These fan activities will thus be a recurring topic throughout this book. Yet what we say about the spread of entertainment content also increasingly applies to news, branding and advertising, political messages, religious messages, and a range of other materials, and we will draw on a variety of these examples to provide a multidimensional picture of the current media environment.

To start, let's contrast a U.S. "broadcast" phenomenon with a widespread entertainment clip. The finale of the 2009 season of

American Idol drew 32 million viewers in the U.S., making it one of the year's most viewed two-hour blocks on broadcast television. In comparison, a video of Scottish woman Susan Boyle auditioning for *Britain's Got Talent* was viewed more than 77 million times on YouTube. This latter figure reflects only the viewership of the original upload; YouTube is a space where success often encourages duplication. A cursory survey showed more than 75 different copies of Boyle's audition performance of "I Dreamed a Dream" available on the site when we conducted our research, with versions uploaded from users in Brazil, Japan, the Netherlands, the U.S., and various parts of the U.K. We found edited copies, high-definition copies, and copies with closed captioning and subtitles in various languages. Many of these versions have themselves been viewed millions of times. Even this scan of the Boyle phenomenon considers YouTube alone, ignoring other large online video-sharing platforms such as Chinese site Tudou (where a quick glance showed at least 43 copies of the original performance) or Dailymotion (where there were 20 easily found copies of her first audition video).

Since any of these videos can be watched more than once by the same person, it is difficult, if not impossible, to reduce these views to a raw "eyeball" count equivalent to television ratings. No matter how you look at it, however, the viewership of the widely spread Susan Boyle clip dwarfs that of the highest-rated show on U.S. broadcast television. The Boyle video was broadcast content made popular through grassroots circulation.

The Susan Boyle audition was the result of mainstream commercial media production, to be sure. The original video was professionally produced and edited to maximize its emotional impact. One segment introduced a character and set up ridiculing expectations, while the next swept the rug out from under those expectations with a spectacular performance of a popular West End song, followed by the emotional responses of the overwhelmed judges and audience. Audience enjoyment of the event was shaped by people's general familiarity with the genre conventions of reality television and/or by particular perception of an investment in Simon Cowell's tough judge character, whose schoolboy grin at the segment's end represents the ultimate payoff for her spectacular performance. And, once the video had been widely spread, the visibility of Boyle was amplified through mainstream media coverage; she was, for instance, interviewed on *Good Morning America* and spoofed on the *Tonight Show*.

Nevertheless, Boyle's international success was not driven by broadcast distribution. Fans found Susan Boyle before media outlets did. The most popular Susan Boyle YouTube video reached 2.5 million views in the first 72 hours and drew 103 million views on 20 different websites within the first nine days of its release. Meanwhile, Boyle's Wikipedia page attracted nearly half a million views within a week of its creation.

While the performance was part of a mainstream television program in the U.K., it was not commercially available at all to viewers in the

U.S. and many other countries. Instead, the video was circulated and discussed through a variety of networks online. Her entry into the U.S. market and her spread around the Internet was shaped by the conscious decisions of millions of everyday people functioning as grassroots intermediaries, each choosing to pass her video along to friends, family members, colleagues, and fellow fans. The Susan Boyle phenomenon would not have played out in the same way if not for the relationships and communities facilitated by social network sites, media sharing tools, and microblogging platforms.

Part of what allowed the Susan Boyle video to travel as far and as fast as it did was the fact it *could* travel so far so fast. People had the right tools and knew what to do with them. Sites such as YouTube make it simple to embed material on blogs or share it through social network sites. Services such as bitly allow people to share links quickly and efficiently. Platforms such as Twitter and Facebook facilitate instantaneous sharing to one's social connections. All of these technical innovations made it that much easier for the Susan Boyle video to spread.

However, the mere existence of individual technologies to facilitate the sharing of the clip does little to explain how the Susan Boyle performance was spread. We must consider the integrated system of participatory channels and practices at work that support an environment where content could be circulated so widely. For instance, uses of particular services should not be viewed in isolation but rather in connection, as people embrace a range of technologies based on if and when a particular platform best supports the cultural practices in which they want to engage.

But, more fundamentally, we have to understand the cultural practices that have both fueled the rise of these sharing technologies and evolved as people discover how these platforms might be used. For instance, the Susan Boyle video was widely shared because the participating public is more collectively and individually literate about social networking online; because people are more frequently and more broadly in contact with their networks of friends, family, and acquaintances; and because people increasingly interact through sharing meaningful bits of media content.

Taken together, this set of social and cultural practices, and the related technological innovations which grew up around them, constitute what we call a "networked culture." These cultural practices were certainly not created by new technologies. We've long known that news stories generate conversations; many of us have a cousin or grandmother who (still!) clips newspaper articles to put on the refrigerator, in an album, or in the mail to us. Social historian Ellen Gruber Garvey (2003), for example, has offered a glimpse into how circulation and value were connected in the scrapbook culture of nineteenth-century U.S. women. Their primary activity was sifting through newspapers, magazines, and other periodicals, gathering material to archive. In an era when news publications themselves actively engaged in "recirculation"—local papers reprinted stories originally published elsewhere if they seemed of interest to local readers—scrapbook collectors stored the most appealing of these ephemeral accounts for future generations. In turn, newspapers sometimes capitalized on this early form of "user-generated content," publishing retrospectives featuring reader-curated material. These archival practices accelerated with the twentieth-century rise of photocopiers, which facilitated easier reproduction and sharing of found material.

However, what happened in a predigital world now occurs with exponentially greater speed and scope, thanks to the affordances of online social tools. According to a CNN research project ("Shared News" 2010), the average global Internet user receives 26 news stories per week via social media or email and shares 13 news stories online. According to a report from the Pew Research Center (Purcell et al. 2010), 75 percent of respondents received news forwarded through email or posted on social network sites, and 52 percent shared links to news with others via those means.

This news gathering is shaped by a strong desire to contribute to ongoing conversations with friends, family, and co-workers. Of the respondents to the Pew study, 72 percent said they follow the news because they enjoy talking with others about what is happening in the world, and 50 percent said they rely to some degree on people around them to tell them the news they need to know. All of this suggests a world where citizens count on each other to pass along compelling bits of news, information, and entertainment, often many times over the course of a given day.

In this networked culture, we cannot identify a single cause for why people spread material. People make a series of socially embedded decisions when they choose to spread any media text: Is the content worth engaging with? Is it worth sharing with others? Might it be of interest to specific people? Does it communicate something about me or my relationship with those people? What is the best platform to spread it through? Should it be circulated with a particular message attached? Even if no additional commentary is appended, however, just receiving a story or video from someone else imbues a range of new potential meanings in a text. As people listen, read, or view shared content, they think not only—often, not even primarily—about what the producers might have meant but about what the person who shared it was trying to communicate.

Indeed, outside the U.K., most people probably encountered the Susan Boyle video because someone sent a link or embedded it in a Facebook update or blog: many people shared the video to boast their accomplishment of discovery. They could anticipate sharing the video with people who hadn't seen it, precisely because the material was not widely available on television. Some may have heard conversations about it and searched on YouTube; for many more, the message came in the midst of other social exchanges, much as an advertisement comes as part of the commercial television flow. Yet, while an advertisement might feel like an intrusion or interruption, people often welcome spreadable media content from friends (at least discerning ones) because it reflects shared interests.

It is apparent that some people were passing Boyle's performance along as a gesture of friendship to build interpersonal relationships, while others used the material to contribute to a community organized around a key interest. This difference is a key distinction: between friendship-based and interest-based networks (Ito et al. 2009). An avowed Christian, Boyle became the focus of online prayer circles. Science blogs discussed how someone with her body could produce such a sound. Karaoke singers debated her technique, reporting an incident when she was thrown out of a karaoke bar because she was now viewed as a professional performer. Reality-television blogs debated whether her success would have been possible on U.S. television given that *American Idol* excludes people her age from competing. Fashion blogs critiqued and dissected the makeover she was given for subsequent television appearances. Boyle's video spread, then, as a result of the many conversations it enabled people to have with each other, whether among friends or within communities of common interest. (And, of course, many may have done some of both.)

From a commercial perspective, *American Idol* had a full season to build public interest in its finale yet failed to attract the scale of attention the seven-minute clip of Boyle sparked. Contrary to speculation that the Boyle phenomenon would be short-lived, her debut album released by Columbia Records months later enjoyed groundbreaking advance sales, surpassing The Beatles and Whitney Houston on Amazon's charts (Lapowsky 2009). The album sold more than 700,000 copies in its first week, the largest opening-week sales of any album released that year. As Columbia Records chair Steve Barnett explained, "People wanted to get it and own it, to feel like they're a part of it" (Sisario 2009). Of course, those who helped circulate the video already felt they were "a part of it."

While such success makes for an impressive business story, the initial international popularity of the Susan Boyle moment wasn't driven by a plan for counting impressions and raking in the cash. Most of the many millions of people who streamed the Boyle clip were part of a "surplus audience" for whom producers had not built a business model. Boyle's performance was part of a British program with no commercial distribution in most other countries, so the majority of people sharing the video couldn't turn on a television network—cable or broadcast—and watch the next installment of *Britain's Got Talent*. They couldn't stream the show legally online. They couldn't buy episodes from iTunes. Despite relationships with multiple television networks, FremantleMedia couldn't get the show into commercial distribution quickly enough for transnational viewers to catch up with the Brits. Given the global circulation of information about Susan Boyle online, anyone who wanted to know what happened on *Britain's Got Talent* heard about it within seconds of its airing. In short, market demand dramatically outpaced supply.

The spread of Susan Boyle demonstrates how content not designed to circulate beyond a contained market or timed for rapid global distribution can gain much greater visibility than ever before, thanks to the active circulation of various grassroots agents, while television networks and production companies struggle to keep up with such unexpected, rapidly escalating demand.

The case also allows us to challenge the commonplace assertion that, in the era of Web 2.0, user-generated content has somehow displaced mass media in the cultural lives of everyday people. Lucas Hilderbrand notes, "For mass audiences, broadcast, cable and satellite television still dominate, [. . .] and network content will continue to feed these streams. And I suspect that for many audiences, network content—new or old—still drives users to YouTube, and amateur content is discovered along the way, through the suggested links, alternative search results, or forwarded emails" (2007, 50). What Hilderbrand's account misses, though, is that much of the mass-media content encountered on YouTube and other such platforms is unauthorized—not so much user-generated content as user-circulated content. While audiences' sharing and spreading of Susan Boyle's video may still fit within the broad logic of capitalism, the capacity of audiences to alter the circulation of content is nevertheless causing consternation for companies and artists trying to figure out how to reshape broadcast business and marketing models or to design new business altogether. In cases where bottom-up activities have not been ordained by content creators, various corporate entities have labeled many of these activities "piracy" or "infringement"—even when unauthorized forms of sharing create value for both the people circulating the material and those who created it, as was clearly the case with the Boyle video.

Piracy is a concept that will surface repeatedly throughout the book, and every reader will probably draw the line between "appropriate" and "inappropriate" practices at different points. In fact, one of the problems of the current use of "piracy" is that it shortcuts important conversations we should all be having about the economic and cultural impact of different types of media sharing. Such discussions might draw on legal notions that consider the nature of the use (commercial or noncommercial, education or entertainment), the degree to which the use is transformative, the portion of the work being taken, and so forth in determining what constitutes piracy.

As a rule, though, we are reserving the term "pirate" in this book for people who profit economically from the unauthorized sale of content produced by others. This is not a legal distinction but a moral one that matters for many of those whose activities we will discuss. Yet, as the Boyle example suggests, piracy is as much a consequence of the market failures of media companies to make content available in a timely and desirable manner as it is a consequence of the moral failure of audience members seeking meaningful content by hook or by crook if it is not legally available. We will thus make the case that the appropriation and recirculation of even entire works may sometimes work in the best interests of not only the culture at large but also of the rights holders.

One can only speculate whether Boyle's album and career could have been even more successful or whether *Britain's Got Talent* could have been a transnational hit had the show's producers been prepared to react quickly to this clip's spread. The failure to reconceptualize the way *Britain's Got Talent* circulates reduced what could have been a season-long event into one discrete moment: a single video. For instance, one imagines that few viewers of Boyle's audition video know that multiethnic dance troupe Diversity won the season rather than Boyle. This case not only demonstrates the cultural and technological system at the core of a networked culture but also the inability of the media industries—whose structure and models are still largely configured to a "broadcast" and "sticky" mentality—to actively listen and respond to unanticipated interest in their material.

We've Found a Cure for Viral Media!

As we question how and why content circulates today, it is all too easy to accept an inadequate answer, a theory of media distribution that makes a media text sound more like a smallpox-infected blanket. Many observers described the Susan Boyle phenomenon as an example of "viral media," a term whose popularity has been fueled by the rapid rise of social network sites alongside declining advertising rates and an extremely fragmented audience for broadcast media.

Viral metaphors do capture the speed with which new ideas circulate through the Internet. The top-down hierarchies of the broadcast era now coexist with the integrated system of participatory channels described earlier in the chapter which have increased access to tools for communication and publishing. As marketers and media companies struggle to make sense of this transformed media landscape, one of the most common explanations is that media content now disseminates like a pandemic—spreading through audiences by infecting person after person who comes into contact with it. Even if the media industries must accept the shift from an environment where people congregate around media texts to a context where audiences do the circulating, they hope to preserve creator control. The promise is simple, if deceptive: create a media virus, and success will be yours. Thus, marketers and media distributors that are unsure of how to reach audiences through traditional "broadcast" or "sticky" methods now pray material will "go viral."

The term "viral" first appeared in science fiction stories, describing (generally bad) ideas that spread like germs. Something of the negative consequences of this simplified understanding of the viral are suggested by this passage from Neal Stephenson's science fiction novel *Snow Crash*: "We are all susceptible to the pull of viral ideas. Like mass hysteria. Or a tune that gets into your head that you keep on humming all day until you spread it to someone else. Jokes. Urban Legends. Crackpot religions. Marxism. No matter how smart we get, there is always this deep irrational part that makes us potential hosts for self-replicating information" (1992, 399). Here, the viral is linked to the "irrational," the public is described as "susceptible" to its "pull," and participants become unknowing "hosts" of the information they carry across their social networks.

Echoing this theme, Douglas Rushkoff's 1994 book *Media Virus* argues that media material can act as a Trojan horse, spreading without the user's conscious consent; people are duped into passing a hidden agenda while circulating compelling content. Rushkoff writes that certain "media events are not *like* viruses. They *are* viruses," and such a virus seeks "to spread its own code as far and wide as possible—from cell to cell and from organism to organism" (1994, 9; emphasis in original). There is an implicit and often explicit proposition that the spread of ideas and messages can occur without users' consent and perhaps actively against their conscious resistance; people are duped into passing a hidden agenda while circulating compelling content.

This notion of the media *as* virus taps a larger discussion that compares systems of cultural distribution to biological systems. Rushkoff describes the culture through which modern U.S. residents navigate as a "datasphere" or "mediaspace"—"a new territory for human interaction, economic expansion, and especially social and political machination"—that has arisen because of the rapid expansion of communication and media technologies (1994, 4). He writes,

> Media viruses spread through the datasphere the same way biological ones spread through the body or a community. But, instead of traveling along an organic circulatory system, a media virus travels through the networks of the mediaspace. The "protein shell" of a media virus might be an event, invention, technology, system of thought, musical riff, visual image, scientific theory, sex scandal, clothing style or even a pop hero—as long as it can catch our attention. Any one of these media virus shells will search out the receptive nooks and crannies in popular culture and stick on anywhere it is noticed. Once attached, the virus injects its more hidden agendas into the datastream in the form of ideological code—not genes, but a conceptual equivalent we now call "memes." (9–10)

This theme of comparing the spread of cultural material to biological processes extends beyond the "virus" metaphor. In the 1976 book *The Selfish Gene*, famed British evolutionary biologist Richard Dawkins introduced the "meme," which was to become both an incredibly important and incredibly overused idea, just like its viral companion. The meme is a cultural equivalent to the gene—the smallest evolutionary unit. "Cultural transmission is analogous to genetic transmission," Dawkins argues (1976, 189), writing,

> Just as genes propagate themselves in the gene pool by leaping from body to body via sperms or eggs, so memes propagate themselves in the meme pool by leaping from brain to brain via a process which, in the broad sense, can be called imitation. If a scientist hears, or reads about, a good idea, he passes it one to his colleagues and students. He mentions it in his articles and his lectures. If the idea catches on, it can be said to propagate itself, spreading from brain to brain. (192)

Dawkins notes in later editions (1989, 2006) that the notion of the meme has itself spread in memelike fashion—it provides a compelling way to understand the dispersion of cultural movements, especially when seemingly innocuous or trivial trends spread and die in rapid fashion. In a moment when the meme pool—the cultural soup which Dawkins describes as the site where memes grow—is overflowing with ideas, being able to create or harness a meme seems to promise anyone the chance to ride the waves of participatory culture.

However, while the idea of the meme is a compelling one, it may not adequately account for how content circulates through participatory culture. While Dawkins stresses that memes (like genes) aren't wholly independent agents, many accounts of memes and viral media describe media texts as "self-replicating." This concept of "self-replicating" culture is oxymoronic, though, as culture is a human product and replicates through human agency.

Simplified versions of these discussions of "memes" and "media viruses" have given the media industries a false sense of security at a time when the old attention economy has been in flux. Such terms promise a pseudoscientific model of audience behavior. The way these terms are now used mystify the way material spreads, leading professional communicators on quixotic quests to create "viral content."

The term "viral marketing" was first popularized in relation to Hotmail in 1995, after the creators of the service used the phrase to describe why their service gained millions of users within months (Jurvetson and Draper 1997). At the bottom of every email sent, a marketing message appeared which offered, "Get your free Web-based email at Hotmail." The term described the process well. People communicated and—in the process—sent along a marketing message, often without realizing it had happened.

Yet the viral metaphor does little to describe situations in which people actively assess a media text, deciding who to share it with and how to pass it along. People make many active decisions when spreading media, whether simply passing content to their social network, making a word-of-mouth recommendation, or posting a mash-up video to YouTube. Meanwhile, active audiences have shown a remarkable ability to circulate advertising slogans and jingles against their originating companies or to hijack popular stories to express profoundly different interpretations from those of their authors.

"Viral marketing," stretched well beyond its original meanings, has been expected to describe all these phenomena in the language of passive and involuntary transmission. Its precise meaning no longer clear, "viral media" gets invoked in discussions about buzz marketing and building brand recognition while also popping up in discussions about guerrilla marketing, exploiting social network sites, and mobilizing audiences and distributors.

Ironically, this rhetoric of passive audiences becoming infected by a media virus gained widespread traction at the same time as a shift toward greater acknowledgment that audience members are active participants in making meaning within networked media. Shenja van der Graaf maintains that viral marketing is "inherently social": "the main feature of viral marketing is that it heavily depends on interconnected peers" (2005, 8); van der Graaf uses "viral" to describe content that circulates in ways linked to network behavior, citing participation within a socially networked system as a central requirement of "viral" behavior. This focus on how audiences pass material along, however, is distorted by the metaphor of infection that "viral" invokes.

Confusion about viral media will not be easily resolved. The term is at once too encompassing and too limiting, creating false assumptions about how culture operates and distorted understandings of the power relations between producers and audiences. As we have been making this argument over the past few years while working on this project, we have found a growing number of marketers and media professionals also challenging the term. (See, for instance, Yakob 2008; Arauz 2008; Caddell 2009b; Askwith 2010; Hasson 2010; Chapman 2010.) The term even received the most nominations for elimination in Lake Superior State University's annual "List of Banished Words from the Queen's English for Mis-use, Over-use, and General Uselessness" (2010). Bluntly put, an antidote for the viral needs to be discovered; we hope this book contributes to that growing charge.

In contrast, the concept of "spreadability" preserves what was useful about earlier communication models—the idea that the effectiveness and impact of messages is increased and expanded by their movement from person to person and community to community. Spreadability recognizes the ways later theorists such as van der Graaf have revised the earliest, relatively static and passive conceptions of "viral" to reflect the realities of the new social web, while suggesting that this emerging paradigm is so substantively different from the initial examples that it requires adopting new terminology. Our use of "spreadable media" avoids the metaphors of "infection" and "contamination," which overestimate the power of media companies and underestimate the agency of audiences. In this emerging model, audiences play an active role in "spreading" content rather than serving as passive carriers of viral media: their choices, investments, agendas, and actions determine what gets valued.

However, while this book combats the use of "viral" to describe many processes in which people are actively involved in circulating and shaping the meaning of content, we want to acknowledge that there still remain examples of "viral marketing." Ilya Vedrashko (2010b) argues that, as marketers (hopefully) shift away from "viral marketing" as a catch-all term, they cannot forget that there are still literal examples of viral marketing which do not seek to engage audiences but rather deploy automated ways to induce audience members to unwittingly pass along their marketing messages.

As Iain Short (2010) points out, for instance, many applications for Twitter and Facebook send automated marketing updates to a person's followers without a user actively passing this material along. Thus, downloading an app might cause a Facebook user's friends to get pinged with a message encouraging them to join, or buying an animal on Farmville might send an update to all of a user's Facebook friends (whether or not they play the game). In the instance of Facebook's Open Graph feature, users receive notice that a friend is reading a particular story or watching a certain video in his or her Facebook news feed. In order to see the content, users have to download an application for that publisher, which then starts sharing what they read to their friends' feeds. In all these cases, messages are sent "from the user," without the user crafting the messages or often even being aware the message has been generated.

The use of "viral marketing" should be reserved only for those marketing concepts that really do not rely on the agency of audience members to circulate media texts for their own purposes and through their own relationships. Vedrashko writes,

> The entire debate over the terminology might look to a marketing practitioner like an Ivory Tower nitpicking but it is an important one because metaphor-based terms rely on our understanding of the underlying concepts to guide our actions. An attempt to create a "viral" video will be informed by what one knows about viruses, which among marketing professionals isn't a lot, anyway. On the other hand, a creator of a "spreadable" video will be drawing upon an entirely different body of knowledge, perhaps a theory about *why people gossip*, or the related *theory of social capital*. (2010b)

As Vedrashko suggests, the choice of metaphors sets expectations. If viral success means elements of a campaign have to be spread rapidly among audiences in pandemic proportions, then many companies are likely to be disappointed by the distribution they achieve. For instance, a 2007 JupiterResearch report found that only 15 percent of marketers launching viral campaigns were successful in "prompting their consumers to promote their messages for them." By using the term "spreadable media," we refer to (and draw on cases that describe) not just those texts which circulate broadly but also those that achieve particularly deep engagement within a niche community. In many cases, such content does not obtain the type of scale that would qualify for many people's definition of "viral success," yet the text beçame highly spread among the particular audiences the product hoped to reach.

Further, if companies set out thinking they will make media texts that do something to audiences (infect them) rather than for audiences to do something with (spread it), they may delude themselves into thinking they control people. Conversely, understanding spreadability will allow audiences and activists to form new connections and communities through their active role in shaping the circulation of media content. The concept of spreadability also gives these groups new means to mobilize and respond to decisions made by companies and governments in ways that challenge decisions that adversely effect them and to exploit gaps in the system which may allow them to serve their own needs.

"Comcast Must Die"

Companies are not just worried about making their content "go viral," though. Marketers have also been using the metaphor to make sense of how their customers' communication about a company now has the potential to circulate widely.

Fifteen years ago, the degree to which audiences had direct access to brands, and vice versa, was limited. Direct mail may have targeted messages at particular customers. Brands with retail outlets had a direct customer touchpoint, but the brand ambassadors in this case—retail employees—were (and remain) among the least respected, trained, and compensated members of the organization. Some companies had sales forces that aggressively contacted potential customers but often only through a one-way message, as during the "telemarking craze." The most robust site of contact between customer and company was customer service, a division in most companies that has been marginalized and is often measured by efficiency—how quickly employees can get customers off the phone—rather than any prioritization of customer engagement (Yellin 2009). Thus, most correspondence between brand and company was one-way, providing little room for the customer to shape the experience.

These conditions persist. However, when corporate websites emerged by the mid-1990s, no one fully realized how substantially they would shift a company's relationship with its audiences. Few of the companies creating brochure-like websites at the time completely considered that brands had the opportunity to tell their stories directly to the audience outside the constraints of advertising spots on television and radio and without going through the third-party voice of journalists. There would be a fundamental shift in how everyone "consumes," as interested people could seek content from companies when they wanted it—to juxtapose and assess corporate messages directly from the source and to publish what they find online for family, friends, colleagues, and strangers to see.

Brands and entertainment properties cannot return to the one-directional communication flows of the broadcast era, when they had the perception of control, so companies must listen to and learn from their audiences if they want to enjoy long-term success.

This "lack of control" is particularly noticeable when it comes to customer complaints. In a world of spreadable media, what were once considered solely "customer service" issues are increasingly "public relations" issues as well (which is ironic, considering "customer service" was, in the early twentieth century, once called "public relations" [Yellin 2009, 22]), as customers spread their own stories about companies.

Comcast, the largest cable operator in the U.S., has learned this lesson with particular pain. Cable operators have long struggled with customer complaints and dissatisfaction, displeasure well illustrated by a 2006 video of a Comcast technician falling asleep on customer Brian Finkelstein's couch while on hold with the company's own help line. Finkelstein's video spread rapidly and widely and received coverage in a variety of traditional media outlets as well. The drowsy technician was fired, and Comcast received a steady stream of negative publicity online as frustrated customers added their own commentary to the video.

The sleepy Comcast technician was only one of their spreading troubles. For instance, there was the much-recounted tale of LaChania Govan, the Illinois Comcast customer whose repeated attempts to resolve a customer service issue in 2005 led to employees changing her account name—and bill—to "Bitch Dog," Similar attention was heaped on 75-year-old Virginia Comcast customer Mona Shaw, who became so angered at her customer service treatment in 2007 that she smashed up the office with a hammer (Yellin 2009, 2–8). Journalist Bob Garfield (2007) shared his own "Hell on Earth" story about Comcast customer service, beginning his *Advertising Age* column with the declaration "Comcast must die." Garfield started a campaign against the cable operator on the site ComcastMustDie.com. And amid these videos, stories, and campaigns were the myriad individual complaints that Comcast customers increasingly voiced across blogs, microblogging platforms, and discussion forums.

Companies now face building pressure to use their online presence not just to communicate their own messages but to respond to the demands of disgruntled customers as well. Comcast listened to some degree, one could argue out of necessity, over time creating a specific department to respond to issues raised online. In February 2008, Comcast Executive Support Manager Frank Eliason (who had been with the company six months) was named the company's "Director of Digital Care." The department Eliason created now reaches out to bloggers, Twitterers, and other online discussants, attempting to proactively resolve their problems. In the process, the "Comcast Cares" initiative has addressed thousands of customers and simultaneously generated significant publicity. *BusinessWeek*, for instance, named Eliason (who has since gone on to work for financial services company Citi as its head of social media) "the most famous customer service manager in the U.S." (Reisner 2009). Although in 2009 Bob Garfield still called Comcast "a vast, greedy, blundering, tone-deaf corporate colossus," he noted that the company "has heard our angry voices and taken concrete steps in the process of putting customers first." Meanwhile, many people in customer service and communications look to Comcast's online customer service response as an exemplar that companies should follow to create online communication platforms which respond to customer questions and reach out to those who complain.

Despite the praise, Comcast's customer service remains far from ideal. Its pioneering work using social media platforms to listen and respond to negative customer experiences still serves as a quick fix to the larger issues that plague service providers. In 2010, for example, Gizmodo published a letter received by a customer who was told his service would be disconnected if he didn't pay the $0.00 he owed (Golijan 2010), while another customer who praised Comcast's Twitter communication shared his ongoing frustrations once he was connected to others within the company (Paul 2010). These are only two of a regular stream of customers expressing frustrations with the company's traditional communication modes.

Further, the "Comcast Cares" initiative, and the general perspective that customer service issues become a higher priority when customers have their own online presence, means that some customers get better treatment than others. See, for instance, this account from *Slate*:

> People with more clout seem to get better service. One Twitterer with fewer than 20 followers told me that though he's tweeted about Comcast frequently, the company has responded only to tell him its customer-service phone number. Another—with about 300 followers—told a better story: When she complained about a service problem, Comcast made special arrangements for a refund. And Glenn Fleishman, a tech journalist with more than 1,600 followers, got the best deal of all. [He] quickly got a call from an executive in the escalation department, who offered to waive [a $1,300 early-cancellation] fee. (Manjoo 2009)

As long as companies treat customer service issues online with some degree of concern about whether the customer is "an influencer," customers will receive different levels of response based on their perceived "public relations threat" (not to mention the lack of recourse for those who lack easy access to these communication platforms). And, in devoting significant energy to responding to those customers who complain loudest, without fixing underlying customer service issues companies might, if anything, encourage people to "spread their complaint" as their first course of action, influenced by the horror stories of phone trees and endless hold times awaiting them at a customer call center.

Even though Comcast and all large companies still have miles to go in fairly and fully prioritizing customer service, the spreadable media environment has made listening to audiences a greater priority for many marketers and media companies. Public relations and corporate communication departments are increasingly using their online presence to address the messages customers are circulating, a sign of the power which visible and socially connected audience members have to shape the agendas of companies through the messages they spread. In other words, companies are feeling more pressure to think not just about how audiences might spread messages about a brand (and content from the brand) but also about how their own corporate presence might "spread" to connect with the messages audiences are circulating about them.

Participatory Culture Reconsidered

Spreadability assumes a world where mass content is continually repositioned as it enters different niche communities. When material is produced according to a one-size-fits-all model, it imperfectly fits the needs of any given audience. Instead, audience members have to retrofit it to better serve their interests. As material spreads, it gets remade: either literally, through various forms of sampling and remixing, or figuratively, via its insertion into ongoing conversations and across various platforms. This continuous process of repurposing and recirculating is eroding the perceived divides between production and consumption.

Whitney Phillips's doctoral work at the University of Oregon focuses on the cultural practices, productions, and performances associated with 4Chan, an online community that actively encourages behavior which is often described as "antisocial" or "troll-like." Phillips argues that even disrespectful remixing is generative. In our enhanced book, she argues that 4Chan members have adopted a distinctive model for thinking about the "contributions" they make to culture, actively seizing on memes as tools for creativity and production:

> As understood by trolls, memes are not passive and do not follow the model of biological infection. Instead, trolls see (though perhaps "experience" is more accurate) memes as microcosmic nests of evolving content. [. . .] Memes spread—that is, they are actively engaged and/or remixed into existence—because something about a given image or phrase or video or whatever lines up with an already-established set of linguistic and cultural norms. In recognizing this connection, a troll is able to assert his or her cultural literacy and to bolster the scaffolding on which trolling as a whole is based, framing every act of reception as an act of cultural production.

For 4Chan members, the concept of the meme as a self-perpetuating phenomenon beyond human control might contribute to the spontaneity and disruption the group hopes to achieve. Phillips (2009) has argued elsewhere that 4Chan may have been the birthplace for widely spread images that represented U.S. President Barack Obama as Batman character The Joker, which some supporters of the U.S. conservative Tea Party movement adopted for protest signs during their public opposition to President Obama's national health care plan.

While the *Los Angeles Times* (Grad 2009) identified the artist of one of the most widely spread versions as college student Firas Alkhateeb, the image emerged from a larger series of remixes by the 4Chan community as they toyed with marketing material produced for the 2008 Batman film *The Dark Knight*. Other remixes included transforming John McCain into The Joker, along with Sarah Palin, Hillary Clinton, various pop stars, and, of course, pictures of cute cats. While most of these remixes didn't circulate broadly outside 4Chan, some members of the Tea Party found particular resonance in the image of Obama as the antisocial joker. Within 4Chan, memes serve as themes for ongoing conversations and fodder for creative activity, with each variation demonstrating and requiring particular cultural knowledge. Much as 4Chan hijacked images from Christopher Nolan's movie, the Tea Party poached these images from 4Chan, changing their political valances yet again. All of this suggests the ways that the appropriation, remixing, and recirculation of content via the mechanisms of participatory culture are increasingly impacting conversations far removed from what once might have been seen as niche communities. As this happens, we are seeing the erosion of traditional boundaries—between fans and activists, creativity and disruption, niche and mainstream in the 4Chan example, or between commercial and grassroots, fan and producer in some of the examples we will consider later in this section.

This book will suggest a range of groups who are strongly motivated to produce and circulate media materials as parts of their ongoing social interactions, among them activists who seek to change public perceptions of an issue of concern to the group; religious groups who seek to spread "the Word"; supporters of the arts—especially of independent media—who seek to build a base to bolster alternative forms of cultural expression; enthusiasts for particular brands that have become signposts for people's identities and lifestyles; bloggers who seek to engage others about the needs of local communities; collectors and retro audiences seek greater access to residual materials; members of subcultures seeking to construct alternative identities; and so forth.

In particular, we will frequently use entertainment fandom as a reference point because fan groups have often been innovators in using participatory platforms to organize and respond to media texts. As early as the mid-nineteenth century, amateur publishers began to print newsletters about shared interests and to circulate them across the country, ultimately leading to the formation of the Amateur Press Association (Petrik 1992). The rise of science fiction fandom in the 1920s and 1930s (Ross 1991) built on this foundation, representing one of the most prominent and enduring examples of organized fan communities.

Television fandom, in turn, has provided a supportive context through which many women, excluded from the male-only club that science fiction fandom had largely become, could develop their skills and hone their talents. By the 1970s, many women were remixing television footage to create their own fanvids, writing and editing their own zines, creating elaborate costumes, singing original folk songs, and painting images, all inspired by their favorite television series (Bacon-Smith 1992; Jenkins 1992; Coppa 2008). With the rise of networked computing, these fan communities did important work, providing their female participants with access to new skills and technologies as their members took their first steps into cyberspace, reversing early conceptions about the gendering of digital culture as a space only for masculine mastery. In particular, female fans were early adopters of social network technologies such as LiveJournal and Dreamwidth, using the resources offered by new media technologies (podcasting, mp3s, video-sharing sites) to create their own distinctive forms of participatory culture.

These types of communities have embraced new technologies as they emerged, particularly when such tools offered them new means of social and cultural interactions. Rather than looking at platforms such as YouTube and Twitter as "new," we consider these sites where multiple existing forms of participatory culture—each with its own historical trajectory, some over a century old—come together, which is part of what makes such platforms so complex to study. The popularity of Twitter, for instance, was driven by how efficiently the site facilities the types of resource sharing, conversation, and coordination that communities have long engaged in. The site's early success owes little to official brand presence; big-name entertainment properties, companies, and celebrities began flocking to the microblogging platform only after its success was considered buzzworthy (a few exceptional early adopters notwithstanding, of course). Launched at the 2007 South by Southwest Interactive festival, a favorite event for people in media-related industries, Twitter quickly enabled individual marketers to build their personal brands, to connect with one another, to demonstrate their social networking abilities, and to share their "thought leadership." Marketers, advertisers, and public relations professionals constituted a good portion of the early professionals using the site at a time when the rules of marketing were rapidly changing and a new crop of professionals were cementing their status and demonstrating their prowess in the "digital era."

The same year Twitter launched, so too did *Mad Men*, AMC's multi-Emmy-award-winning series about 1960s advertising agency Sterling Cooper. *Mad Men* celebrates what many people consider a "golden era" of U.S. mass marketing. The series serves as both a retrospective on the broadcast era and an exploration of another time in marketing when the rules were in flux and new advertising practices were developing around an increasingly important new media form (in this case, television).

It almost seems inevitable now that Twitter would prove a natural extension for the drama of *Mad Men*. Since season one, ad man Don Draper and fellow Sterling Cooper employees Pete Campbell, Joan Holloway, and Roger Sterling (or, rather, someone performing their identities) had been providing advice to readers through a Tumblr blog. However, on August 12, 2008, in the midst of the series's second season, Draper showed up on Twitter, gaining several thousand followers in a few days. Soon, Pete, Joan, Roger, and almost the full cast of *Mad Men* characters arrived. During and between episodes, their followers could watch the characters interact and even join conversations with them. Some wholly new creations began to appear in the Twitter/*Mad Men* narrative as well, including Sterling Cooper mailroom employee Bud Melman and the office's Xerox copy machine.

The *Mad Men* characters on Twitter were often playful and self-referential. Despite the obvious questions about how characters from the 1960s were using a modern communication platform, why they would share personal thoughts publicly, or how a Xerox machine could tweet, the interaction largely fit within the parameters of the show's storyline, deepening engagement with existing stories rather than challenging the narrative or taking it in new directions. Some tweets referenced facts the audience knew but most characters didn't, such as the closeted homosexuality of art director Sal. Others alluded to contemporary political events in relation to developments on the show, such as the rise to prominence of Joe "the plumber" Wurzelbacher as the quintessential middle-class citizen during the 2008 U.S. presidential election (King 2009).

A growing number of high-profile bloggers, especially in the fan and brand spheres, praised AMC's marketing prowess. This praise was somewhat misdirected, however: as it turned out, the tweeting *Mad Men* (like their Tumblr forebears) were not affiliated with AMC or the show. Instead, fans of the show had inhabited the identities of favorite characters. As the popularity of these virtual versions of *Mad Men*'s characters escalated, AMC contacted Twitter to ascertain who was behind the accounts. Twitter interpreted this inquiry as a copyright challenge from AMC and suspended several user accounts, under the guise of the Digital Millennium Copyright Act, on August 26, 2008, about two weeks after Draper's first tweet.

Twitter's suspension of the accounts fit a narrative that media fans and marketers alike knew well. Cease-and-desist orders have become an all-too-familiar means of correspondence between brands and their audiences in an era when prohibitionist corporate attitudes have collided with the collaborative nature of online social networks. There was immediate outcry against AMC for disrespecting its fans, pointing out that this activity had become an engine for generating interest and deepening engagement in a niche cable show with high critical praise but underwhelming ratings.

Part of AMC's ambivalence about *Mad Men*'s Twitter popularity was likely driven by marketers' uncertainty about ceding control, in some ways paralleling *Mad Men* creator Matthew Weiner's own reputation as a self-professed "control freak" who "approves every actor, costume, hairstyle and prop" (Witchel 2008). Weiner's reputation for tight control has extended beyond careful monitoring of the production; he has spoken out vehemently against ways of viewing or experiencing the show of which he disapproves. Says Weiner, "I met this guy who was creating software where you could watch *Mad Men* and you could chat with your friend while you're watching it, and things would pop up, and facts would pop up, and I said 'You're a human battery. Turn the fucking thing off! You're not allowed to watch the show anymore. You're missing the idea of sitting in a dark place and having an experience'" (quoted in Jung 2009). Weiner's response is emotional rather than legal, but both his complaint and AMC's actions in response to tweeting fans reflect a desire on the part of the media industries to maintain a tight grip on the reception and circulation of content. While the attention to detail that Weiner and his staff consistently display is part of what drives the show's reputation and its audience's enjoyment, expanding that tight control over how *Mad Men* is viewed, discussed, and spread restricts the show's circulation and dampens audience enthusiasm.

In many cases, however, the people writing as *Mad Men* characters had professional as well as personal interest in the show. Several were marketers themselves (Draper, for instance, was performed by strategist Paul Isakson with digital agency space150), and these fans drew on their professional identities to lobby for account reinstatement. Strategist Bud Caddell (who created the original character Bud Melman on Twitter) launched WeAreSterlingCooper.org to act as "command central" for the community of fans participating in the Twitter fan fiction and to articulate their rights to continue posting. The site issued "a rallying cry to brands and fans alike to come together and create together":

> Fan fiction. Brand hijacking. Copyright misuse. Sheer devotion. Call it what you will, but we call it the blurred line between content creators and content consumers, and it's not going away. We're your biggest fans, your die-hard proponents, and when your show gets cancelled we'll be among the first to pass around the petition. Talk to us. Befriend us. Engage us. But please, don't treat us like criminals. (Caddell 2008)

In the midst of the controversy, marketer Carri Bugbee, who had tweeted as @peggyolson, opened up new Twitter account @Peggy_Olson to continue writing. She started with, "I worked hard. I did my job. But the boys at Twitter are just as churlish as the boys at Sterling Cooper. Such a pity that they're so petty" (quoted in Siegler 2008). As fan tweeting and public discussion about the controversy increased, AMC did a swift about-face. Reportedly, AMC was following advice from its digital marketing agency Deep Focus, which itself had suffered criticism from marketers for preaching the value of social media while working with a client blatantly stomping on fans' passion and expressions (Learmonth 2008). More visible after the suspension controversy, the Sterling Cooper Twitterers returned to their posts.

Perhaps the *Mad Men* snafu resulted from the continued prevalence of "stickiness" as the chief way to measure success. If AMC evaluated the success of promoting *Mad Men* only by the easily measurable traffic through its official channels, then discouraging anything that might distract people from these destinations makes sense. From that mindset, fan-created material off official *Mad Men* channels is in competition with the show, and any traffic those outlets receive dilutes the reach of the show's official presence. This approach assigns no value to how fan-created-and-circulated content might drive awareness and engagement in a show indirectly, because it cannot be easily quantified.

Beyond the lingering desire to cling to a stickiness model, companies are often just uncertain about audiences spreading material for their own purposes. Though marketers idealize a dream audience that will passively pass along official (viral) messages, they know that the reality is much messier: fans who create new material or pass along existing media content ultimately want to communicate something about themselves. Fans may seek to demonstrate their own technical prowess, to gain greater standing within a niche community, to speculate about future developments, or to make new arguments using texts already familiar to their own audiences. As the *Mad Men* Twitter example proves, content often gains traction when people are given the latitude to use "official" media texts to communicate something about themselves.

The clash of professional concerns and fan enthusiasm within the *Mad Men* Twitter community caused particular consternation. Since the *Mad Men* Twitterers were marketers, professional motivations also drove their fan creation. Because of this, Deep Focus initially indicated that the Twitterers shouldn't be considered fans (Caddell 2008), suggesting their professions removed them from the logics of fandom, locating them instead squarely within the economics of "corporate America."

Further, Caddell describes infighting among the Twitterers as their popularity grew, with multiple contenders vying to portray popular characters and some more secretive members concerned that, if their true identities were "outed," their professional standing could be compromised. Meanwhile, some of these fans used their role in this controversy to demonstrate their own knowledge about Twitter and their understanding of fan enthusiasm, building recognition within the marketing community. After the controversy subsided, Caddell published the report "Becoming a Mad Man"; Bugbee built a new agency, Big Deal PR—drawing, in part, on the controversy and the Shorty Award she won for her Twitter portrayal of Peggy Olson; and several others have drawn on their participation in this fan activity through professional publications or conference presentations. In the process, tension over who claimed ownership of the fan activity and which Twitterers took credit for this moment of success became public. For instance, when Bugbee created a South by Southwest Interactive panel about the *Mad Men*/Twitter phenomenon, Caddell (2009a) publicly discussed the politics of panelist selection, blogging about the omission of himself and other prominent "fans" who were pivotal in the movement.

The circulation of media content within participatory culture can serve a range of interests, some cultural (such as promoting a particular genre or performer), some personal (such as strengthening social bonds between friends), some political (such as critiquing the construction of gender and sexuality within mass media), some economic (such as those which serve the immediate needs of everyday individuals, as well as those which serve the needs of media companies). We are not arguing that fans are somehow resisting consumer capitalism and its intellectual property regimes through these various processes and practices, as many of even these unauthorized activities might indirectly profit media companies and brands. Whatever audiences' motivations, they may discover new markets, generate new meanings, renew once-faded franchises, support independent producers, locate global content which was never commercially introduced in a local market, or disrupt and reshape the operations of contemporary culture in the process. In some cases, these outcomes are the direct goal of participatory culture; in others, they are a byproduct. Companies that tell audiences to keep their hands off a brand's intellectual property cut themselves off from these processes, many of which might create and prolong the value of media texts.

The media industries understand that culture is becoming more participatory, that the rules are being rewritten and relationships between producers and their audiences are in flux. Few companies, however, are willing to take what may be seen as substantial risks with potentially valuable intellectual property. Fans' desires and corporate interests sometimes operate in parallel, yet they never fully coincide, in part because even companies that embrace the ideals of audience engagement are uncertain about how much control to abdicate. Watching AMC and Deep Focus sometimes reject and sometimes embrace the efforts of their fans to promote *Mad Men*, regardless of these fans' alternative motivations, provides a glimpse into the limits of current industry understanding of what we call spreadable media. The fans in the *Mad Men* case are themselves part of the branded entertainment industry, using their recreational time to consider how this new cultural economy might operate. Some have publicly acknowledged that their actions crossed the lines which normally separate producers from their audiences, while others were wary to speak out, unsure what was at risk as they ventured into this uncertain terrain. However, these marketers/fans and their fictional characters articulated audience desires to participate more actively in producing and circulating media and professional desires to make marketing and media texts more participatory.

Corporate interests will never fully align with those of participatory culture, and frictions will frequently emerge. For instance, people are deeply ambivalent about how media companies and corporate communicators participate in such an environment. With audiences' greater autonomy, they seek more explicit acknowledgment from companies but are concerned with how the active participation of corporations might distort communities or that corporations will only embrace audience practices in the ways they can most easily profit from them. Participatory culture is not synonymous with the business practices that have been labeled Web 2.0. We are all struggling over the shape our culture(s) will take in the coming decades, a struggle being tackled on uneven terms and with unequal resources. We see participatory culture as a relative term—culture is more participatory now than it was under older regimes of media power in many places. Yet we are a long way away from anything approaching full participation.

All of this suggests ways we are revising the concept of participatory culture to reflect the realities of a dramatically altered and still-evolving mediascape. We are moving from an initial focus on fandom as a particular subculture to a larger model that accounts for many groups that are gaining greater communicative capacity within a networked culture and toward a context where niche cultural production is increasingly influencing the shape and direction of mainstream media. We are moving from focusing on the oppositional relationship between fans and producers as a form of cultural resistance to understanding those roles as increasingly and complexly intertwined. We are moving from a celebration of the growth of participatory opportunities toward a view tempered by concern for the obstacles blocking many people from meaningful participation. We will return throughout the book to debates about the terms of our participation, about how our participation is valued or blocked through various corporate policies and practices, and about which participants are welcomed, marginalized, and excluded.

Papyrus and Marble

The innovations, and struggles, of participatory culture that take place within the broad interplay between top-down institutional and bottom-up social forces have shaped the spread of media within and across cultures. There is a long history of such cultural exchanges, conducted through various channels and practices. The rise of networked computing and the ways its components have been absorbed into participatory culture and deployed through social network sites represents a new configuration of long-existing practices. (MIT media historian William Uricchio traces some key chapters of that history in our enhanced book, showing how media from coins to printed books have flowed within and across cultures.) Even if grassroots channels of communication may have disruptive effects on existing monopolies of knowledge, spreadable media needs to be understood in evolutionary rather than revolutionary terms.

How media circulates has been a central concern of media studies at least since the 1951 publication of Harold Innis's *The Bias of Communication*. In Innis's formulation, the dominant means of communication in a given society influences the production and control of information. Calling for an approach to media studies centered on "the dissemination of knowledge over space and over time," Innis note that some media (stone or marble, for example) are "heavy and durable," preserving information for long periods but also leading to top-down control over what information is preserved. Other media (papyrus, for example) are "light and easily transported," allowing for their quick and easy spread across a geographically dispersed area (1951, 33). Often, those media that enable mobility are also low cost, allowing for their deployment by and among more people and resulting in more decentralized communication.

Innis argues that ongoing tension between durability and mobility—between marble and papyrus—has determined what kinds of information gained visibility in its own time and what has been preserved for subsequent generations. In his account, shifts in the technological infrastructure have the potential to construct or undermine "monopolies of knowledge" closely associated with other sources of institutional power. Innis's focus on how different configurations of technologies may enable or constrain the circulation of information has been taken up by more recent writers seeking to explain the rise of phenomena such as digital rights management systems (DRM) as attempts to shape audience behavior. Tarleton Gillespie describes the system of constraints determining how users can engage with and share digital media texts:

> Constructing technology to regulate human activity, such that it limits all users in a fair and effective way, is never simply a technical matter. It is a heterogeneous effort in which the material artifacts, the institutions that support them, the laws that give them teeth, and the political and cultural mechanisms that give them legitimacy, must all be carefully aligned into a loosely regimented but highly cohesive, hybrid network. (2006, 652)

Different technological choices, then, can shape the uses the public makes of media content, facilitating some while constraining others, but technologies can never be designed to absolutely control how material gets deployed within a given social and cultural context. Indeed, both popular and niche uses of technology always emerge far outside anything foreseen by the designer.

Yet the more companies and governments roadblock the spread of media texts, the more grassroots circulation requires advanced technical skills to work around those obstacles. In the process, many people are shut out of being able to meaningfully shape the circulation process. Gillespie describes user agency as a mixture of technical capacities (being able to "act with a tool and on that tool") and social capacities ("the user's perception of their ability and right to do so") (2006, 661). Using transportation as an example, Gillespie discusses the range of cultural resources, economic incentives, and technological innovations which have encouraged some users to fix their own cars, even as he describes ways current car design has made this less likely than in the past and has limited which groups of people feel able to do so without causing more damage than they are fixing. Spreadability is coming to a head right now because a complex set of changes has made it easier for grassroots communities to circulate content than ever before, yet the requirements of skills and literacies, not to mention access to technologies, are not evenly distributed across the population, an issue which we will examine throughout this book.

However, we again do not wish to ascribe too much power to any particular technology or platform. While Innis's formulation presumes there will always be a dominant communication medium "biasing" society in one direction or another, this present moment of media convergence is one when there are multiple (sometimes competing and sometimes complementary) media systems whose intersections provide the infrastructure for contemporary communication (as the Susan Boyle and *Mad Men* examples suggest about the interplay between broadcast and digital networks). Some of these structures (such as the digital rights management systems Gillespie describes) seek the weight and authority prescribed to previous durable media. Often, such structures seek to lock down content, limiting or controlling its circulation. Other current platforms (such as YouTube, which makes it easy to embed its content elsewhere) have the freedom and mobility once ascribed to papyrus, enabling their rapid circulation across a range of social networks. Some media texts are made to last, while others (such as Twitter) are intended to be timely and disposable.

If various platforms offer divergent opportunities for participation, preservation, and mobility—and each system of communication sustains different relations between producers and citizens—then the established geopolitical system also creates hierarchies which make it harder for some groups (and some nations) to participate than others. Anthropologist Arjun Appadurai, a leading theorist of globalization, is another who has followed in Innis's footsteps. Appadurai observes that "cultural objects, including images, languages, and hairstyles, now move ever more swiftly across regional and national boundaries. This acceleration is a consequence of the speed and spread of the Internet and the simultaneous, comparative growth in travel, cross-cultural media and global advertising" (2010, 4). Appadurai sees this accelerated flow of information and culture being facilitated not simply by the efforts of multinational capitalism but also through the expansion of illegal and unauthorized markets. These markets often cobble together systems of exchange that support the spread of media content and cultural values (but also guns and drugs) outside official and commercial channels. Often, he suggests, these underground, grassroots circuits—which serve the needs of less-affluent or marginalized peoples—"ride on" older systems of exchange which emerge from even more longstanding processes of globalization.

Appadurai's model concedes fundamental inequalities in terms of which countries have access to these different forms of circulation, which face roadblocks that make it difficult to meaningfully participate in such exchanges, and how these inequalities of participation shape which ideas get put into circulation. There are, as Appadurai's work demonstrates, many different kinds of networks which reach many different layers of societies and which travel between many different nodes in the system. While our book details the potentials of spreadability as a means of ensuring that more people have access to the means of cultural circulation, we believe it's crucial to always be cognizant that not everyone has equal access to the technologies and to the skills needed to deploy them.

Despite (or perhaps because of) these inequalities, though, we are seeing some spectacular shifts in the flow of information across national borders and, as a consequence, in the relations between the peoples of different countries. As Appadurai notes, "This volatile and exploding traffic in commodities, styles, and information has been matched by the growth of both flows of cultural politics, visible most powerfully in the discourse of human rights, but also in the new languages of radical Christianity and Islam, and the discourse of civil society activists, who wish to promote their own versions of global equity, entitlement, and citizenship" (2010, 5).

Journalists, bloggers, and other cyber-enthusiasts have celebrated the use of sites such as Twitter, Facebook, and YouTube by protesters across the Muslim world and their supporters from the West as a decisive sign that grassroots communicators might be able to route around government censors and that citizen journalists might be able to force international concerns onto the agenda of the professional news media. Consider, for example, the role such technologies played in the aftermath of Iran's hotly contested summer 2009 elections. Between June 7 and June 26, the Web Ecology Project (2009) at Harvard University recorded 2,024,166 tweets about the Iranian election, involving 480,000 people. Meanwhile, CNN's iReport received more than 1,600 citizen-produced reports from Iran (Carafano 2009), mostly photographs but including videos of the actions in the street, recorded and transmitted via mobile phones. (Our enhanced book features a more involved discussion by Henry Jenkins on how "spreadability" applies to these events in Iran and the 2011 Arab Spring movements as well as the Occupy Wall Street movement in the United States.)

Sean Aday et al.'s 2010 report *Blogs and Bullets: New Media in Contentious Politics* argues that Twitter participation inside Iran was too low to have made much difference on the ground (estimating that as few as 100 people may have produced most of the Twitter traffic out of the country) and that the regime in power likewise used social network tools to monitor the behavior of protesters and often to circulate counterrevolutionary materials. However, the report concludes, "Where Twitter and other new media clearly did matter is how they conveyed information about the protests to the outside world. Traditional media were at a disadvantage in covering events inside Iran because of restrictions placed on journalists, and thus ended up relying on new media for content. Hence, the outside world's perceptions of the protests were crucially shaped by Twitter (as conveyed through blogs and other means), amateur videos uploaded to YouTube and Facebook, and other sources" (22). In Innis's terms, what happened challenged two "monopolies of knowledge" which potentially regulated the flow of information from Tehran to the United States: the Iranian government's desire to contain news of the protest and the mainstream news media's ability to determine the priority it gave to covering specific events. For Appadurai, the same data might have illustrated continued inequalities in the speed and spread of communication, such that people struggling for power within Iran were forced to rely on influence and attention from the Western world to shape events within their own country.

Clay Shirky has argued that Twitter's impact in this instance was more affective than informational: "As a medium gets faster, it gets more emotional. We feel faster than we think. [. . .] Twitter makes us empathize. It makes us part of it. Even if it's just retweeting, you're aiding the goal that dissidents have always sought: the awareness that the outside world is paying attention is really valuable" (2009). These strong emotions reflected the cumulative effect of an ongoing but always fragile flow of messages from the streets of Tehran. Much as daily digital communication about mundane matters led to people using social network sites feeling stronger personal ties to their friends, the flow of political messages through Twitter helped make them feel more directly implicated by the protest. Global citizens (including a strong diasporic community in North America and western Europe) helped the Iranian protesters evade potential censorship and technical roadblocks, translated their thoughts into English and other Western languages, flagged reliable information from rumors, passed what they had learned onto others, and rallied news outlets to pay closer attention.

Newsrooms are still struggling to figure out what their new roles may be in an environment where the demand for information can be driven by affect and shaped by what happens within online communities, where citizens may make demands on what journalists cover and may cobble together information from a range of resources if traditional news outlets fail to provide desired information. While smooth relations between grassroots and commercial media can be rare, the two can coexist within a more layered media environment, each holding the other accountable for its abuses, each scanning the other for potentially valuable content that might otherwise fall through the cracks.

However, one could argue that these acts of circulation (and discussions of circulation) substituted for actual political action. Jodi Dean contends in an essay on what she calls "communicative capitalism" that the expansion of the public's capacity to circulate messages has too often been fetishized as an end in itself, often at the expense of real debate or action on the ground that might seek to directly change the struggles taking place:

> Today, the circulation of content in the dense, intensive networks of global communications relieves top-level actors (corporate, institutional and governmental) from the obligation to respond. Rather than responding to messages sent by activists and critics, they counter with their own contributions to the circulating flow of communications, hoping that sufficient volume (whether in terms of number of contributions or the spectacular nature of a contribution) will give their contributions dominance or stickiness. [. . .] Under conditions of the intensive and extensive proliferation of media, messages are more likely to get lost as mere contributions to the circulation of content. (2005, 54)

Dean raises an important caveat about how means can become ends in themselves, especially amid the techno-euphoria that has surrounded the expansion of communications capacities. Twitter (as a new company seeking to increase its visibility in the marketplace) benefited, from what happened in this case as much or more than the Tehran protestors did. Yet we feel that Dean goes too far in dismissing the meaningfulness of popular acts of circulation. She writes, "Messages are contributions to circulating content—not actions to elicit responses. [. . .] So, a new message is no longer primarily a message from a sender to a receiver. Uncoupled from contexts of action and application—as on the Web or in print and broadcast media—the message is simply part of a circulating data stream. Its particular content is irrelevant" (59). For Dean, meaningful participation is a fantasy used to sell products and services rather than a description of contemporary political and economic realities. We disagree. Web 2.0 companies may often seek to sell longstanding cultural practices back to the communities where they originated, but Dean's argument is every bit as disempowering as corporate versions of "viral media" and ultimately fatalistic in its conclusions. Rather than seeing circulation as the empty exchange of information stripped of context and meaning, we see these acts of circulation as constituting bids for meaning and value.

We feel that it very much matters who sends the message, who receives it, and, most importantly, what messages get sent. Acts of circulation shape both the cultural and political landscape in significant ways, as we will demonstrate throughout this book. What happened with Iran was not revolutionary, in the sense that it led to a regime change, but it was profound, in the sense that it made people around the world more aware of the political dynamics on the ground in Tehran and left many of us feeling closer to a group of people who, for most of our lives, we had been told to hate and fear.

What's Next

Innis's distinction between marble and papyrus, storage and mobility, is helpful for considering the ways a more spreadable media culture breaks with the assumptions of both the broadcast paradigm and the "stickiness" model. Both broadcast and stickiness represent different kinds of "monopoly" structures, locking down access and limiting participation. Under the conditions we've been describing here, media content that remains fixed in location and static in form fails to generate sufficient public interest and thus drops out of these ongoing conversations. Throughout this chapter, we've detailed many examples of spreadability at work, including those from the realm of entertainment (Susan Boyle, *Mad Men*), news and politics (Iran), and marketing/customer service (Comcast). Insofar as spreadability becomes an attribute of the contemporary media landscape, it has the potential to dramatically reshape how central cultural and political institutions operate.

If we all accept that the media industries and marketing worlds are moving toward a model of circulation based on the logic of spreadability, and if we also accept that concepts such as the meme and the virus often distort the human agency involved in spreading media content, how might we better understand the ways in which material travels within a networked culture? This core question will structure the rest of this book.

First, we consider the economic and social logics shaping this spreadable media landscape. Chapter 1 critiques the rhetoric and mindset of Web 2.0, examining what gets lost in contemporary businesses' own economic gain and exploring some of the gaps emerging between the social logic that often shapes noncommercial production and the commodity logic that informs much of commercial culture. Chapter 2 digs further into the processes used to evaluate and appraise media content from yesteryear, examining the residual meanings and potential new value for content and brands as they move between commercial and noncommercial exchange.

Second, we consider ways the media industries have begun to re-conceptualize their audiences as active participants whose labor helps determine the value of branded entertainment. Chapter 3 focuses on how the television industry is rethinking audience measurement as it seeks new business models built on audience engagement. In particular, we explore how transmedia entertainment has emerged as an alternative strategy for courting and mobilizing audiences behind media franchises. Chapter 4 directs attention toward the nature of participation, suggesting a need to move from the broadcast era's focus on individual audience members to an emphasis on socially active and networked audiences. Along the way, we consider which forms of participation are and are not valued within current business models. We make the case for a greater focus on processes of deliberation rather than aggregation and on the value of "listening" to what audience members say rather than simply "hearing" that a brand or media property has been mentioned. And we examine the gaps in access and participation that persist in our culture.

Third, in Chapter 5, we explore why some types of media content spread more widely and more quickly than others. In focusing specifically on marketing (in the first part of the chapter) and on activist and civic media (in the second), we seek to link the spread of material with the social needs of online communities. We draw on John Fiske's (1989b) notion of "producerly" media texts to explore how networked communities transform mass-produced media into "resources" which fuel their ongoing conversations with each other.

Finally, our book explores how spreadable practices may support a more diverse array of media options than the old broadcast paradigm—focusing on independent and Christian media in Chapter 6 and transnational media flows in Chapter 7. In Chapter 6, we examine how independent media makers from film, publishing, music, comics, and games are building new kinds of relations with their audiences. While these practices may not match the economic advantages enjoyed by mass-media producers, they have allowed independent artists to expand access to and increase the visibility of their productions. Chapter 7 argues that a combination of pirates, immigrants, and pop cosmopolitans have helped circulate more media content beyond geographic borders than ever before. Much like the creations of independent media makers, these cultural goods often still operate from a position of marginality, unable to compete directly with dominant media industries. Yet there are signs that their cultural and economic impact is increasing, thanks to their ability to travel through grassroots media channels.

REFERENCES

Aday, Sean, Henry Farrell, Marc Lynch, John Sides, John Kelly, and Ethan Zuckerman. 2010. *Blogs and Bullets: New Media in Contentious Politics.* Washington, DC: United State Institute of Peace/Peaceworks.

Appadurai, Arjun. 2010. "How Histories Make Geographies: Circulation and Context in a Global Perspective." *Transcultural Studies* 1:4-13.

Arauz, Mike. 2008. "Pass-along is Made of People! Peeeeeeeeopllllle!" *Mike Arauz* (blog), Dec. 1. http://www.mikearauz.com/2008/12/pass-along-is-made-of-people.html.

Askwith, Ivan. 2010. "Stop Spreading Viruses and Start Giving Gifts." In *Society of Digital Agencies Two Thousand and Ten Digital Marketing Outlook*, 47-48. http://www.scribd.com/doc/25441346/Two-Thousand-and-Ten-Digital-Marketing-Outlook.

Bacon-Smith, Camille. 1992. *Enterprising Women: Television Fandom and the Creation of Popular Myth.* Philadelphia: University of Pennsylvania Press.

Caddell, Bud. 2008. "Becoming a Mad Man." *We Are Sterling Cooper*. http://wearesterlingcooper.org/becoming-a-mad-man.pdf.

_____. 2009a. "Mad Men on Twitter at SXSW." *What Consumes Me* (blog), March 2. http://whatconsumesme.com/2009/what-im-writing/mad-men-on-twitter-at-sxsw/.

_____. 2009b. "Stop Saying Viral Video." *What Consumes Me* (blog), Dec. 10. http://whatconsumesme.com/1009/posts-ive-written/will-i-share-your-branded-content/.

Carafano, James Jay. 2009. "All a Twitter: How Social Networking Shaped Iran's Election Profile." *Backgrounder* (Heritage Foundation), July 20.

Chapman, C.C. 2010. "The Going Viral Myth." *C.C. Chapman* (blog). Nov. 19. http://www.ccchapman.com/2010/11/19/the-going-viral-myth/.

Coppa, Francesca. 2008. "Women, *Star Trek* and the Early Development of Fannish Viding." *Transformative Works and Cultures* 1. http://journal.transformativeworks.org/index.php/twc/article/view/44/64.

Dawkins, Richard. 1976. *The Selfish Gene.* Oxford: Oxford University Press.

_____. 1989. *The Selfish Gene 2nd ed.* Oxford: Oxford University Press.

Dean, Jodi. 2002. *Publicity's Secret: How Technoculture Capitalizes on Democracy.* Ithaca: Cornell University Press.

Garfield, Bob. 2007. "Comcast Must Die." *Advertising Age*, Sept. 9. http://adage.com/garfieldtheblog/post?article_id=120338.

Garvey, Ellen Gruber. 2003. "Scissoring and Scrapbooks: Nineteenth-Century Reading, Remaking, and Recirculating." In Lisa Gitelman and Geoffrey B. Pingree (eds.), *New Media*, 1740-1915, 207-225. Cambridge: MIT Press

Gillespie, Tarleton. 2006. "Designed to 'Effectively Frustrate': Copyright, Technology, and the Agency of Users." *New Media & Society* 8 (4): 651-669.

Gladwell, Malcolm. 2000. *The Tipping Point: How Little Things Can Make a Big Difference.* Boston: Little, Brown.

Golijan, Rosa. 2010. "Comcast to Customer: Pay Us $0.00 or We'll Cancel Your Service." *Gizmodo*, July 28. http://gizmodo.com/5599103/comcast-to-customer-pay-us-000-or-well-cancel-your-service.

Grad, Shelby. 2009. "Sorting Out the Facts in Obama-Joker 'Socialist' Posters around L.A." *L.A. Now* (blog), *Los Angeles Times,* Aug. 3. http://latimesblogs.latimes.com/lanow/2009/08/sorting-out-the-facts-in-obamajoker-socialist-posters-around-la.html.

Hassan, Eva. 2010. "Stop Saying Viral—A Case for Spreadable Media." *SlideShare*, March 23. http://www.slideshare.net/evahasson/stop-saying-viral-a-case-for-spreadable-media-3517863.

Hilderbrand, Lucas. 2007. "YouTube: Where Cultural Memory and Copyright Converge." *Film Quarterly 6*(1): 48-57.

Innis, Harold. 1951. *The Bias of Communication*. Toronto: University of Toronto Press.

Ito, Mizuko, Sonia Baumer, Matteo Bittani, danah boyd, Rachel Cody, Becky Herr-Stephenson, Heather A. Horst, Patricia G. Lange, Dilan Mahendran, Katynka Z. Martinez, C. J. Pascoe, Dan Perkel, Laura Robinson, Christo Sims, and Lisa Tripp. 2009. *Hanging Out, Messing Around, and Geeking Out: Kids Living and Learning with New Media.* Cambridge: MIT Press.

Jenkins, Henry. 1992. *Textual Poachers: Television Fans and Participatory Culture*. New York: Routledge.

Jung. Helen. 2009. "Mad Men Creator Matthew Weiner Goes Off on the Internet." *New York Magazine Vulture,* Oct. 18.http://nymag.com/daily/entertainment/2009/10/mad_men_creator_matthew_weiner_goes.html.

Jurvetson, Steve, and Tim Draper. 1997. "Viral Marketing: Viral Marketing Phenomenon Explained." *Netscape M-Files* newsletter, Jan. 1.

King, Lindy. 2009. "The Dual Universe of the Twitter Mad Men—they're alive!" *Examiner.com,* July 19. http://www.examiner.com/mad-men-in-national/the-dual-universe-of-the-twitter-mad-men-they-re-alive.

Lake Superior State University. 2010. "LSSU's 36th Annual List of Banished Words Goes Viral." Dec. 31. http://www.lssu.edu/whats_new/articles.php?articleid=2135.

Lapowsky, Issie. 2009. "Susan Boyle's Upcoming Debut Album Bigger than the Beatles and Whitney, Hits No. 1 on Amazon List." *New York Daily News*, Sept. 4. http://www.nydailynews.com/entertainment/music/2009/09/04/2009-09-04_susan_boyles_upcoming_debut_album_bigger_than_the_beatles_and_whitney_hits_no_1.html.

Learmonth, Michael. 2008. "Twitter, AMC, Wise Up, Restore 'Mad Men' Accounts." *Silicon Alley Insider, Business Insider,* Aug. 26. http://www.businessinsider.com/2008/8/twitter-amc-wise-up-restore-mad-men-.

Manjoo, Farhad. 2009. "Tweeting Avengers: Does Venting Consumer Outrage on Twitter Actually Work?" *Slate*, Sept. 1. http://www.slate.com/id/2226927/pagenum/all/.

Paul, Keith. 2010. "Comcast (Still) Doesn't Care." *Keith Paul* (blog), Dec. 2. http://keithpaul.net/2010/12/comcast-doesnt-car/.

Petrik, Paula. 1992. "The Youngest Fourth Estate: The Novelty Toy Printing Press and Adolescense, 1870–1886." In Elliot West and Paula Petrik (eds.), *Small Worlds: Childrens and Adolescents in America, 1850-1950.* Kansas City: University Press of Kansas.

Phillips, Whitney. 2009. "'Why So Socialist?': Unmasking the Joker." *Confessions of an Aca-Fan* (blog), Aug. 14. http://www.henryjenkins.org/2009/08/unmasking_the_joker.html.

Purcell, Kristen, Lee Rainie, Amy Mitchell, Tom Rosenthal, and Kenny Olmstead. 2010. *Understanding the Participatory News Consumer.* Pew Center for Internet and American Life. March 1. http://pewinternet.org/Reports/2010/Online-News/summary-of-Findings.aspx.

Reisner, Rebecca. 2009. "Comcast's Twitter Man." *BusinessWeek*, Jan. 13. http://www.businessweek.com/managing/content/jan2009/ca20090113_373506.htm.

Ross, Andrew. 1991. *Strange Weather: Culture, Science and Technology in the Age of Limits.* London: Verso.

Rushkoff, Douglas. 1994. *Media Virus: Hidden Agendas in Popular Culture*. New York: Ballantine.

"Shared News Matters More," Say Results from CNN's First International Study into Social Media Recommendation." 2010. *CNN International*, Oct. 7. http://cnninternational.presslift.com/socialmediaresearch.

Shirky, Clay. 2009. "Q&A with Clay Shirky on Twitter and Iran." Talk at TEDGlobal 2005 in Oxford, England, July 14. http://www.ted.com/talks/clay_shirky_on_institutions_versus_collaboration.html.

Short, Iain. 2010. "Viral Marketing vs. Spreadable Media." *EngageSciences*, Aug. 24. http://www.engagesciences.com/readytoland/2010/08/viral-marketing-vs-spreadable-media.

Siegler, MG. 2008. "DMCA Takedown Notice Forces Twitter to Blacklist Mad Men Characters." *Venture Beat DigitalBeat*, Aug. 25. http://venturebeat.com/2008/08/25/twitter-blacklists-mad-men characters-some-of-them-.

Sisario, Ben. 2009. "Susan Boyle, Top Seller, Shakes Up CD Trends." *New York Times*, Dec. 1. http://www.nytimes.com/2009/12/03/arts/music/03sales.html.

Stephenson, Neal. 1992. *Snow Crash*. New York: Bantam.

Van der Graaf, Shenja. 2005. "Viral Experiences: Do You Trust Your Friends?" In Sandeep Krishnamurthy (ed.), *Contemporary Research in E-Marketing*, vol. 1, 166-185. Hershey, PA: Idea.

Vedrashko, Ilya. 2010. "The Spreadable War on Viral Media." *Marketshare* (blog), *Forbes*, June 17. http://blogs.forbes.com/marketshare/2010/06/17/the-spreadable-war-on-viral-media/.

Web Ecology Project. 2009. *The Iranian Election on Twitter: The First Eighteen Days.* June 26. http//www.webecologyproject.org/2009/06/iran-election-on-twitter/.

Witchel, Alex. 2008. "Mad men Has Its Moment." *New York Times Magazine,* June 22. http://www.nytimes.com/2008/06/22/magazine/22madmen-t.html.

Yakob, Faris. 2006. "Transmedia Planning." *Talent Imitates, Genius Steals* (blog), Oct. 3. http://farisyakob.typepad.com/blog/2006/10/transmedia_plan.html.

_____. 2008. "Spreadable Media." *Talent Imitates, Genius Steals* (blog), Nov. 25. http:farisyakob.typepad.com/blog/2008/11/spreadable-media.html.

Yellin, Emily. 2009. *Your Call Is (Not That) Important to Us: Customer Service and What It Reveals about Our World and Our Lives*. New York: Free Press.

Google and the Future of Books

By Robert Darnton

For the last four years, Google has been digitizing millions of books, including many covered by copyright, from the collections of major research libraries, and making the texts searchable online. This project, known as Google Book Search, triggered a suit by a group of authors and publishers who claimed that Google was violating their copyrights. After lengthy negotiations, the plaintiffs and Google agreed on a settlement, which could have a profound effect on the world of books for the foreseeable future. What will that future be?

No one knows, because the settlement is so complex that it is difficult to perceive the legal and economic contours in the new lay of the land. But those of us who are responsible for research libraries have a clear view of a common goal: we want to open up our collections and make them available to readers everywhere. How to get there? The only workable tactic may be vigilance: see as far ahead as you can; and while you keep your eye on the road, remember to look in the rearview mirror.

When I look backward, I fix my gaze on the eighteenth century, the Enlightenment, its faith in the power of knowledge, and the world of ideas in which it operated—what the enlightened referred to as the Republic of Letters.

The eighteenth century imagined the Republic of Letters as a realm with no police, no boundaries, and no inequalities other than those determined by talent. Anyone could join it by exercising the two main attributes of citizenship, writing and reading. Writers formulated ideas, and readers judged them. Thanks to the power of the printed word, the judgments spread in widening circles, and the strongest arguments won.

The word also spread by written letters, for the eighteenth century was a great era of epistolary exchange. Read through the correspondence of Voltaire, Rousseau, Franklin, and Jefferson—each filling about fifty volumes—and you can watch the Republic of Letters in operation. All four writers debated all the issues of their day in a steady stream of letters, which crisscrossed Europe and America in a transatlantic information network.

I especially enjoy the exchange of letters between Jefferson and Madison. They discussed everything, notably the American Constitution, which Madison was helping to write in Philadelphia while Jefferson was representing the new republic in Paris. They often wrote about books, for Jefferson loved to haunt the bookshops in the capital of the Republic of Letters, and he frequently bought books for his friend. The purchases included Diderot's *Encyclopédie*, which Jefferson thought that he had got at a bargain price, although he had mistaken a reprint for a first edition.

Two future presidents discussing books through the information network of the Enlightenment—it's a stirring sight. But before this picture of the past fogs over with sentiment, I should add that the Republic of Letters was democratic only in principle. In practice, it was dominated by the wellborn and the rich. Far from being able to live from their pens, most writers had to court patrons, solicit sinecures, lobby for appointments to state-controlled journals, dodge censors, and wangle their way into salons and academies, where reputations were made. While suffering indignities at the hands of their social superiors, they turned on one another. The quarrel between Voltaire and Rousseau illustrates their temper. After reading Rousseau's *Discourse on the Origins of Inequality* in 1755, Voltaire wrote to him, "I have received, Monsieur, your new book against the human race. . . . It makes one desire to go down on all fours." Five years later, Rousseau wrote to Voltaire, "Monsieur, . . . I hate you."

The personal conflicts were compounded by social distinctions. Far from functioning like an egalitarian agora, the Republic of Letters suffered from the same disease that ate through all societies in the eighteenth century: privilege. Privileges were not limited to aristocrats. In France, they applied to everything in the world of letters, including printing and the book trade, which were dominated by exclusive guilds, and the books themselves, which could not appear legally without a royal privilege and a censor's approbation, printed in full in their text.

One way to understand this system is to draw on the sociology of knowledge, notably Pierre Bourdieu's notion of literature as a power field composed of contending positions within the rules of a game that itself is subordinate to the dominating forces of society at large. But one needn't subscribe to Bourdieu's school of sociology in order to acknowledge the connections between literature and power. Seen from the perspective of the players, the realities of literary life contradicted the lofty ideals of the Enlightenment. Despite its principles, the Republic of Letters, as it actually operated, was a closed world, inaccessible to the underprivileged. Yet I want to invoke the Enlightenment in an argument for openness in general and for open access in particular.

If we turn from the eighteenth century to the present, do we see a similar contradiction between principle and practice—right here in the world of research libraries? One of my colleagues is a quiet, diminutive lady, who might call up the notion of Marian the Librarian. When she meets people at parties and identifies herself, they sometimes say condescendingly, "A librarian, how nice. Tell me, what is it like to be a librarian?" She replies, "Essentially, it is all about money and power."

We are back with Pierre Bourdieu. Yet most of us would subscribe to the principles inscribed in prominent places in our public libraries. "Free to All," it says above the main entrance to the Boston Public Library; and in the words of Thomas Jefferson, carved in gold letters on the wall of the Trustees' Room of the New York Public Library: "I look to the diffusion of light and education as the resource most to be relied on for ameliorating the condition promoting the virtue and advancing the happiness of man." We are back with the Enlightenment.

Our republic was founded on faith in the central principle of the eighteenth-century Republic of Letters: the diffusion of light. For Jefferson, enlightenment took place by means of writers and readers, books and libraries—especially libraries, at Monticello, the University of Virginia, and the Library of Congress. This faith is embodied in the United States Constitution. Article 1, Section 8, establishes copyright and patents "for limited times" only and subject to the higher purpose of promoting "the progress of science and useful arts." The Founding Fathers acknowledged authors' rights to a fair return on their intellectual labor, but they put public welfare before private profit.

How to calculate the relative importance of those two values? As the authors of the Constitution knew, copyright was created in Great Britain by the Statute of Anne in 1710 for the purpose of curbing the monopolistic practices of the London Stationers' Company and also, as its title proclaimed, "for the encouragement of learning." At that time, Parliament set the length of copyright at fourteen years, renewable only once. The stationers attempted to defend their monopoly of publishing and the book trade by arguing for perpetual copyright in a long series of court cases. But they lost in the definitive ruling of *Donaldson v. Beckett* in 1774.

When the Americans gathered to draft a constitution thirteen years later, they generally favored the view that had predominated in Britain. Twenty-eight years seemed long enough to protect the interests of authors and publishers. Beyond that limit, the interest of the public should prevail. In 1790, the first copyright act—also dedicated to "the encouragement of learning"—followed British practice by adopting a limit of fourteen years renewable for another fourteen.

How long does copyright extend today? According to the Sonny Bono Copyright Term Extension Act of 1998 (also known as the "Mickey Mouse Protection Act," because Mickey was about to fall into the public domain), it lasts as long as the life of the author plus seventy years. In practice, that normally would mean more than a century. Most books published in the twentieth century have not yet entered the public domain. When it comes to digitization, access to our cultural heritage generally ends on January 1, 1923, the date from which great numbers of books are subject to copyright laws. It will remain there—unless private interests take over the digitizing, package it for consumers, tie the packages up by means of legal deals, and sell them for the profit of the shareholders. As things stand now, for example, Sinclair Lewis's *Babbitt*, published in 1922, is in the public domain, whereas Lewis's *Elmer Gantry*, published in 1927, will not enter the public domain until 2022.[1]

To descend from the high principles of the Founding Fathers to the practices of the cultural industries today is to leave the realm of Enlightenment for the hurly-burly of corporate capitalism. If we turned the sociology of knowledge onto the present—as Bourdieu himself did—we would see that we live in a world designed by Mickey Mouse, red in tooth and claw.

Does this kind of reality check make the principles of Enlightenment look like a historical fantasy? Let's reconsider the history. As the Enlightenment faded in the early nineteenth century, professionalization set in. You can follow the process by comparing the *Encyclopédie* of Diderot, which organized knowledge into an organic whole dominated by the faculty of reason, with its successor from the end of the eighteenth century, the *Encyclopédie méthodique*, which divided knowledge into fields that we can recognize today: chemistry, physics, history, mathematics, and the rest. In the nineteenth century, those fields turned into professions, certified by PhDs and guarded by professional associations. They metamorphosed into departments of universities, and by the twentieth century they had left their mark on campuses—chemistry housed in this building, physics in that one, history here, mathematics there, and at the center of it all, a library, usually designed to look like a temple of learning.

Along the way, professional journals sprouted throughout the fields, subfields, and sub-subfields. The learned societies produced them, and

1 The 1998 Copyright Term Extension Act retroactively lengthened protection by twenty years for books copyrighted after January 1, 1923. Unfortunately, the copyright status of books published in the twentieth century is complicated by legislation that has extended copyright eleven times during the last fifty years. Rightsholders had to renew their copyrights until a 1992 congressional act removed that requirement for books published between 1964 and 1977, when, according to the Copyright Act of 1976, their copyrights would last for the author's life plus fifty years. The 1998 act extended that protection to the author's life plus seventy years. Therefore, all books published after 1963 remain in copyright, and an unknown number—owing to inadequate information about the deaths of authors and the owners of copyright—published between 1923 and 1964 are also protected. See Paul A. Davis and Jared Rubin, "Restricting Access to Books on the Internet: Some Unanticipated Effects of U.S. Copyright Legislation," Review of Economic Research on Copyright Issues, Vol. 5, No. 1 (2008).

the libraries bought them. This system worked well for about a hundred years. Then commercial publishers discovered that they could make a fortune by selling subscriptions to the journals. Once a university library subscribed, the students and professors came to expect an uninterrupted flow of issues. The price could be ratcheted up without causing cancellations, because the libraries paid for the subscriptions and the professors did not. Best of all, the professors provided free or nearly free labor. They wrote the articles, refereed submissions, and served on editorial boards, partly to spread knowledge in the Enlightenment fashion, but mainly to advance their own careers.

The result stands out on the acquisitions budget of every research library: the *Journal of Comparative Neurology* now costs $25,910 for a year's subscription; *Tetrahedron* costs $17,969 (or $39,739, if bundled with related publications as a *Tetrahedron* package); the average price of a chemistry journal is $3,490; and the ripple effects have damaged intellectual life throughout the world of learning. Owing to the skyrocketing cost of serials, libraries that used to spend 50 percent of their acquisitions budget on monographs now spend 25 percent or less. University presses, which depend on sales to libraries, cannot cover their costs by publishing monographs. And young scholars who depend on publishing to advance their careers are now in danger of perishing.

Fortunately, this picture of the hard facts of life in the world of learning is already going out of date. Biologists, chemists, and physicists no longer live in separate worlds; nor do historians, anthropologists, and literary scholars. The old map of the campus no longer corresponds to the activities of the professors and students. It is being redrawn everywhere, and in many places the interdisciplinary designs are turning into structures. The library remains at the heart of things, but it pumps nutrition throughout the university, and often to the farthest reaches of cyberspace, by means of electronic networks.

The eighteenth-century Republic of Letters had been transformed into a professional Republic of Learning, and it is now open to amateurs—amateurs in the best sense of the word, lovers of learning among the general citizenry. Openness is operating everywhere, thanks to "open access" repositories of digitized articles available free of charge, the Open Content Alliance, the Open Knowledge Commons, OpenCourseWare, the Internet Archive, and openly amateur enterprises like Wikipedia. The democratization of knowledge now seems to be at our fingertips. We can make the Enlightenment ideal come to life in reality.

At this point, you may suspect that I have swung from one American genre, the jeremiad, to another, utopian enthusiasm. It might be possible, I suppose, for the two to work together as a dialectic, were it not for the danger of commercialization. When businesses like Google look at libraries, they do not merely see temples of learning. They see potential assets or what they call "content," ready to be mined. Built up over centuries at an enormous expenditure of money and labor, library collections can be digitized en masse at relatively little cost—millions of dollars, certainly, but little compared to the investment that went into them.

Libraries exist to promote a public good: "the encouragement of learning," learning "Free to All." Businesses exist in order to make money for their shareholders—and a good thing, too, for the public good depends on a profitable economy. Yet if we permit the commercialization of the content of our libraries, there is no getting around a fundamental contradiction. To digitize collections and sell the product in ways that fail to guarantee wide access would be to repeat the mistake that was made when publishers exploited the market for scholarly journals, but on a much greater scale, for it would turn the Internet into an instrument for privatizing knowledge that belongs in the public sphere. No invisible hand would intervene to correct the imbalance between the private and the public welfare. Only the public can do that, but who speaks for the public? Not the legislators of the Mickey Mouse Protection Act.

You cannot legislate Enlightenment, but you can set rules of the game to protect the public interest. Libraries represent the public good. They are not businesses, but they must cover their costs. They need a business plan. Think of the old motto of Con Edison when it had to tear up New York's streets in order to get at the infrastructure beneath them: "Dig we must." Libraries say, "Digitize we must." But not on any terms. We must do it in the interest of the public, and that means holding the digitizers responsible to the citizenry.

It would be naive to identify the Internet with the Enlightenment. It has the potential to diffuse knowledge beyond anything imagined by Jefferson; but while it was being constructed, link by hyperlink, commercial interests did not sit idly on the sidelines. They want to control the game, to take it over, to own it. They compete among themselves, of course, but so ferociously that they kill each other off. Their struggle for survival is leading toward an oligopoly; and whoever may win, the victory could mean a defeat for the public good.

Don't get me wrong. I know that businesses must be responsible to shareholders. I believe that authors are entitled to payment for their creative labor and that publishers deserve to make money from the value they add to the texts supplied by authors. I admire the wizardry of hardware, software, search engines, digitization, and algorithmic relevance ranking. I acknowledge the importance of copyright, although I think that Congress got it better in 1790 than in 1998.

But we, too, cannot sit on the sidelines, as if the market forces can be trusted to operate for the public good. We need to get engaged, to mix it up, and to win back the public's rightful domain. When I say "we," I mean we the people, we who created the Constitution and who should make the Enlightenment principles behind it inform the everyday realities of the information society. Yes, we must digitize. But more important, we must democratize. We must open access to our cultural heritage. How? By rewriting the rules of the game, by subordinating private interests to the public good, and by taking inspiration from the early republic in order to create a Digital Republic of Learning.

What provoked these jeremianic-utopian reflections? Google Book Search. Four years ago, Google began digitizing books from research libraries, providing full-text searching and making books in the public domain available on the Internet at no cost to the viewer. For example, it is now possible for anyone, anywhere, to view and download a digital copy of the 1871 first edition of *Middlemarch* that is in the collection of the Bodleian Library at Oxford. Everyone profited, including Google, which collected revenue from some discreet advertising attached to the service. Google also digitized an ever-increasing number of library books that were protected by copyright in order to provide search services that displayed small snippets of the text. In September and October 2005, a group of authors and publishers brought a class-action suit against Google, alleging violation of copyright. On October 28, 2008, after long and secret negotiations, the opposing parties announced agreement on a settlement, which is subject to approval by the US District Court for the Southern District of New York.[2]

The settlement creates an enterprise known as the Book Rights Registry to represent the interests of the copyright holders. Google will sell access to a gigantic data bank composed primarily of copyrighted, out-of-print books digitized from research libraries. Colleges, universities, and other organizations will be able to subscribe by paying for an "institutional license" providing access to the data bank. A "public access license" will make this material available to public libraries, where Google will provide free viewing of the digitized books on one computer terminal. And individuals also will be able to access and print out digitized versions of the books by purchasing a "consumer license" from Google, which will cooperate with the registry for the distribution of all the revenue to copyright holders. Google will retain 37 percent, and the registry will distribute 63 percent among the rightsholders.

Meanwhile, Google will continue to make books in the public domain available for users to read, download, and print, free of charge. Of the seven million books that Google reportedly had digitized by November 2008, one million are works in the public domain; one million are in copyright and in print; and five million are in copyright but out of print. It is this last category that will furnish the bulk of the books to be made available through the institutional license.

Many of the in-copyright and in-print books will not be available in the data bank unless the copyright owners opt to include them. They will continue to be sold in the normal fashion as printed books and also could be marketed to individual customers as digitized copies, accessible through the consumer license for downloading and reading, perhaps eventually on e-book readers such as the Sony Reader.

2 The full text of the settlement can be found at www.googlebooksettlement.com/agreement.html.

After reading the settlement and letting its terms sink in—no easy task, as it runs to 134 pages and 15 appendices of legalese—one is likely to be dumbfounded: here is a proposal that could result in the world's largest library. It would, to be sure, be a digital library, but it could dwarf the Library of Congress and all the national libraries of Europe. Moreover, in pursuing the terms of the settlement with the authors and publishers, Google could also become the world's largest book business—not a chain of stores but an electronic supply service that could out-Amazon Amazon.

An enterprise on such a scale is bound to elicit reactions of the two kinds that I have been discussing: on the one hand, utopian enthusiasm; on the other, jeremiads about the danger of concentrating power to control access to information.

Who could not be moved by the prospect of bringing virtually all the books from America's greatest research libraries within the reach of all Americans, and perhaps eventually to everyone in the world with access to the Internet? Not only will Google's technological wizardry bring books to readers, it will also open up extraordinary opportunities for research, a whole gamut of possibilities from straightforward word searches to complex text mining. Under certain conditions, the participating libraries will be able to use the digitized copies of their books to create replacements for books that have been damaged or lost. Google will engineer the texts in ways to help readers with disabilities.

Unfortunately, Google's commitment to provide free access to its database on one terminal in every public library is hedged with restrictions: readers will not be able to print out any copyrighted text without paying a fee to the copyright holders (though Google has offered to pay them at the outset); and a single terminal will hardly satisfy the demand in large libraries. But Google's generosity will be a boon to the small-town, Carnegie-library readers, who will have access to more books than are currently available in the New York Public Library. Google can make the Enlightenment dream come true.

But will it? The eighteenth-century philosophers saw monopoly as a main obstacle to the diffusion of knowledge—not merely monopolies in general, which stifled trade according to Adam Smith and the Physiocrats, but specific monopolies such as the Stationers' Company in London and the booksellers' guild in Paris, which choked off free trade in books.

Google is not a guild, and it did not set out to create a monopoly. On the contrary, it has pursued a laudable goal: promoting access to information. But the class-action character of the settlement makes Google invulnerable to competition. Most book authors and publishers who own US copyrights are automatically covered by the settlement. They can opt out of it; but whatever they do, no new digitizing enterprise can get off the ground without winning their assent one by one, a practical impossibility, or without becoming mired down in another class-action suit. If approved by the court—a process that could take as much as two years—the settlement will give Google control over the digitizing of virtually all books covered by copyright in the United States.

This outcome was not anticipated at the outset. Looking back over the course of digitization from the 1990s, we now can see that we missed a great opportunity. Action by Congress and the Library of Congress or a grand alliance of research libraries supported by a coalition of foundations could have done the job at a feasible cost and designed it in a manner that would have put the public interest first. By spreading the cost in various ways—a rental based on the amount of use of a database or a budget line in the National Endowment for the Humanities or the Library of Congress—we could have provided authors and publishers with a legitimate income, while maintaining an open access repository or one in which access was based on reasonable fees. We could have created a National Digital Library—the twenty-first-century equivalent of the Library of Alexandria. It is too late now. Not only have we failed to realize that possibility, but, even worse, we are allowing a question of public policy—the control of access to information—to be determined by private lawsuit.

While the public authorities slept, Google took the initiative. It did not seek to settle its affairs in court. It went about its business, scanning books in libraries; and it scanned them so effectively as to arouse the appetite of others for a share in the potential profits. No one should dispute the claim of authors and publishers to income from rights that properly belong to them; nor should anyone presume to pass quick judgment on the contending parties of the lawsuit. The district court judge will pronounce on the validity of the settlement, but that is primarily a matter of dividing profits, not of promoting the public interest.

As an unintended consequence, Google will enjoy what can only be called a monopoly—a monopoly of a new kind, not of railroads or steel but of access to information. Google has no serious competitors. Microsoft dropped its major program to digitize books several months ago, and other enterprises like the Open Knowledge Commons (formerly the Open Content Alliance) and the Internet Archive are minute and ineffective in comparison with Google. Google alone has the wealth to digitize on a massive scale. And having settled with the authors and publishers, it can exploit its financial power from within a protective legal barrier; for the class action suit covers the entire class of authors and publishers. No new entrepreneurs will be able to digitize books within that fenced-off territory, even if they could afford it, because they would have to fight the copyright battles all over again. If the settlement is upheld by the court, only Google will be protected from copyright liability.

Google's record suggests that it will not abuse its double-barreled fiscal-legal power. But what will happen if its current leaders sell the company or retire? The public will discover the answer from the prices that the future Google charges, especially the price of the institutional subscription licenses. The settlement leaves Google free to negotiate deals with each of its clients, although it announces two guiding principles: "(1) the realization of revenue at market rates for each Book and license on behalf of the Rightsholders and (2) the realization of broad access to the Books by the public, including institutions of higher education."

What will happen if Google favors profitability over access? Nothing, if I read the terms of the settlement correctly. Only the registry, acting for the copyright holders, has the power to force a change in the subscription prices charged by Google, and there is no reason to expect the registry to object if the prices are too high. Google may choose to be generous in its pricing, and I have reason to hope it may do so; but it could also employ a strategy comparable to the one that proved to be so effective in pushing up the price of scholarly journals: first, entice subscribers with low initial rates, and then, once they are hooked, ratchet up the rates as high as the traffic will bear.

Free-market advocates may argue that the market will correct itself. If Google charges too much, customers will cancel their subscriptions, and the price will drop. But there is no direct connection between supply and demand in the mechanism for the institutional licenses envisioned by the settlement. Students, faculty, and patrons of public libraries will not pay for the subscriptions. The payment will come from the libraries; and if the libraries fail to find enough money for the subscription renewals, they may arouse ferocious protests from readers who have become accustomed to Google's service. In the face of the protests, the libraries probably will cut back on other services, including the acquisition of books, just as they did when publishers ratcheted up the price of periodicals.

No one can predict what will happen. We can only read the terms of the settlement and guess about the future. If Google makes available, at a reasonable price, the combined holdings of all the major U..S libraries, who would not applaud? Would we not prefer a world in which this immense corpus of digitized books is accessible, even at a high price, to one in which it did not exist?

Perhaps, but the settlement creates a fundamental change in the digital world by consolidating power in the hands of one company. Apart from Wikipedia, Google already controls the means of access to information online for most Americans, whether they want to find out about people, goods, places, or almost anything. In addition to the original "Big Google," we have Google Earth, Google Maps, Google Images, Google Labs, Google Finance, Google Arts, Google Food, Google Sports, Google Health, Google Checkout, Google Alerts, and many more Google enterprises on the way. Now Google Book Search promises to create the largest library and the largest book business that have ever existed.

Whether or not I have understood the settlement correctly, its terms are locked together so tightly that they cannot be pried apart. At this point, neither Google, nor the authors, nor the publishers, nor the district court is likely to modify the settlement substantially. Yet this is also a tipping point in the development of what we call the information society. If we get the balance wrong at this moment, private interests may outweigh the public good for the foreseeable future, and the Enlightenment dream may be as elusive as ever.

The Ecstasy of Influence: A Plagiarism

Jonathan Lethem

> All mankind is of one author, and is one volume; when one man dies, one chapter is not torn out of the book, but translated into a better language; and every chapter must be so translated....
>
> —John Donne

Love and Theft

Consider this tale: a cultivated man of middle age looks back on the story of an *amour fou,* one beginning when, traveling abroad, he takes a room as a lodger. The moment he sees the daughter of the house, he is lost. She is a preteen, whose charms instantly enslave him. Heedless of her age, he becomes intimate with her. In the end she dies, and the narrator—marked by her forever—remains alone. The name of the girl supplies the title of the story: *Lolita.*

The author of the story I've described, Heinz von Lichberg, published his tale of Lolita in 1916, forty years before Vladimir Nabokov's novel. Lichberg later became a prominent journalist in the Nazi era, and his youthful works faded from view. Did Nabokov, who remained in Berlin until 1937, adopt Lichberg's tale consciously? Or did the earlier tale exist for Nabokov as a hidden, unacknowledged memory? The history of literature is not without examples of this phenomenon, called cryptomnesia. Another hypothesis is that Nabokov, knowing Lichberg's tale perfectly well, had set himself to that art of quotation that Thomas Mann, himself a master of it, called "higher cribbing." Literature has always been a crucible in which familiar themes are continually recast. Little of what we admire in Nabokov's *Lolita* is to be found in its predecessor; the former is in no way deducible from the latter. Still: did Nabokov consciously borrow and quote?

"When you live outside the law, you have to eliminate dishonesty." The line comes from Don Siegel's 1958 film noir, *The Lineup,* written by Stirling Silliphant. The film still haunts revival houses, likely thanks to Eli Wallach's blazing portrayal of a sociopathic hit man and to Siegel's long, sturdy auteurist career. Yet what were those words worth—to Siegel, or Silliphant, or their audience—in 1958? And again: what was the line worth when Bob Dylan heard it (presumably in some Greenwich Village repertory cinema), cleaned it up a little, and inserted it into "Absolutely Sweet Marie"? What are they worth now, to the culture at large?

Appropriation has always played a key role in Dylan's music. The songwriter has grabbed not only from a panoply of vintage Hollywood films but from Shakespeare and F. Scott Fitzgerald and Junichi Saga's *Confessions of a Yakuza.* He also nabbed the title of Eric Lott's study of minstrelsy for his 2001 album *Love and Theft.* One imagines Dylan liked the general resonance of the title, in which emotional misdemeanors stalk the sweetness of love, as they do so often in Dylan's songs. Lott's title is, of course, itself a riff on Leslie Fiedler's *Love and Death in the American Novel,* which famously identifies the literary motif of the interdependence of a white man and a dark man, like Huck and Jim or Ishmael and Queequeg—a series of nested references to Dylan's own appropriating, minstrel-boy self. Dylan's art offers a paradox: while it famously urges us not to look back, it also encodes a knowledge of past sources that might otherwise have little home in contemporary culture, like the Civil War poetry of the Confederate bard Henry Timrod, resuscitated in lyrics on Dylan's newest record, *Modern Times.* Dylan's originality and his appropriations are as one.

The same might be said of *all* art. I realized this forcefully when one day I went looking for the John Donne passage quoted above. I know the lines, I confess, not from a college course but from the movie version of *84, Charing Cross Road* with Anthony Hopkins and Anne Bancroft. I checked out *84, Charing Cross Road* from the library in the hope of finding the Donne passage, but it wasn't in the book. It's alluded to in the play that was adapted from the book, but it isn't reprinted. So I rented the movie again, and there was the passage, read in voiceover by Anthony Hopkins but without attribution. Unfortunately, the line was also abridged so that, when I finally turned to the Web, I found myself searching for the line "all mankind is of one volume" instead of "all mankind is of one author, and is one volume."

My Internet search was initially no more successful than my library search. I had thought that summoning books from the vasty deep was a matter of a few keystrokes, but when I visited the website of the Yale library I found that most of its books don't yet exist as computer text. As a last-ditch effort I searched the seemingly more obscure phrase "every chapter must be so translated." The passage I wanted finally came to me, as it turns out, not as part of a scholarly library collection but simply because someone who loves Donne had posted it on his homepage. The lines I sought were from Meditation 17 in *Devotions upon Emergent Occasions,* which happens to be the most famous thing Donne ever wrote, containing as it does the line "never send to know for whom the bell tolls; it tolls for thee." My search had led me from a movie to a book to a play to a website and back to a book. Then again, those words may be as famous as they are only because Hemingway lifted them for his book title.

Literature has been in a plundered, fragmentary state for a long time. When I was thirteen I purchased an anthology of Beat writing. Immediately, and to my very great excitement, I discovered one William S. Burroughs, author of something called *Naked Lunch,* excerpted there in all its coruscating brilliance. Burroughs was then as radical a literary man as the world had to offer. Nothing, in all my experience of literature since, has ever had as strong an effect on my sense of the sheer possibilities of writing. Later, attempting to understand this impact, I discovered that Burroughs had incorporated snippets of other writers' texts into his work, an action I knew my teachers would have called plagiarism. Some of these borrowings had been lifted from American science fiction of the Forties and Fifties, adding a secondary shock of recognition for me. By then I knew that this "cut-up method," as Burroughs called it, was central to whatever he thought he was doing, and that he quite literally believed it to be akin to magic. When he wrote about his process, the hairs on my neck stood up, so palpable was the excitement. Burroughs was interrogating the universe with scissors and a paste pot, and the least imitative of authors was no plagiarist at all.

Contamination Anxiety

In 1941, on his front porch, Muddy Waters recorded a song for the folklorist Alan Lomax. After singing the song, which he told Lomax was entitled "Country Blues," Waters described how he came to write it. "I made it on about the eighth of October '38," Waters said. "I was fixin' a puncture on a car. I had been mistreated by a girl. I just felt blue, and the song fell into my mind and it come to me just like that and I started singing." Then Lomax, who knew of the Robert Johnson recording called "Walkin' Blues," asked Waters if there were any other songs that used the same tune. "There's been some blues played like that," Waters replied. "This song comes from the cotton field and a boy once put a record out—Robert Johnson. He put it out as named 'Walkin'

Blues.' I heard the tune before I heard it on the record. I learned it from Son House." In nearly one breath, Waters offers five accounts: his own active authorship: he "made it" on a specific date. Then the "passive" explanation: "it come to me just like that." After Lomax raises the question of influence, Waters, without shame, misgivings, or trepidation, says that he heard a version by Johnson, but that his mentor, Son House, taught it to him. In the middle of that complex genealogy, Waters declares that "this song comes from the cotton field."

Blues and jazz musicians have long been enabled by a kind of "open source" culture, in which pre-existing melodic fragments and larger musical frameworks are freely reworked. Technology has only multiplied the possibilities; musicians have gained the power to *duplicate* sounds literally rather than simply approximate them through allusion. In Seventies Jamaica, King Tubby and Lee "Scratch" Perry deconstructed recorded music, using astonishingly primitive pre-digital hardware, creating what they called "versions." The recombinant nature of their means of production quickly spread to DJs in New York and London. Today an endless, gloriously impure, and fundamentally social process generates countless hours of music.

Visual, sound, and text collage—which for many centuries were relatively fugitive traditions (a cento here, a folk pastiche there)—became explosively central to a series of movements in the twentieth century: futurism, cubism, Dada, musique concrete, situationism, pop art, and appropriationism. In fact, collage, the common denominator in that list, might be called *the* art form of the twentieth century, never mind the twenty-first. But forget, for the moment, chronologies, schools, or even centuries. As examples accumulate—Igor Stravinsky's music and Daniel Johnston's, Francis Bacon's paintings and Henry Darger's, the novels of the Oulipo group and of Hannah Crafts (the author who pillaged Dickens's *Bleak House* to write *The Bondwoman's Narrative),* as well as cherished texts that become troubling to their admirers after the discovery of their "plagiarized" elements, like Richard Condon's novels or Martin Luther King Jr.'s sermons—it becomes apparent that appropriation, mimicry, quotation, allusion, and sublimated collaboration consist of a kind of sine qua non of the creative act, cutting across all forms and genres in the realm of cultural production.

In a courtroom scene from *The Simpsons* that has since entered into the television canon, an argument over the ownership of the animated characters Itchy and Scratchy rapidly escalates into an existential debate on the very nature of cartoons. "Animation is built on plagiarism!" declares the show's hot-tempered cartoon-producer-within-a-cartoon, Roger Meyers Jr. "You take away our right to steal ideas, where are they going to come from?" If nostalgic cartoonists had never borrowed from *Fritz the Cat,* there would be no *Ren & Stimpy Show;* without the Rankin/Bass and Charlie Brown Christmas specials, there would be no *South Park;* and without *The Flintstones*—more or less *The Honeymooners* in cartoon loincloths—*The Simpsons* would cease to exist. If those don't strike you as essential losses, then consider the remarkable series of "plagiarisms" that links Ovid's "Pyramus and Thisbe" with Shakespeare's *Romeo and Juliet* and Leonard Bernstein's *West Side Story,* or Shakespeare's description of Cleopatra, copied nearly verbatim from Plutarch's life of Mark Antony and also later nicked by T. S. Eliot for *The Waste Land.* If these are examples of plagiarism, then we want more plagiarism.

Most artists are brought to their vocation when their own nascent gifts are awakened by the work of a master. That is to say, most artists are converted to art by art itself. Finding one's voice isn't just an emptying and purifying oneself of the words of others but an adopting and embracing of filiations, communities, and discourses. Inspiration could be called inhaling the memory of an act never experienced. Invention, it must be humbly admitted, does not consist in creating out of void but out of chaos. Any artist knows these truths, no matter how deeply he or she submerges that knowing.

What happens when an allusion goes unrecognized? A closer look at *The Waste Land* may help make this point. The body of Eliot's poem is a vertiginous melange of quotation, allusion, and "original" writing. When Eliot alludes to Edmund Spenser's "Prothalamion" with the line "Sweet Thames, run softly, till I end my song," what of readers to whom the poem, never one of Spenser's most popular, is unfamiliar? (Indeed, the Spenser is now known largely because of Eliot's use of it.) Two responses are possible: grant the line to Eliot, or, later discover the source and understand the line as plagiarism. Eliot evidenced no small anxiety about these matters; the notes he so carefully added to *The Waste Land* can be read as a symptom of modernism's contamination anxiety. Taken from this angle, what exactly is postmodernism, except modernism without the anxiety?

Surrounded by Signs

The surrealists believed that objects in the world possess a certain but unspecifiable intensity that had been dulled by everyday use and utility. They meant to reanimate this dormant intensity, to bring their minds once again into close contact with the matter that made up their world. Andre Breton's maxim "Beautiful as the chance encounter of a sewing machine and an umbrella on an operating table" is an expression of the belief that simply placing objects in an unexpected context reinvigorates their mysterious qualities.

This "crisis" the surrealists identified was being simultaneously diagnosed by others. Martin Heidegger held that the essence of modernity was found in a certain technological orientation he called "enframing." This tendency encourages us to see the objects in our world only in terms of how they can serve us or be used by us. The task he identified was to find ways to resituate ourselves vis-a-vis these "objects," so that we may see them as "things" pulled into relief against the ground of their functionality. Heidegger believed that art had the great potential to reveal the "thingness" of objects.

The surrealists understood that photography and cinema could carry out this reanimating process automatically; the process of framing objects in a lens was often enough to create the charge they sought. Describing the effect, Walter Benjamin drew a comparison between the photographic apparatus and Freud's psychoanalytic methods. Just as Freud's theories "isolated and made analyzable things which had heretofore floated along unnoticed in the broad stream of perception," the photographic apparatus focuses on "hidden details of familiar objects," revealing "entirely new structural formations of the subject."

It's worth noting, then, that early in the history of photography a series of judicial decisions could well have changed the course of that art: courts were asked whether the photographer, amateur or professional, required permission before he could capture and print an image. Was the photographer *stealing* from the person or building whose photograph he shot, pirating something of private and certifiable value? Those early decisions went in favor of the pirates. Just as Walt Disney could take inspiration from Buster Keaton's *Steamboat Bill, Jr.*, the Brothers Grimm, or the existence of real mice, the photographer should be free to capture an image without compensating the source. The world that meets our eye through the lens of a camera was judged to be, with minor exceptions, a sort of public commons, where a cat may look at a king.

Novelists may glance at the stuff of the world too, but we sometimes get called to task for it. For those whose ganglia were formed pre-TV, the mimetic deployment of pop-culture icons seems at best an annoying tic and at worst a dangerous vapidity that compromises fiction's seriousness by dating it out of the Platonic Always, where it ought to reside. In a graduate workshop I briefly passed through, a certain gray eminence tried to convince us that a literary story should always eschew "any feature which serves to date it" because "serious fiction must be Timeless." When we protested that, in his own well-known work, characters moved about electrically lit rooms, drove cars, and spoke not Anglo-Saxon but postwar English—and further, that fiction he'd himself ratified as great, such as Dickens, was liberally strewn with innately topical, commercial, and time bound references—he impatiently amended his proscription to those explicit references that would date a story in the "frivolous Now." When pressed, he said of course he meant the "trendy mass-popular-media" reference. Here, transgenerational discourse broke down.

I was born in 1964; I grew up watching Captain Kangaroo, moon landings, zillions of TV ads, the Banana Splits, *M*A*S*H*, and *The Mary Tyler Moore Show.* I was born with words in my mouth—"Band-Aid," "Q-tip," "Xerox"—object-names as fixed and eternal in my logosphere as "taxicab" and "toothbrush." The world is a home littered with pop-culture products and their emblems. I also came of age swamped by parodies that stood for originals yet mysterious to me—I knew Monkees before Beatles, Belmondo before Bogart, and "remember" the movie *Summer of '42* from a *Mad* magazine satire, though I've still never seen the film itself. I'm not alone in having been born backward into an incoherent realm of texts, products, and images, the commercial and cultural environment with which we've both supplemented and blotted out our natural world. I can no more claim it as "mine" than the sidewalks and forests of the world, yet I do dwell in it, and for me to stand a chance as either artist or citizen, I'd probably better be permitted to name it.

Consider Walker Percy's *The Moviegoer:*

> Other people, so I have read, treasure memorable moments in their lives: the time one climbed the Parthenon at sunrise, the summer night one met a lonely girl in Central Park and achieved with her a sweet and natural relationship, as they say in books. I too once met a girl in Central Park, but it is not much to remember. What I remember is the time John Wayne killed three men with a carbine as he was falling to the dusty street in *Stagecoach*, and the time the kitten found Orson Welles in the doorway in *The Third Man.*

Today, when we can eat Tex-Mex with chopsticks while listening to reggae and watching a YouTube rebroadcast of the Berlin Wall's fall—i.e., when damn near everything presents itself as familiar—it's not a surprise that some of today's most ambitious art is going about trying to *make the familiar strange*. In so doing, in reimagining what human life might truly be like over there across the chasms of illusion, mediation, demographics, marketing, imago, and appearance, artists are paradoxically trying to restore what's taken for "real" to three whole dimensions, to reconstruct a univocally round world out of disparate streams of flat sights.

Whatever charge of tastelessness or trademark violation may be attached to the artistic appropriation of the media environment in which we swim, the alternative—to flinch, or tiptoe away into some ivory tower of irrelevance—is far worse. We're surrounded by signs; our imperative is to ignore none of them.

Usemonopoly

The idea that culture can be property—*intellectual* property—is used to justify everything from attempts to force the Girl Scouts to pay royalties for singing songs around campfires to the infringement suit brought by the estate of Margaret Mitchell against the publishers of Alice Randall's *The Wind Done Gone.* Corporations like Celera Genomics have filed for patents for human genes, while the Recording Industry Association of America has sued music downloaders for copyright infringement, reaching out-of-court settlements for thousands of dollars with defendants as young as twelve. ASCAP bleeds fees from shop owners who play background music in their stores; students and scholars are shamed from placing texts facedown on photocopy machines. At the same time, copyright is revered by most established writers and artists as a birthright and bulwark, the source of nurture for their infinitely fragile practices in a rapacious world. Plagiarism and piracy, after all, are the monsters we working artists are taught to dread, as they roam the woods surrounding our tiny preserves of regard and remuneration.

A time is marked not so much by ideas that are argued about as by ideas that are taken for granted. The character of an era hangs upon what needs no defense. In this regard, few of us question the contemporary construction of copyright. It is taken as a law, both in the sense of a universally recognizable moral absolute, like the law against murder, and as naturally inherent in our world, like the law of gravity. In fact, it is neither. Rather, copyright is an ongoing social negotiation, tenuously forged, endlessly revised, and imperfect in its every incarnation.

Thomas Jefferson, for one, considered copyright a necessary evil: he favored providing just enough incentive to create, nothing more, and thereafter allowing ideas to flow freely, as nature intended. His conception of copyright was enshrined in the Constitution, which gives Congress the authority to "promote the Progress of Science and useful Arts, by securing for limited Times to Authors and Inventors the exclusive Right to their respective Writings and Discoveries." This was a balancing act between creators and society as a whole; second comers might do a much better job than the originator with the original idea.

But Jefferson's vision has not fared well, has in fact been steadily eroded by those who view the culture as a market in which everything of value should be owned by someone or other. The distinctive feature of modern American copyright law is its almost limitless bloating—its expansion in both scope and duration. With no registration requirement, every creative act in a tangible medium is now subject to copyright protection: your email to your child or your child's finger painting, both are automatically protected. The first Congress to grant copyright gave authors an initial term of fourteen years, which could be renewed for another fourteen if the author still lived. The current term is the life of the author plus seventy years. It's only a slight exaggeration to say that each time Mickey Mouse is about to fall into the public domain, the mouse's copyright term is extended.

Even as the law becomes more restrictive, technology is exposing those restrictions as bizarre and arbitrary. When old laws fixed on reproduction as the compensable (or actionable) unit, it wasn't because there was anything fundamentally invasive of an author's rights in the making of a copy. Rather it was because copies were once easy to find and count, so they made a useful benchmark for deciding when an owner's rights had been invaded. In the contemporary world, though, the act of "copying" is in no meaningful sense equivalent to an infringement—we make a copy every time we accept an emailed text, or send or forward one—and is impossible anymore to regulate or even describe.

At the movies, my entertainment is sometimes lately preceded by a dire trailer, produced by the lobbying group called the Motion Picture Association of America, in which the purchasing of a bootleg copy of a Hollywood film is compared to the theft of a car or a handbag—and, as the bullying supertitles remind us, "You wouldn't steal a handbag!" This conflation forms an incitement to quit thinking. If I were to tell you that pirating DVDs or downloading music is in no way different from loaning a friend a book, my own arguments would be as ethically bankrupt as the MPAA's. The truth lies somewhere in the vast gray area between these two overstated positions. For a car or a handbag, once stolen, no longer is available to its owner, while the appropriation of an article of "intellectual property" leaves the original untouched. As Jefferson wrote, "He who receives an idea from me, receives instruction himself without lessening mine; as he who lights his taper at mine, receives light without darkening me."

Yet industries of cultural capital, who profit not from creating but from distributing, see the sale of culture as a zero-sum game. The piano-roll publishers fear the record companies, who fear the cassette-tape manufacturers, who fear the online vendors, who fear whoever else is next in line to profit most quickly from the intangible and infinitely reproducible fruits of an artist's labor. It has been the same in every industry and with every technological innovation. Jack Valenti, speaking for the MPAA: "I say to you that the VCR is to the American film producer and the American public as the Boston Strangler is to the woman home alone."

Thinking clearly sometimes requires unbraiding our language. The word "copyright" may eventually seem as dubious in its embedded purposes as "family values," "globalization," and, sure, "intellectual property." Copyright is a "right" in no absolute sense; it is a government-granted monopoly on the use of creative results. So let's try calling it that—not a right but a *monopoly* on *use,* a "usemonopoly"—and then consider how the rapacious expansion of monopoly rights has always been counter to the public interest, no matter if it is Andrew Carnegie controlling the price of steel or Walt Disney managing the fate of his mouse. Whether the monopolizing beneficiary is a living artist or some artist's heirs or some corporation's shareholders, the loser is the community, including living artists who might make splendid use of a healthy public domain.

The Beauty of Second Use

A few years ago someone brought me a strange gift, purchased at MoMA's downtown design store: a copy of my own first novel, *Gun, With Occasional Music,* expertly cut into the contours of a pistol. The object was the work of Robert The, an artist whose specialty is the reincarnation of everyday materials. I regard my first book as an old friend, one who never fails to remind me of the spirit with which I entered into this game of art and commerce—that to be allowed to insert the materials of my imagination onto the shelves of bookstores and into the minds of readers (if only a handful) was a wild privilege. I was paid $6,000 for three years of writing, but at the time I'd have happily published the results for nothing. Now my old friend had come home in a new form, one I was unlikely to have imagined for it myself. The gun-book wasn't readable, exactly, but I couldn't take offense at that. The fertile spirit of stray connection this appropriated object conveyed back to me—the strange beauty of its second use—was a reward for being a published writer I could never have fathomed in advance. And the world makes room for both my novel and Robert The's gun-book. There's no need to choose between the two.

In the first life of creative property, if the creator is lucky, the content is sold. After the commercial life has ended, our tradition supports a second life as well. A newspaper is delivered to a doorstep, and the next day wraps fish or builds an archive. Most books fall out of print after one year, yet even within that period they can be sold in used bookstores and stored in libraries, quoted in reviews, parodied in magazines, described in conversations, and plundered for costumes for kids to wear on Halloween. The demarcation between various possible uses is beautifully graded and hard to define, the more so as artifacts distill into and repercuss through the realm of culture into which they've been entered, the more so as they engage the receptive minds for whom they were presumably intended.

Active reading is an impertinent raid on the literary preserve. Readers are like nomads, poaching their way across fields they do not own—artists are no more able to control the imaginations of their audiences than the culture industry is able to control second uses of its artifacts. In the children's classic *The Velveteen Rabbit,* the old Skin Horse offers the Rabbit a lecture on the practice of textual poaching. The value of a new toy lies not it its material qualities (not "having things that buzz inside you and a stick-out handle"), the Skin Horse explains, but rather in how the toy is used. "Real isn't how you are made….It's a thing that happens to you. When a child loves you for a long, long time, not just to play with, but REALLY loves you, then you become Real." The Rabbit is fearful, recognizing that consumer goods don't become "real" without being actively reworked: "Does it hurt?" Reassuring him, the Skin Horse says: "It doesn't happen all at once….You become. It takes a long time….Generally, by the time you are Real, most of your hair has been loved off, and your eyes drop out and you get loose in the joints and very shabby." Seen from the perspective of the toymaker, the Velveteen Rabbit's loose joints and missing eyes represent vandalism, signs of misuse and rough treatment; for others, these are marks of its loving use.

Artists and their surrogates who fall into the trap of seeking recompense for every possible second use end up attacking their own best audience members for the crime of exalting and enshrining their work. The Recording Industry Association of America prosecuting their own record-buying public makes as little sense as the novelists who bristle at autographing used copies of their books for collectors. And artists, or their heirs, who fall into the trap of attacking the collagists and satirists and digital samplers of their work are attacking the next generation of creators for the crime of being influenced, for the crime of responding with the same mixture of intoxication, resentment, lust, and glee that characterizes all artistic successors. By doing so they make the world smaller, betraying what seems to me the primary motivation for participating in the world of culture in the first place: to make the world larger.

Source Hypocrisy, or, Disnial

The Walt Disney Company has drawn an astonishing catalogue from the work of others: *Snow White and the Seven Dwarfs, Fantasia, Pinocchio, Dumbo, Bambi, Song of the South, Cinderella, Alice in Wonderland, Robin Hood, Peter Pan, Lady and the Tramp, Mulan, Sleeping Beauty, The Sword* in *the Stone, The Jungle Book,* and, alas, *Treasure Planet,* a legacy of cultural sampling that Shakespeare, or De La Soul, could get behind. Yet Disney's protectorate of lobbyists has policed the resulting cache of cultural materials as vigilantly as if it were Fort Knox—threatening legal action, for instance, against the artist Dennis Oppenheim for the use of Disney characters in a sculpture, and prohibiting the scholar Holly Crawford from using any Disney-related images including artwork by Lichtenstein, Warhol, Oldenburg, and others—in her monograph *Attached* to *the Mouse: Disney and Contemporary Art.*

This peculiar and specific act—the enclosure of commonwealth culture for the benefit of a sole or corporate owner—is close kin to what could be called *imperial plagiarism,* the free use of Third World or "primitive" artworks and styles by more privileged (and better-paid) artists. Think of Picasso's *Les Demoiselles d'Avignon,* or some of the albums of Paul Simon or David Byrne: even without violating copyright, those creators have sometimes come in for a certain skepticism when the extent of their outsourcing became evident. And, as when Led Zeppelin found themselves sued for back royalties by the bluesman Willie Dixon, the act can occasionally be an expensive one. *To live outside the law, you must be honest:* perhaps it was this, in part, that spurred David Byrne and Brian Eno to recently launch a "remix" website, where anyone can download easily disassembled versions of two songs from *My Life in the Bush of Ghosts,* an album reliant on vernacular speech sampled from a host of sources. Perhaps it also explains why Bob Dylan has never refused a request for a sample.

Kenneth Koch once said, "I'm a writer who likes to be influenced." It was a charming confession, and a rare one. For so many artists, the act of creativity is intended as a Napoleonic imposition of one's uniqueness upon the universe—*après moi le déluge* of copycats! And for every James Joyce or Woody Guthrie or Martin Luther King Jr., or Walt Disney, who gathered a constellation of voices in his work, there may seem to be some corporation or literary estate eager to stopper the bottle: cultural debts flow in, but they don't flow out. We might call this tendency "source hypocrisy." Or we could name it after the most pernicious source hypocrites of all time: Disnial.

You Can't Steal a Gift

My reader may, understandably, be on the verge of crying, "Communist!" A large, diverse society cannot survive without property; a large, diverse, and modern society cannot flourish without some form of intellectual property. But it takes little reflection to grasp that there is ample value that the term "property" doesn't capture. And works of art exist simultaneously in two economies, a market economy and a *gift economy.*

The cardinal difference between gift and commodity exchange is that a gift establishes a feeling-bond between two people, whereas the sale of a commodity leaves no necessary connection. I go into a hardware store, pay the man for a hacksaw blade, and walk out. I may never see him again. The disconnectedness is, in fact, a virtue of the commodity mode. We don't want to be bothered, and if the clerk always wants to chat about the family, I'll shop elsewhere. I just want a hacksaw blade. But a gift makes a connection. There are many examples, the candy or cigarette offered to a stranger who shares a seat on the plane, the few words that indicate goodwill between passengers on the late-night bus. These tokens establish the simplest bonds of social life, but the model they offer may be extended to the most complicated of unions—marriage, parenthood, mentorship. If a value is placed on these (often essentially unequal) exchanges, they degenerate into something else.

Yet one of the more difficult things to comprehend is that the gift economies—like those that sustain open-source software—coexist so naturally with the market. It is precisely this doubleness in art practices that we must identify, ratify, and enshrine in our lives as participants in culture, either as "producers" or "consumers." Art that matters to us—which moves the heart, or revives the soul, or delights the senses, or offers courage for living, however we choose to describe the experience—is received as a gift is received.

Even if we've paid a fee at the door of the museum or concert hall, when we are touched by a work of art something comes to us that has nothing to do with the price. The daily commerce of our lives proceeds at its own constant level, but a gift conveys an uncommodifiable surplus of inspiration.

The way we treat a thing can change its nature, though. Religions often prohibit the sale of sacred objects, the implication being that their sanctity is lost if they are bought and sold. We consider it unacceptable to sell sex, babies, body organs, legal rights, and votes. The idea that something should never be commodified is generally known as *inalienability* or *unalienability*—a concept most famously expressed by Thomas Jefferson in the phrase "endowed by their Creator with certain unalienable Rights..." A work of art seems to be a hardier breed; it can be sold in the market and still emerge a work of art. But if it is true that in the essential commerce of art a gift is carried by the work from the artist to his audience, if I am right to say that where there is no gift there is no art, then it may be possible to destroy a work of art by converting it into a pure commodity. I don't maintain that art can't be bought and sold, but that the gift portion of the work places a constraint upon our merchandising. This is the reason why even a really beautiful, ingenious, powerful ad (of which there are a lot) can never be any kind of real art: an ad has no status as gift; i.e., it's never really *for* the person it's directed at.

The power of a gift economy remains difficult for the empiricists of our market culture to understand. In our times, the rhetoric of the market presumes that everything should be and can be appropriately bought, sold, and owned-a tide of alienation lapping daily at the dwindling redoubt of the unalienable. In free-market theory, an intervention to halt propertization is considered "paternalistic," because it inhibits the free action of the citizen, now reposited as a "potential entrepreneur." Of course, in the real world, we know that child-rearing, family life, education, socialization, sexuality, political life, and many other basic human activities require insulation from market forces. In fact, paying for many of these things can ruin them. We may be willing to peek at *Who Wants to Marry a Multimillionaire* or an eBay auction of the ova of fashion models, but only to reassure ourselves that some things are still beneath our standards of dignity.

What's remarkable about gift economies is that they can flourish in the most unlikely places—in rundown neighborhoods, on the Internet, in scientific communities, and among members of Alcoholics Anonymous. A classic example is commercial blood systems, which generally produce blood supplies of lower safety, purity, and potency than volunteer systems. A gift economy may be superior when it comes to maintaining a group's commitment to certain extra-market values.

The Commons

Another way of understanding the presence of gift economies—which dwell like ghosts in the commercial machine-is in the sense of a *public commons.* A commons, of course, is anything like the streets over which we drive, the skies through which we pilot airplanes, or the public parks or beaches on which we dally. A commons belongs to everyone and no one, and its use is controlled only by common consent. A commons describes resources like the body of ancient music drawn on by composers and folk musicians alike, rather than the commodities, like "Happy Birthday to You," for which ASCAP, 114 years after it was written, continues to collect a fee. Einstein's theory of relativity is a commons. Writings in the public domain are a commons. Gossip about celebrities is a commons. The silence in a movie theater is a transitory commons, impossibly fragile, treasured by those who crave it, and constructed as a mutual gift by those who compose it.

The world of art and culture is a vast commons, one that is salted through with zones of utter commerce yet remains gloriously immune to any overall commodification. The closest resemblance is to the commons of a *language:* altered by every contributor, expanded by even the most passive user. That a language is a commons doesn't mean that the community owns it; rather it belongs *between* people, possessed by no one, not even by society as a whole.

Nearly any commons, though, can be encroached upon, partitioned, enclosed. The American commons include tangible assets such as public forests and minerals, intangible wealth such as copyrights and patents, critical infrastructures such as the Internet and government research, and cultural resources such as the broadcast airwaves and public spaces. They include resources we've paid for as taxpayers and inherited from previous generations. They're not just an inventory of marketable assets; they're social institutions and cultural traditions that define us as Americans and enliven us as human beings. Some invasions of the commons are sanctioned because we can no longer muster a spirited commitment to the public sector. The abuse goes unnoticed because the theft of the commons is seen in glimpses, not in panorama. We may occasionally see a former wetland paved; we may hear about the breakthrough cancer drug that tax dollars helped develop, the rights to which pharmaceutical companies acquired for a song. The larger movement goes too much unremarked. The notion of a *commons of cultural materials* goes more or less unnamed.

Honoring the commons is not a matter of moral exhortation. It is a practical necessity. We in Western society are going through a period of intensifying belief in private ownership, to the detriment of the public good. We have to remain constantly vigilant to prevent raids by those who would selfishly exploit our common heritage for their private gain. Such raids on our natural resources are not examples of enterprise and initiative. They are attempts to take from all the people just for the benefit of a few.

Undiscovered Public Knowledge

Artists and intellectuals despondent over the prospects for originality can take heart from a phenomenon identified about twenty years ago by Don Swanson, a library scientist at the University of Chicago. He called it "undiscovered public knowledge." Swanson showed that standing problems in medical research may be significantly addressed, perhaps even solved, simply by systematically surveying the scientific literature. Left to its own devices, research tends to become more specialized and abstracted from the real-world problems that motivated it and to which it remains relevant. This suggests that such a problem may be tackled effectively not by commissioning more research but by assuming that most or all of the solution can already be found in various scientific journals, waiting to be assembled by someone willing to read across specialties. Swanson himself did this in the case of Raynaud's syndrome, a disease that causes the fingers of young women to become numb. His finding is especially striking—perhaps even scandalous—because it happened in the ever-expanding biomedical sciences.

Undiscovered public knowledge emboldens us to question the extreme claims to originality made in press releases and publishers' notices: Is an intellectual or creative offering truly novel, or have we just forgotten a worthy precursor? Does solving certain scientific problems really require massive additional funding, or could a computerized search engine, creatively deployed, do the same job more quickly and cheaply? Lastly, does our appetite for creative vitality require the violence and exasperation of another avant-garde, with its wearisome killing-the-father imperatives, or might we be better off ratifying *the ecstasy of influence*—and deepening our willingness to understand the commonality and timelessness of the methods and motifs available to artists?

Give All

A few years ago, the Film Society of Lincoln Center announced a retrospective of the works of Dariush Mehrjui, then a fresh enthusiasm of mine. Mehrjui is one of Iran's finest filmmakers, and the only one whose subject was personal relationships among the upper-middle-class intelligentsia. Needless to say, opportunities to view his films were—and remain—rare indeed. I headed uptown for one, an adaptation of J.D. Salinger's *Franny and Zooey,* titled *Pari,* only to discover at the door of the Walter Reade Theater that the screening had been canceled: its announcement had brought threat of a lawsuit down on the Film Society. True, these were Salinger's rights under the law. Yet why would he care that some obscure Iranian filmmaker had paid him homage with a meditation on his heroine? Would it have damaged his book or robbed him of some crucial remuneration had the screening been permitted? The fertile spirit of stray connection—one stretching across what is presently seen as the direst of international breaches—had in this case been snuffed out. The cold, undead hand of one of my childhood literary heroes had reached out from its New Hampshire redoubt to arrest my present-day curiosity.

A few assertions, then:

Any text that has infiltrated the common mind to the extent of *Gone With the Wind* or *Lolita* or *Ulysses* inexorably joins the language of culture. A map-turned-to-landscape, it has moved to a place beyond enclosure or control. The authors and their heirs should consider the subsequent parodies, refractions, quotations, and revisions an honor, or at least the price of a rare success.

A corporation that has imposed an inescapable notion—Mickey Mouse, Band-Aid—on the cultural language should pay a similar price.

The primary objective of copyright is not to reward the labor of authors but "to promote the Progress of Science and useful Arts." To this end, copyright assures authors the right to their original expression, but encourages others to build freely upon the ideas and information conveyed by a work. This result is neither unfair nor unfortunate.

Contemporary copyright, trademark, and patent law is presently corrupted. The case for perpetual copyright is a denial of the essential gift-aspect of the creative act. Arguments in its favor are as un-American as those for the repeal of the estate tax.

Art is sourced. Apprentices graze in the field of culture.

Digital sampling is an art method like any other, neutral in itself.

Despite hand-wringing at each technological turn—radio, the Internet—the future will be much like the past. Artists will sell some things but also give some things away. Change may be troubling for those who crave less ambiguity, but the life of an artist has never been filled with certainty.

The dream of a perfect systematic remuneration is nonsense. I pay rent with the price my words bring when published in glossy magazines and at the same moment offer them for almost nothing to impoverished literary quarterlies, or speak them for free into the air in a radio interview. So what are they worth? What would they be worth if some future Dylan worked them into a song? Should I care to make such a thing impossible?

Any text is woven entirely with citations, references, echoes, cultural languages, which cut across it through and through in a vast stereophony. The citations that go to make up a text are anonymous, untraceable, and yet *already read;* they are quotations without inverted commas. The kernel, the soul—let us go further and say the substance, the bulk, the actual and valuable material of all human utterances—is plagiarism. For substantially all ideas are secondhand, consciously and unconsciously drawn from a million outside sources, and daily used by the garnerer with a pride and satisfaction born of the superstition that he originated them; whereas there is not a rag of originality about them anywhere except the little discoloration they get from his mental and moral caliber and his temperament, and which is revealed in characteristics of phrasing. Old and new make the warp and woof of every moment. There is no thread that is not a twist of these two strands. By necessity, by proclivity, and by delight, we all quote. Neurological study has lately shown that memory, imagination, and consciousness itself is stitched, quilted, pastiched. If we cut-and-paste our selves, might we not forgive it of our artworks?

Artists and writers—and our advocates, our guilds and agents—too often subscribe to implicit claims of originality that do injury to these truths. And we too often, as hucksters and bean counters in the tiny enterprises of our selves, act to spite the gift portion of our privileged roles. People live differently who treat a portion of their wealth as a gift. If we devalue and obscure the gift-economy function of our art practices, we turn our works into nothing more than advertisements for themselves. We may console ourselves that our lust for subsidiary rights in virtual perpetuity is some heroic counter to rapacious corporate interests. But the truth is that with artists pulling on one side and corporations pulling on the other, the loser is the collective public imagination from which we were nourished in the first place, and whose existence as the ultimate repository of our offerings makes the work worth doing in the first place.

As a novelist, I'm a cork on the ocean of story, a leaf on a windy day. Pretty soon I'll be blown away. For the moment I'm grateful to be making a living, and so must ask that for a limited time (in the Thomas Jefferson sense) you please respect my small, treasured usemonopolies. Don't pirate my editions; do plunder my visions. The name of the game is Give All. You, reader, are welcome to my stories. They were never mine in the first place, but I gave them to you. If you have the inclination to pick them up, take them with my blessing.

Key: I is Another

This key to the preceding essay names the source of every line I stole, warped, and cobbled together as I "wrote" (except, alas, those sources I forgot along the way). First uses of a given author or speaker are highlighted in red. Nearly every sentence I culled I also revised, at least slightly—for necessities of space, in order to produce a more consistent tone, or simply because I felt like it.

Title

The phrase "the ecstasy of influence," which embeds a rebuking play on Harold Bloom's "anxiety of influence," is lifted from spoken remarks by Professor Richard Dienst of Rutgers.

Love and Theft

"...a cultivated man of middle age..." to "...hidden, unacknowledged memory?" These lines, with some adjustments for tone, belong to the anonymous editor or assistant who wrote the dust-flap copy of Michael Maar's *The Two Lolitas.* Of course, in my own experience, dust-flap copy is often a collaboration between author and editor. Perhaps this was also true for Maar.

"The history of literature..." to "...borrow and quote?" comes from Maar's book itself.

"Appropriation has always..." to "...Ishmael and Queequeg..." This paragraph makes a hash of remarks from an interview with Eric Lott conducted by David McNair and Jayson Whitehead, and incorporates both interviewers' and interviewee's observations. (The text-interview form can be seen as a commonly accepted form of multivocal writing. Most interviewers prime their subjects with remarks of their own—leading the witness, so to speak—and gently refine their subjects' statements in the final printed transcript.)

"I realized this..." to "...for a long time." The anecdote is cribbed, with an elision to avoid appropriating a dead grandmother, from Jonathan Rosen's *The Talmud and the Internet.* I've never seen *84, Charing Cross Road,* nor searched the Web for a Donne quote. For me it was through Rosen to Donne, Hemingway, website, et al.

"When I was thirteen..." to "...no plagiarist at all." This is from William Gibson's "God's Little Toys," in *Wired* magazine. My own first encounter with William Burroughs, also at age thirteen, was less epiphanic. Having grown up with a painter father who, during family visits to galleries or museums, approvingly noted collage and appropriation techniques in the visual arts (Picasso, Claes Oldenburg, Stuart Davis), I was gratified, but not surprised, to learn that literature could encompass the same methods.

Contamination Anxiety

"In 1941, on his front porch..." to "...'this song comes from the cotton field.'" Siva Vaidhyanathan, *Copyrights and Copywrongs.*

"...enabled by a kind...freely reworked." Kembrew McLeod, *Freedom of Expression.* In *Owning Culture,* McLeod notes that, as he was writing, he

> happened to be listening to a lot of old country music, and in my casual listening I noticed that *six* country songs shared *exactly* the same vocal melody, including Hank Thompson's "Wild Side of Life," the Carter Family's "I'm Thinking Tonight of My Blue Eyes," Roy Acuff's "Great Speckled Bird," Kitty Wells's "It Wasn't God Who Made Honkv Tonk Angels," Reno & Smiley's "I'm Using My Bible for a Roadmap," and Townes Van Zandt's "Heavenly Houseboat Blues."... In his extensively researched book, *Country: The Twisted Roots of Rock* 'n' *Roll,* Nick Tosches documents that the melody these songs share is both "ancient and British." There were no recorded lawsuits stemming from these appropriations....

"...musicians have gained...through allusion." Joanna Demers, *Steal This Music.*

"In Seventies Jamaica..." to "...hours of music." Gibson.

"Visual, sound, and text collage..." to "...realm of cultural production." This plunders, rewrites, and amplifies paragraphs from McLeod's *Owning Culture,* except for the line about collage being the art form of the twentieth and twenty-first centuries, which I heard filmmaker Craig

Baldwin say, in defense of sampling, in the trailer for a forthcoming documentary, *Copyright Criminals.*

"In a courtroom scene..." to "...would cease to exist." Dave Itzkoff, *New York Times.*

"...the remarkable series of 'plagiarisms'..." to "...we want more plagiarism." Richard Posner, combined from The Becker-Posner Blog and *The Atlantic Monthly.*

"Most artists are brought..." to "...by art itself." These words, and many more to follow, come from Lewis Hyde's *The Gift*. Above any other book I've here plagiarized, I commend *The Gift* to your attention.

"Finding one's voice ... filiations, communities, and discourses." Semanticist George L. Dillon, quoted in Rebecca Moore Howard's "The New Abolitionism Comes to Plagiarism."

"Inspiration could be...act never experienced." Ned Rorem, found on several "great quotations" sites on the Internet.

"Invention, it must be humbly admitted...out of chaos." Mary Shelley, from her introduction to *Frankenstein.*

"What happens ..." to "...contamination anxiety." Kevin J.H. Dettmar, from "The Illusion of Modernist Allusion and the Politics of Postmodern Plagiarism."

Surrounded by Signs

"The surrealists believed..." to the Walter Benjamin quote. Christian Keathley's *Cinephilia and History,* or *the Wind* in *the Trees,* a book that treats fannish fetishism as the secret at the heart of film scholarship. Keathley notes, for instance, Joseph Cornell's surrealist-influenced 1936 film *Rose Hobart,* which simply records "the way in which Cornell himself watched the 1931 Hollywood potboiler *East of Borneo*, fascinated and distracted as he was by its B-grade star"—the star, of course, being Rose Hobart herself. This, I suppose, makes Cornell a sort of father to computer-enabled fan-creator reworkings of Hollywood product, like the version of George Lucas's *The Phantom Menace* from which the noxious Jar Jar Binks character was purged; both incorporate a viewer's subjective preferences into a revision of a filmmaker's work.

"...early in the history of photography" to "...without compensating the source." From *Free Culture,* by Lawrence Lessig, the greatest of public advocates for copyright reform, and the best source if you want to get radicalized in a hurry.

"For those whose ganglia..." to "...discourse broke down." From David Foster Wallace's essay "E Unibus Pluram," reprinted in A *Supposedly Fun Thing I'll Never Do Again.* I have no idea who' Wallace's "gray eminence" is or was. I inserted the example of Dickens into the paragraph; he strikes me as overlooked in the lineage of authors of "brand-name" fiction.

"I was born...*Mary Tyler Moore Show."* These are the reminiscences of Mark Hosler from Negativland, a collaging musical collective that was sued by U2's record label for their appropriation of "I Still Haven't Found What I'm Looking For." Although I had to adjust the birth date, Hosler's cultural menu fits me like a glove.

"The world is a home ... pop-culture products..." McLeod.

"Today, when we can eat..." to "...flat sights." Wallace.

"We're surrounded by signs, ignore none of them." This phrase, which I unfortunately rendered somewhat leaden with the word "imperative," comes from Steve Erickson's novel *Our Ecstatic Days.*

Usemonopoly

"...everything from attempts..." to "defendants as young as twelve." Robert Boynton, *The New York*

Times Magazine, "The Tyranny of Copyright?"

"A time is marked..." to "...what needs no defense." Lessig, this time from *The Future of Ideas.*

"Thomas Jefferson, for one..." to "'...respective Writings and Discoveries.'" Boynton.

"...second comers might do a much better job than the originator..." I found this phrase in Lessig, who is quoting Vaidhyanathan, who himself is characterizing a judgment written by Learned Hand.

"But Jefferson's vision...owned by someone or other." Boynton.

"The distinctive feature..." to "...term is extended." Lessig, again from *The Future of Ideas.*

"When old laws..." to "...had been invaded." Jessica Litman, *Digital Copyright.*

"'I say to you...woman home alone.'" I found the Valenti quote in Mcl. eod. Now fill in the blank: Jack Valenti is to the public domain as _____ is to _____.

The Beauty of Second Use

"In the first ..." to "...builds an archive." Lessig.

"Most books...one year..." Lessig.

"Active reading is..." to "...do not own..." This is a mashup of Henry Jenkins, from his *Textual Poachers: Television Fans and Participatory Culture,* and Michel de Certeau, whom Jenkins quotes.

"In the children's classic..." to "...its loving use." Jenkins. (Incidentally, have the holders of the copyright to *The Velveteen Rabbit* had a close look at *Toy Story?* There could be a lawsuit there.)

Source Hypocrisy, or, Disnial

"The Walt Disney Company...alas, *Treasure Planet...*" Lessig.

"Imperial Plagiarism" is the title of an essay by Marilyn Randall.

"...spurred David Byrne... *My Life in the Bush of Ghosts...*" Chris Dahlen, *Pitchfork*—though in truth by the time I'd finished, his words were so utterly dissolved within my own that had I been an ordinary cutting-and-pasting journalist it never would have occurred to me to give Dahlen a citation. The effort of preserving another's distinctive phrases as I worked on this essay was sometimes beyond my capacities; this form of plagiarism was oddly hard work.

"Kenneth Koch..." to "...*deluge* of copycats!" Emily Nussbaum, *The New York Times Book Review.*

You Can't Steal a Gift

"You can't steal a gift." Dizzy Gillespie, defending another player who'd been accused of poaching Charlie Parker's style: "You can't steal a gift. Bird gave the world his music, and if you can hear it you can have it."

"A large, diverse society...intellectual property." Lessig.

"And works of art..." to "...marriage, parenthood, mentorship." Hyde.

"Yet one...so naturally with the market." David Bollier, *Silent Theft.*

"Art that matters..." to "...bought and sold." Hyde.

"We consider it unacceptable..." to "'...certain unalienable Rights...'" Bollier, paraphrasing Margaret Jane Radin's *Contested Commodities.*

"A work of art..." to "...constraint upon our merchandising." Hyde.

"This is the reason...person it's directed at." Wallace.

"The power of a gift..." to "...certain extra-market values." Bollier, and also the sociologist Warren O.

Hagstrom, whom Bollier is paraphrasing.

The Commons

"Einstein's theory..." to "...public domain are a commons." Lessig.

"That a language is a commons...society as a whole." Michael Newton, in the London *Review of Books,* reviewing a book called *Echolalias: On the Forgetting of Language* by Daniel Heller-Roazen. The paraphrases of book reviewers are another covert form of collaborative culture; as an avid reader of reviews, I know much about books I've never read. To quote Yann Martel on how he came to be accused of imperial plagiarism in his Booker-winning novel *Life of Pi*,

> Ten or so years ago, I read a review by John Updike in the *New York Times Review of Books* [sic]. It was of a novel by a Brazilian writer, Moacyr Scliar. I forget the title, and John Updike did worse: he clearly thought the book as a whole was forgettable. His review—one of those that makes you suspicious by being mostly descriptive...oozed indifference. But one thing about it struck me: the premise....Oh, the wondrous things I could do with this premise.

Unfortunately, no one was ever able to locate the Updike review in question.

"The American commons..." to "...for a song." Bollier.

"Honoring the commons..." to "...practical necessity." Bollier.

"We in Western...public good." John Sulston, Nobel Prize-winner and co-mapper of the human genome.

"We have to remain..." to "...benefit of a few." Harry S Truman, at the opening of the Everglades National Park. Although it may seem the height of presumption to rip off a president—I found claiming Truman's stolid advocacy as my own embarrassing in the extreme—I didn't rewrite him at all. As the poet Marianne Moore said, "If a thing had been said in the *best* way, how can you say it better?" Moore confessed her penchant for incorporating lines from others' work, explaining, "I have not yet been able to outgrow this hybrid method of composition."

Undiscovered Public Knowledge

"...intellectuals despondent..." to "...quickly and cheaply?" Steve Fuller, *The Intellectual*. There's something of Borges in Fuller's insight here; the notion of a storehouse of knowledge waiting passively to be assembled by future users is suggestive of both "The Library of Babel" and "Kafka and his Precursors."

Give All

"...one of Iran's finest..." to "...meditation on his heroine?" Amy Taubin, *Village Voice*, although it was me who was disappointed at the door of the Walter Reade Theater.

"The primary objective..." to "...unfair nor unfortunate." Sandra Day O'Connor, 1991.

"...the future will be much like the past" to "...give some things away." Open-source film archivist Rick Prelinger, quoted in McLeod.

"Change may be troubling...with certainty." McLeod.

"...woven entirely..." to "...without inverted commas." Roland Barthes.

"The kernel, the soul..." to "...characteristics of phrasing." Mark Twain, from a consoling letter to Helen Keller, who had suffered distressing accusations of plagiarism (!). In fact, her work included unconsciously memorized phrases; under Keller's particular circumstances, her writing could be understood as a kind of allegory of the "constructed" nature of artistic perception. I found the Twain quote in the aforementioned *Copyrights and Copywrongs,* by Siva Vaidhyanathan.

"Old and new..." to "...we all quote." Ralph Waldo Emerson. These guys all sound alike!

"People live differently...wealth as a gift." Hyde.

"...I'm a cork..." to "...blown away." This is adapted from The Beach Boys song "Til I Die," written by Brian Wilson. My own first adventure with song-lyric permissions came when I tried to have a character in my second novel quote the lyrics "There's a world where I can go and/Tell my secrets to/In my room/In my room." After learning the likely expense, at my editor's suggestion I replaced those with "You take the high road/ I'll take the low road/I'll be in Scotland before you," a lyric in the public domain. This capitulation always bugged me, and in the subsequent

British publication of the same book I restored the Brian Wilson lyric, without permission. *Ocean of Story* is the title of a collection of Christina Stead's short fiction.

Saul Bellow, writing to a friend who'd taken offense at Bellow's fictional use of certain personal facts, said: "The name of the game is Give All. You are welcome to all my facts. You know them, I give them to you. If you have the strength to pick them up, take them with my blessing." I couldn't bring myself to retain Bellow's "strength," which seemed presumptuous in my new context, though it is surely the more elegant phrase. On the other hand, I was pleased to invite the suggestion that the gifts in question may actually be light and easily lifted.

Key to the Key

The notion of a collage text is, of course, not original to me. Walter Benjamin's incomplete *Arcades Project* seemingly would have featured extensive interlaced quotations. Other precedents include Graham Rawle's novel *Diary of an Amateur Photographer,* its text harvested from photography magazines, and Eduardo Paolozzi's collage-novel *Kex,* cobbled from crime novels and newspaper clippings. Closer to home, my efforts owe a great deal to the recent essays of David Shields, in which diverse quotes are made to closely intertwine and reverberate, and to conversations with editor Sean Howe and archivist Pamela Jackson. Last year David Edelstein, in *New York* magazine, satirized the Kaavya Viswanathan plagiarism case by creating an almost completely plagiarized column denouncing her actions. Edelstein intended to demonstrate, through ironic example, how bricolage such as his own was ipso facto facile and unworthy. Although Viswanathan's version of "creative copying" was a pitiable one, I differ with Edelstein's conclusions.

The phrase *Je est un autre,* with its deliberately awkward syntax, belongs to Arthur Rimbaud. It has been translated both as "I is another" and "I is someone else," as in this excerpt from Rimbaud's letters:

> For *I* is someone else. If brass wakes up a trumpet, it is not its fault. To me this is obvious: I witness the unfolding of my own thought: I watch it, I listen to it: I make a stroke of the bow: the symphony begins to stir in the depths, or springs on to the stage.
>
> If the old fools had not discovered only the *false* significance of the Ego, we should not now be having to sweep away those millions of skeletons which, since time immemorial, have been piling up the fruits of their one-eyed intellects, and claiming to be, themselves, the authors!

13

Design

This chapter covers all of the design techniques that you'll need to complete your visuals, including basic strategies concerning color, typography, layout, perspective, balance, and other considerations. While this chapter will cover "how" to implement these design practices into your compositions, it will also explain "why" you should use certain design elements and techniques. In other words, the chapter discusses the rhetorical impact that a particular design element will have and how such an element might further your rhetorical goals for making a visual composition in the first place.

Given this chapter is called "design," it may seem clear how the rhetorical tetrahedron ties into its subject matter. However, you also have to think of design in relation to your audience, the text's message, and the medium and genre in which you actualize your design. Since a rhetorical situation is always shifting and in flux, you should think about how your design meets a particular moment (*kairos*) and interacts with the other parts of the rhetorical tetrahedron.

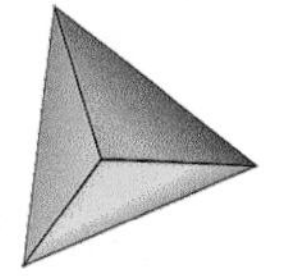

Design Basics

Color

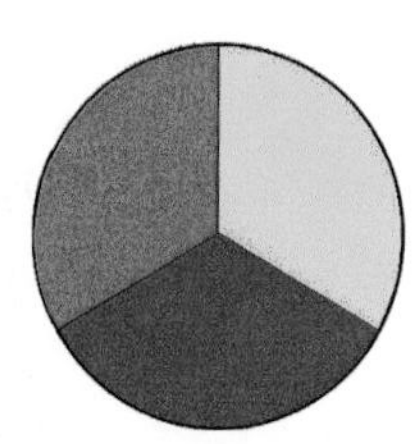

Figure 13-1 This color wheel shows the basic hues of red, blue, and yellow.

While you might think that colors are "red" or "blue," the term "color" more accurately names totality of a color, which is made up of three parts: *hue*, *value*, and *saturation*. Red by itself is really a hue and not a color. As a starting point, consider the classic color (or hue) wheel developed by Sir Isaac Newton (Figure 13-1). This hue wheel is based on the primary hues of red, blue, and yellow, which combine to make other hues.

Figure 13-2 depicts hue wheels with the primary hues and the secondary hues of orange, purple, and green (left wheel). The primary hues mix to make these other hues. For instance, yellow and red make orange, red and blue make purple, and blue and yellow make green.

These hues can be mixed further as depicted by the right wheel in Figure 13-2, producing tertiary hues, so that yellow and orange make yellow-orange or blue and green make blue-green.

However, these three hues—red, blue, and yellow—are mainly used to create other colors when mixing paints. When designing and rendering final projects for print, you'll need to mix colors according to the colors cyan, magenta, yellow, and black, creating the acronym CMYK (Figure 13-3). It's important to make sure any work to be printed by professional printers is created based on this color scheme, as these are the ink hues used by their equipment to produce all the other hues.

Credit: Isaac Newton

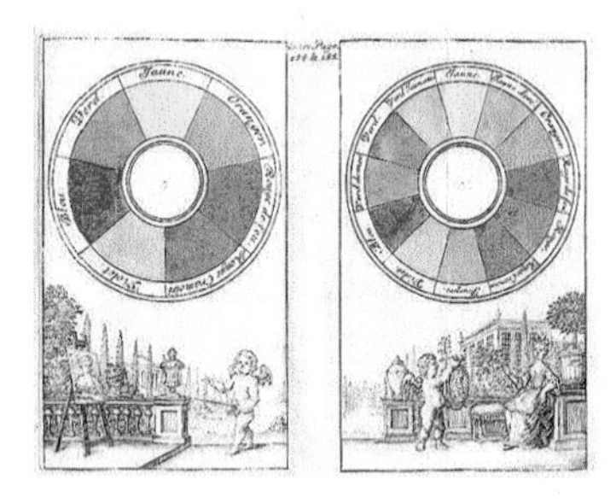

Figure 13-2
The color wheel developed by Isaac Newton has seven colors (left), which can then be mixed to produce even more (right).

Alternatively, colors produced by light, such as theater spotlights or computer monitors, do so according to the colors red, green, and blue (RGB) (Figure 13-4). You should produce work intended for online presentation in this color scheme. In most photo editors and other design software, you'll have the option of creating and saving your work as either a CMYK (print) or RGB (electronic) version.

Another important aspect of color is value, which refers to the lightness or darkness of a hue. Value can help emphasize or deemphasize objects within a design. Elements with similar value will tend to blend together, while those with contrasting values will separate and appear more striking in opposition to each other. This is especially true when using black and white.

Finally, the saturation of a color determines how dominant one of the primary hues is within the color. Look at the color cone in Figure 13-5. The primary hues are located around the outside of the chart, and any of these colors are high in saturation. However, as you move more toward the center, toward white, the colors become desaturated, losing the dominant hue until no hue dominates the color. When adjusting

Figure 13-3
Printing is usually done with cyan, magenta, yellow, and black inks.

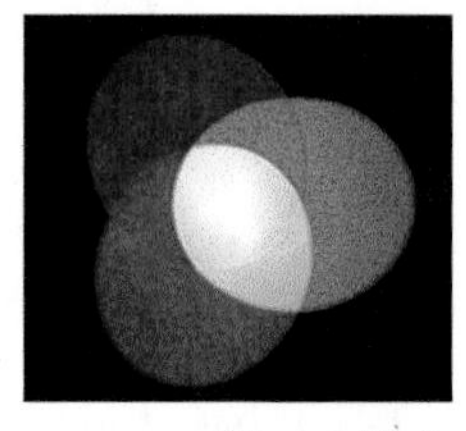

Figure 13-4
Red, Green, and Blue color systems are used for electronic documents.

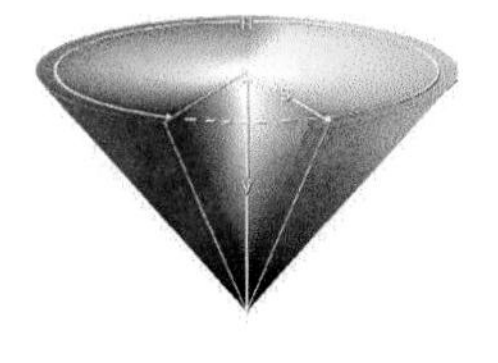

Figure 13-5
This inverted cone shows hue, value, and saturation.

saturation within a photo editor, you are increasing or decreasing the dominance of a particular hue within your design.

When using multiple hues in a design, one of the design goals is that of color harmony. Although this chapter will return to harmony later, especially concerning spatial arrangement, here are a few tips to strike color harmony when designing color palates.

When applying color, two primary methods involve choosing analogous hues or complementary hues. Analogous hues appear close together on the color wheel. For instance, yellow, yellow-orange, and orange are analogous hues. Together they create a color palate where all the hues are similar and blend well together. No one hue clashes with the other, creating a pleasing design.

Credit: Scott Boehm/Getty Images North America

Figure 13-6
The Denver Broncos use complementary colors, while the Green Bay Packers use analogous colors.

Alternatively, complementary hues appear oppositely from each other on the color wheel. Most viewers often consider white and black as complementary or other combinations such as yellow and purple, red and green, or orange and blue. If you look at the colors of different sports teams, many of them use either analogous or complementary color schemes. The Green Bay Packers use green and yellow (analogous), while the Denver Broncos use orange and blue (complementary) (Figure 13-6).

Humans approach color differently, depending on cultural backgrounds and psychological associations, as well as "natural" associations. Colors are often considered natural when they appear universally in the natural world. For instance, most types of vegetation are green, and most oceans are blue (with varying shades, of course). You might expect most people who have seen vegetation or the ocean to agree about how green and blue associate with these elements.

However, colors can mean different things to different groups and individuals. While the United States and many Western nations use the color red to symbolize danger, some Asian countries consider red to symbolize good luck or happiness. In Ireland, green is the color for good luck. The chart in Figure 13-7 analyzes some of the moods associated with different colors in ten cultural contexts.

Credit: David McCandless & AlwaysWithHonor.org

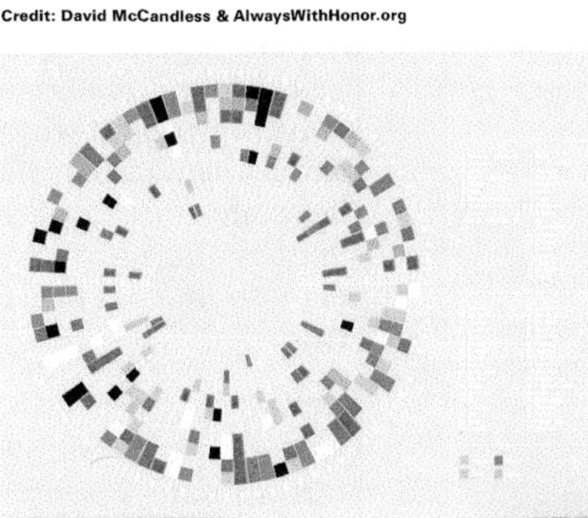

Figure 13-7
Colors mean different things to different cultures.

Love, #53, is represented by red in Western/American, Japanese, and Eastern European countries, green in Hindu, yellow in Native American, and blue in African cultures. Such differences don't preclude you from using any particular color, but you should be attuned to your audience's perceptions and associations about colors when making your selections. Research how your primary and secondary audiences might respond to colors when considering your design choices.

Beyond the color wheel, there are many online tools that you can use to help select color palates for making design choices. Some of these examples include websites such as colorhunter.com, which allows you to upload a picture and provides a color palate based on that image (Figure 13-8). If you happen to have an image that has the color aesthetics you like, this site will give you the colors and HTML codes that you can then use in an HTML or photo editor.

Credit: colorhunter.com

Figure 13-8
By uploading an image, Color Hunter will give you a whole palette of related colors.

Although many ways to use color exist, the guidelines above are meant to suggest some basic color theory when selecting colors for the designs you create. Keep in mind that they are only guidelines and not intended to stifle your design choices; you should feel free to experiment with color. However, the theories above can give you practical reasons why you might choose a certain color scheme and help you to persuade an audience or client about a particular design you might produce for them.

Making Connections

As a Class

Browse through various advertisements online and analyze their color choices. Do these advertisements use colors similar to the product's color? Do they achieve color harmony? Do they use analogous or complementary colors? How do you think the colors in the ads would affect an international audience?

In a Group

Choose four or five company brand marks. Analyze the colors in these brand marks and why you think the companies chose these particular colors. Then, import these images into a photo editor and manipulate the colors. How do such colors change the meaning of the brand mark? Produce alternative versions of these brand marks by changing their colors to create a new meaning, and share them with the rest of the class.

On Your Own

Choose your favorite color and using the chart in Figure 13-7 as a starting point, research as many meanings of this color from as many cultures as you can find. How does this research change your perception of this color? Compose a short report for your instructor that details your findings as well as a Prezi that depicts your report in a visual format and present this to your class.

Typography

Typography refers to how the individual letters are arranged in design, and the letter designs are called typefaces. Usually typefaces are created by professional type designers for specific purposes. The word sometimes substituted for typeface—font—refers to a larger complex that not only includes the typeface, but also variables such as bold, italic, or underlined; Garamond is a typeface, while Garamond-bold-italic is a font (Figure 13-9).

If you've ever used the font drop-down menu in a word editing program, you've noticed that you have hundreds of options when

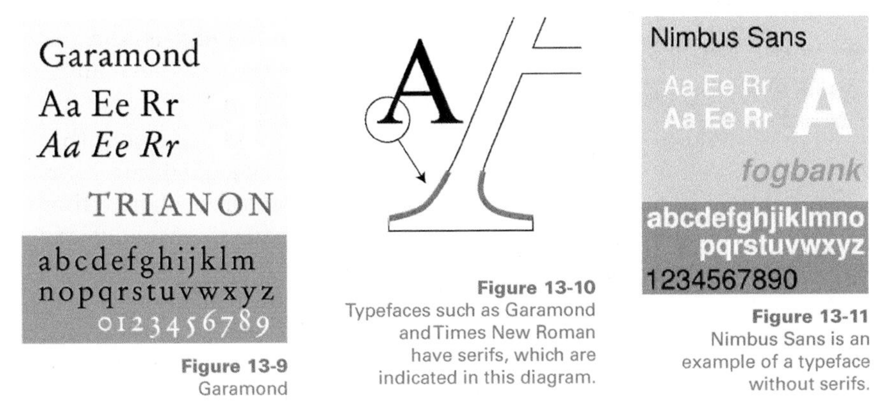

Figure 13-9
Garamond

Figure 13-10
Typefaces such as Garamond and Times New Roman have serifs, which are indicated in this diagram.

Figure 13-11
Nimbus Sans is an example of a typeface without serifs.

selecting a font. This section will provide some general guidelines to help you understand which fonts should be used in particular situations and allow you to filter through the many font options to select the one that's best for your particular project.

One of the basic differences between typefaces are those with serifs—which are the small lines that extend from letters (Figure 13-10) such as the ones in this font—and sans serif typefaces (without serif), which have no serifs, such as Arial or Nimbus Sans (Figure 13-11). In general, choose serif typefaces for most of your large blocks of texts since the serifs help the audience by making reading easier, blending one letter into the next.

Sans serif typefaces are better used for any text elements you want to stand out, such as headers or titles, since the letters are more distinct. These are just some guidelines, but when you do select a font, research the intended use for which it was designed. Some fonts display better on paper stock, while some are designed specifically for reading on a computer monitor. These details about a typeface may help confirm your choice or may give you pause to alter it. Either way, it will also provide some evidence if you have to justify your typeface choice to a client.

Point size simply refers to the size of the font, which is usually presented numerically, such as Arial 12, which indicates the typeface Arial at a 12-point size. For selecting a point size, consider how readable it will be for an audience and where it appears in a document. If the reader will be physically close to the document, such as a website or printed page, then 12-point font will probably be large enough. However, this same point size on a poster, or even something larger like a billboard, will probably be unreadable. For these genres, you should select a larger point size that can be read from a distance.

Point size should also change depending on the part of the document. While paragraphs of text can be set at 10-12 point, titles, headers, and other elements demand more emphasis; increasing the font size can make these features stand out from the rest of the page. Of course, other tools for emphasis, such as boldface and italics, can do this as well.

Credit: fontstruct

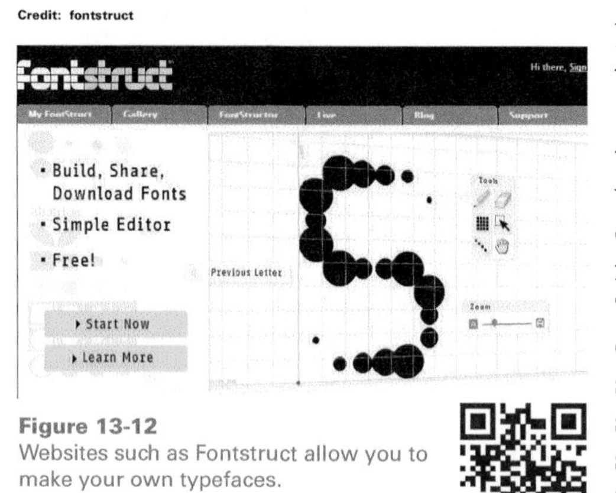

Figure 13-12
Websites such as Fontstruct allow you to make your own typefaces.

You might find that the typefaces loaded into your word editor or photo editor don't have the best options for your project. By entering "font" into an Internet search engine, you will find many sites that offer free fonts, such as Dafont.com. Also, sites such as fontstruct.com (Figure 13-12) allow you to design your own typeface for more custom applications.

Making Connections

As a Class

Scroll through the list of typefaces on a word processor, then analyze and discuss each font design. Consider what rhetorical situations might call for each typeface design.

In a Group

Locate a series of advertisements that feature text. Analyze the typeface used on the advertisement and discuss whether you think the typeface is effective.

On Your Own

Choose a typeface design from the list of fonts on your word processor. Research the history of the typeface, noting why the typeface was designed in a particular way and for what purposes. Share your findings with the class.

Contrast

Figure 13-13
Black and white offer the greatest contrast.

In the context of visual rhetoric, contrast is the technique used to separate a particular part of an image from its background and other objects within the image. While many methods may be used to create contrast, the most important design feature to achieve effective contrast is to make any differences obvious. For instance, using black and white will achieve a high level of contrast, but using white with a cream color probably won't (Figure 13-13).

Besides emphasizing some elements over others, contrast can help you direct your audience's attention, showing them how to read your document. If you use size to create contrast, you're encouraging your audience to read the largest element first since this element will usually grab their attention before the smaller elements. This is one reason why the title on a poster or flyer usually appears larger than other textual elements.

Contrast also emphasizes importance. On a movie poster, the title of the movie is usually more important than who stars in the movie, which is in turn more important (to a typical movie viewer) than the casting company, which probably appears in very small print at the bottom.

However, you can have too much contrast by making a particular element too large. While one key is to make the contrasting element sufficiently different, you should also try to achieve balance between the different objects in an image so that your rhetorical goals are achieved.

Scale

As indicated above, contrasting with scale is an easy way to emphasize some elements over others. Until one object appears next to another in a design, that object only has a size, some absolute value (which may be in millimeters, inches, feet, or miles). Only when another object is introduced can you compare the two in size, and this creates a scale between the objects. This difference (or similarity) in scale can be used to contrast the elements, which can be smaller and larger images, smaller and larger fonts, or a combination of text and images at different sizes.

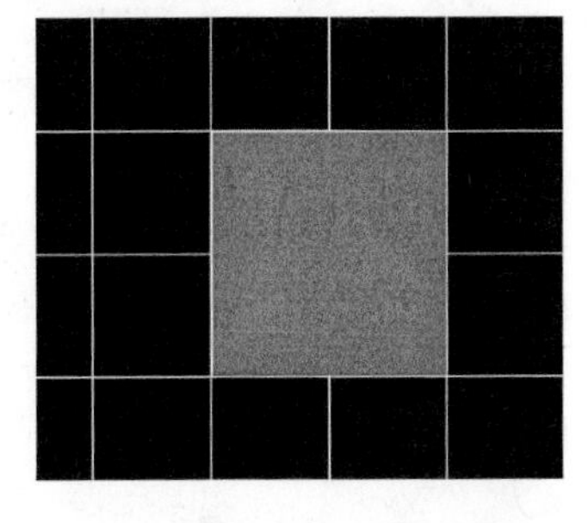

Figure 13-14
This image offers contrast through both the size of the squares and their colors.

Color

As discussed earlier in the chapter, juxtaposing colors can create contrast (Figure 13-14). Black and white is usually considered to produce the most striking contrast. However, many colors will contrast against these two colors, such as red and white, or yellow and black. In addition, *complementary colors* on the color wheel also contrast with each other while analogous colors may fail to achieve any meaningful contrast. It's also possible to use too much color. If every object in an image has a different color, then no single object gains emphasis. Instead, try to use color to achieve rhetorical emphasis—to guide your reader toward a particular interpretation. Consider your reason and specific purposes for using color and why you want to make a part of your visual stand out.

Value

Also discussed in the section on color, value refers to the darkness or lightness of an image. When contrasting different images, the further apart in value—that is, a darker value juxtaposed with a lighter value—the more contrast you'll achieve.

Type

Typography can create contrast in all the ways discussed above. You might use different size fonts, different colors, use both serif or sans serif typefaces, or use bold and italics. However, just as with color, size, or any of the techniques already mentioned, choose only a few methods to create contrast, otherwise you may confuse your audience about what exactly you're trying to contrast.

You can apply numerous other techniques to images to create contrast. For example, you can add texture or filters to different objects within an image by using a photo editor equipped with these tools. You can also contrast information using shapes, such as a circle and square. You might also align objects differently by placing some in the center and others in a corner. Such placement can also create direction and movement that will guide your reader through the document in particular ways.

The contrast controls in photo editors work according to these principles as well. Increasing the contrast makes the individual colors (or gray scales) more distinct from each other. Decreasing the contrast washes the color from the photo, making the elements blend together. Often, you'll only need to adjust the contrast slightly, otherwise the image may become significantly distorted.

Consider the contrast in the movie poster (a kind of flyer) for *Transformers* (Figure 13-15). The designer has contrasted several elements here, beginning with the transformers Optimus Prime and Bumblebee appearing opposite of each other. In terms of color, Optimus

Figure 13-15
This poster for the movie *Transformers* uses many kinds of contrast.

Prime has blues and reds, while Bumblebee is depicted mostly with shades of yellow.

Regarding scale, viewers see the enormous size of the transformers which dwarf the size of the human characters. Finally, the text appears at the bottom with the first part of the title (which also happens to be the brand name) more prominent in size than the subtitle. This single poster uses numerous levels and techniques to create contrast.

Making Connections

As a Class

Visit sites that most students visit regularly, such as Facebook. Discuss how the site uses contrast in its design. What are the rhetorical reasons for creating contrast in these sites?

In a Group

Locate a series of advertisements or flyers and analyze how the documents use contrast. Do they use scale, color, or type? Do they use contrast effectively? Why or why not? Discuss these questions and share your results with the class.

On Your Own

Open a photo in a photo editor and adjust the contrast. Note how the image changes as you make adjustments. What kinds of emphasis change as you adjust contrast? How does the meaning of the image change? Share the results of this experiment with the class.

Perspective

You may recognize the man in Figure 13-16 as the "Head Crusher" from the TV program *Kids in the Hall*. As you can see, his hobby is "crushing" the heads of people who pass him on the street. Try it yourself: Close one eye, and then place your fingers near the open eye. Notice that objects in the distance (like heads) appear much smaller than your fingers. Now "crush" them. You've probably noticed this phenomenon before; the closer something is to you, the larger it appears, and the further something is from you, the smaller it appears.

Credit: CBC Television

Figure 13-16
Head Crusher from *Kids in the Hall*.
http://www.youtube.com/watch?v=8t4pmlHRokg

Most of you know that objects look larger or smaller depending on proximity, but this knowledge lets you do more than just crush the head of a passerby. Artists and designers can reproduce the effects of this phenomenon using linear perspective. The basic rules of linear perspective can help you to add a sense of depth and a touch of realism to your designs.

This section will introduce you to the concept of linear perspective and show you how you can use linear perspective when you create your own images. If you read this section carefully and work through the examples provided, you will be able to use scale and position to make images that appear to be three-dimensional.

Perspective refers to the position from which a viewer looks at an image. Perspective also relates to the sizes and positions of objects in relation to one another, as the Head Crusher has shown. The positions of objects (such as fingers and heads) and the position of the viewer (Head Crusher) can change the relative sizes of objects, making relatively small objects like fingers appear much larger than relatively large objects like heads. If you know how much the relative sizes of objects appear to change with proximity in real three-dimensional life, you can represent this change in size on a two-dimensional surface, like a computer screen. In other words, if you know how to use the rules of perspective, you can make a two-dimensional image appear three-dimensional.

When you create an image on a two-dimensional surface, you can often assume that the viewer will be positioned in front of the image, looking at the image as if looking through a window. Because you know the viewer's position, you can reproduce the viewer's perspective using the geometrical principles of linear perspective.

Linear perspective was first demonstrated during the Italian Renaissance by architect Filippo Brunelleschi (Figure 13-17). Renaissance painters were the first to think of the painting as a kind of window that the viewer looks through to see the image in the painting. The metaphor of a painting as a window is now commonplace, and it has been transferred to other visual media like photos, TVs, and computer screens. The metaphor has become such a part of the experience of

Credit: Lorenzo di Pietro di Giovanni Vecchietta

Figure 13-17
This painting (*St Bernardino Preaching*) achieves perspective by placing the vanishing point on the cross in the background.

visual media that the text you are reading right might appear in a computer "window."

While the idea of looking at visual media through a window is common now, it was revolutionary during the Renaissance because it led directly to the use of linear perspective in painting. Since painters knew the relative perspective of the viewer to the image, they could create realistic paintings from that perspective.

Because viewers approach visual media as windows looking into space, you can design images so that they approximate that perspective, creating realistic-looking depth in the images. The most common ways to create realistic depth are to use one-point perspective and two-point perspective. Other types of multipoint perspective, such as three-point perspective, can be tricky for beginners and can sometimes distort images so that they don't look as realistic. For those reasons, this section will focus on one-point and two-point perspective.

One-Point Perspective

Here's how one-point linear perspective works.

Just as the horizon is always at eye level when you look into the distance outside, a horizon line runs across the image at the eye level of the viewer. The horizon line may be obscured by other objects in an image, but images created with linear perspective at least start with a visible horizon line. The horizon line runs parallel to the page or screen and runs across it as a straight line.

All lines that are parallel to the surface of the window and the horizon will appear parallel to each other.

All lines that are perpendicular to the window appear to move closer together as they move further from the viewer. These perpendicular lines are called orthogonal lines. Orthogonals continue to look like they are closer together until they converge at a point on the horizon called the vanishing point.

Figure 13-18 (on page 222) demonstrates one-point perspective. In this photo, the railroad tracks run along parallel orthogonal lines that converge at a vanishing point at the horizon. Notice that the tracks look smaller as they recede into the distance. When drawing an image, making one part of an object larger than another part of that object is called foreshortening. In Figure 13-19, the horizon is marked by a blue line. You can now see that the horizon line runs across the image, parallel to the "window" of the photo.

In Figure 13-20, the orthogonal lines of the tracks are marked with green lines. You can see that the green lines along the tracks meet on the horizon. The point where they appear to meet is the vanishing point, marked as a red dot.

All orthogonals meet at the vanishing point, and all parallel lines share the same vanishing point. You can see in Figure 13-21 that all the

Figure 13-18

Figure 13-19

Figure 13-20

Figure 13-21

lines parallel to the railroad tracks, such as the fences and the gravel road beside the tracks, also converge on the same vanishing point.

Using orthogonal lines that merge at a vanishing point, image-makers can create the sense that some objects in the image are closer to or farther away from the viewer.

Figure 13-20 of the railroad tracks is in one-point perspective because all parallel lines run toward a single vanishing point.

Two-Point Perspective

Another common use of linear perspective is two-point perspective. Like one-point perspective, two-point perspective starts with a horizon line but uses two sets of parallel orthogonal lines that merge into two different vanishing points.

Figure 13-22 shows a building in two-point perspective. You can see in this image that the horizon line is visible on the road and partially obscured by the building. In Figure 13-23, the horizon line is marked in yellow, and the two sets of orthogonals are marked in green and blue. Each set of parallel orthogonal lines runs toward a different vanishing point, marked in red.

If you know how to use orthogonals and vanishing points in one-point and two-point perspective, you can learn to scale and position the objects

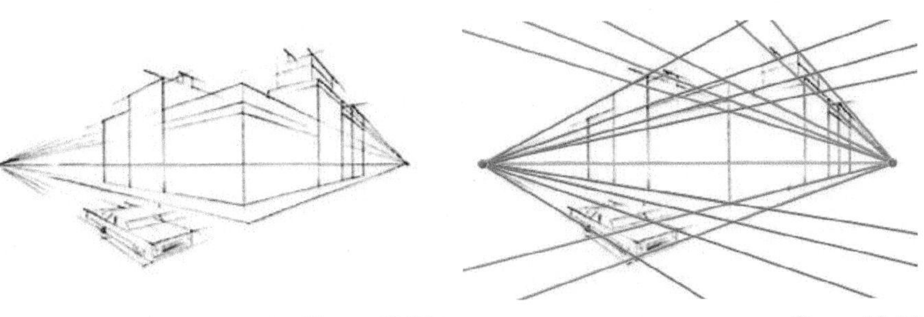

Figure 13-22

Figure 13-23

in your images so that they have realistic depth. The next two sections show you how to draw a simple geometrical figure, a box, to give you practice working with basic linear proportion. Follow these guides for drawing a box in one-point and two-point perspective and then practice using orthogonals to scale the objects in an image to create a scene with depth.

Drawing a Box in One-Point Perspective

First, draw a horizontal line across the page or screen, near the top. This will be the horizon line (Figure 13-24).

Figure 13-24

Next, place a vanishing point somewhere on the left half of the horizon line (Figure 13-25). If you are using paper, you may want to draw this point fairly lightly, so you can erase it later. If you are using a computer to draw, you will be able to erase the point later.

Figure 13-25

Draw a square near the bottom right corner of the screen (Figure 13-26).

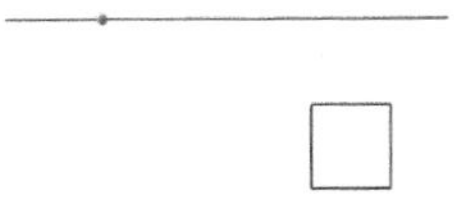

Figure 13-26

Next draw light lines from the vanishing point to each of the three closest corners of the square (Figure 13-27). These are the orthogonal lines. You will erase the orthogonal lines after the boxes are drawn.

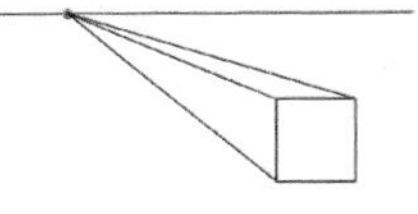

Figure 13-27

Draw a horizontal line between the two orthogonals to the right, and draw a vertical line between the two orthogonals to the left (Figure 13-28). The square is now becoming a box, and these lines are the sides and top of the box.

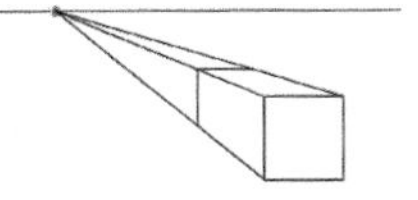

Figure 13-28

With the orthogonal lines in place, you can continue drawing boxes that appear to recede into the distance. When you have finished, you can erase the vanishing point and orthogonal lines (Figure 13-29, page 224).

When making an image with one-point perspective, use only a single vanishing point in the image. To draw other boxes in other locations in this image, draw another square, then draw orthogonals from that square to the same vanishing point used to make the first box (Figure 13-30).

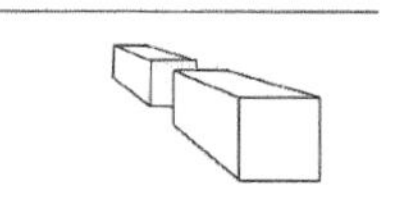

Figure 13-29

Figure 13-30

Drawing a Box in Two-Point Perspective

Draw a horizontal line in the top one-third of your page or screen (Figure 13-31). This is the horizon line.

Place two vanishing points near the ends of your horizon line (Figure 13-32).

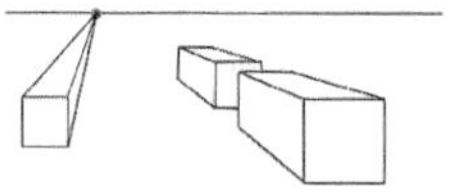

Place a vertical line near the bottom of the screen between the vanishing points. This line will be the front edge of the box (Figure 13-33).

Draw orthogonal lines from each vanishing point to both ends of the vertical line. If you are using paper, draw lightly, because you will erase all orthogonal lines when you are finished (Figure 13-34).

Draw a vertical line between the orthogonal lines to the right of the first vertical line (Figure 13-35). This will be the right edge of the box. Draw orthogonal lines from the left vanishing point to the top and bottom of the new vertical line.

Figure 13-31

Repeat the last step on the opposite side. Start with a vertical line between the original orthogonal lines to the left of the first vertical line. Then draw orthogonal lines from the vanishing point on the right side to the top and bottom of the newest vertical line (Figure 13-36).

Figure 13-32

Fill in the lines that make up the top and bottom edges of the box, and then erase the orthogonal lines and vanishing points, leaving you with a box in two-point perspective (Figure 13-37).

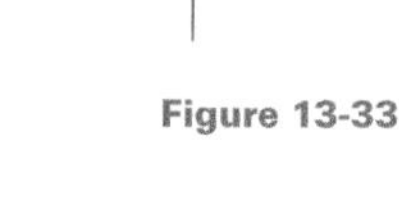

Figure 13-33

Creating a Scene in Perspective

With just a horizon line and three different images, you can see how to use vanishing points and orthogonal lines to create a sense of depth (Figure 13-38).

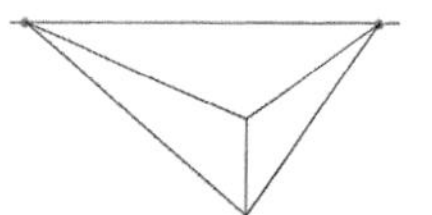

Figure 13-34

Decide which object should be in the foreground. Once that object is in scale and position, draw (or imagine) a square/rectangle around it (Figure 13-39). Draw orthogonal lines from the corners of the rectangle to a vanishing point. You can see now how large that object would be if it were moved away from the viewer, closer to the horizon line. This can help you decide the proper scale when trying to draw distance.

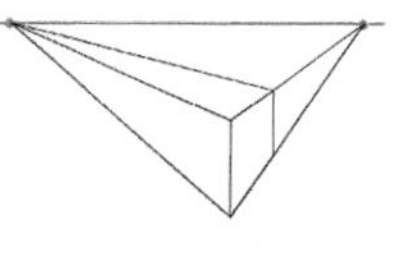

Figure 13-35

In Figure 13-40, you should assume that the two aliens are about the same size when standing side-by-side. In order to keep the purple alien in the foreground but move the other behind it, scale the image of the second alien until it fits within the orthogonal lines at the preferred distance.

Now you can move the second alien to the left or right, staying on the blue horizontal line that marks its distance from the purple alien (Figure 13-41).

Let's assume the alien tree is about twice the height of both aliens. You can place the tree in the orthogonals noting the point where the top orthogonal lines cross the tree (Figure 13-42).

If you want to move the tree further back, then scale it to fit within the orthogonal lines, being sure that the top orthogonals cross the tree in the same spot noted in the last step (Figure 13-43).

Now you can move the tree horizontally, keeping it in the appropriate vertical position for its new scale (Figure 13-44).

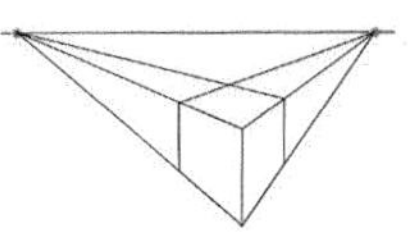

Figure 13-36

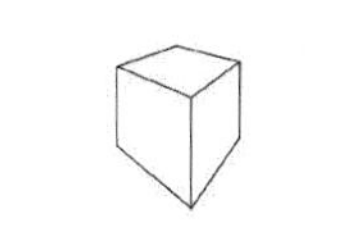

Figure 13-37

Using the same principles, you could scale and position the images differently. The orthogonal lines in this image extend from the vanishing point past the image of the purple alien. Now you can scale the image of the green alien in order to make it appear closer to the viewer than the purple alien (Figure 13-45).

The resulting scene now carries a different meaning, achieved only by scaling objects using the principles of linear perspective (Figure 13-46).

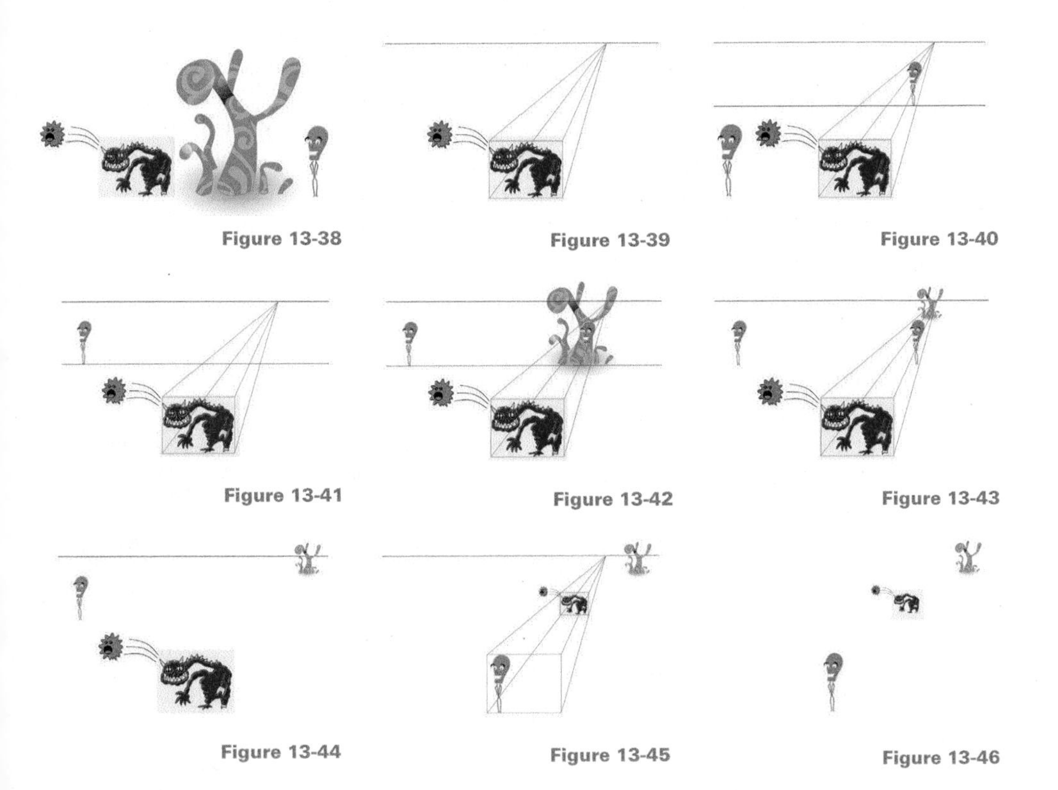

Figure 13-38

Figure 13-39

Figure 13-40

Figure 13-41

Figure 13-42

Figure 13-43

Figure 13-44

Figure 13-45

Figure 13-46

Making Connections

As a Class

Search online for the term "perspective" and locate images showing the use of perspective. Which techniques do the images use to achieve perspective in their designs?

In a Group

Locate other uses of perspective and analyze the rhetorical effect created by this technique. What does the design "argue" by using perspective in these particular ways?

On Your Own

Find three different images using an online search engine and save them to your computer. Resize the images and position them to create a scene using linear perspective. This assignment can also be done by cutting out images from different pages in a magazine and positioning them so that they appear to be in correct linear perspective. If you are using a computer, be sure to prepare two images, one with the orthogonals and vanishing point highlighted and one with those guiding lines erased. If using paper and magazine photos, lightly draw the orthogonals with a pencil and a ruler.

Emphasis

Often you need to direct the audience's attention to a particular visual element just as you might emphasize a particular word or phrase when speaking. Emphasizing a visual element within a larger composition creates a focal point, a point in the composition where you want a viewer to direct her or his gaze. The focal point is often the most important element in the design, and you should keep in mind the rhetorical reasons why you might include a particular focal point in your own compositions. Three main techniques can create emphasis: contrast, isolation, and placement.

Contrast

As discussed above, contrast distinguishes different parts of a design, separating elements so that the audience can better understand the various pieces and how they fit together. For emphasis, you can use any of the contrasting techniques already discussed. For instance, if you use a single element of color among black and white, then the colored element will draw the audience's attention and create the focal point (Figure 13-47). Also, a large element inserted amongst other small elements will draw attention as will a difference in shape.

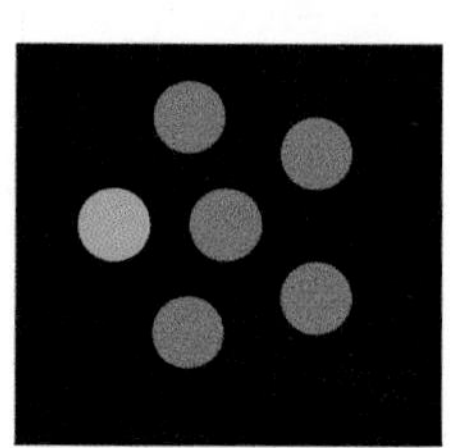

Figure 13-47 This image uses different colors to achieve emphasis.

Isolation

You can also emphasize an object by isolating it from other objects in the composition's frame. Whitespace is one method to achieve this kind of isolation, or you could use borders or boxes. The illustration in Figure 13-48 uses a combination of techniques. Whitespace separates the dot from the other shapes, but the single dot draws the audience's gaze because it is isolated from a larger group and thus becomes a focal point.

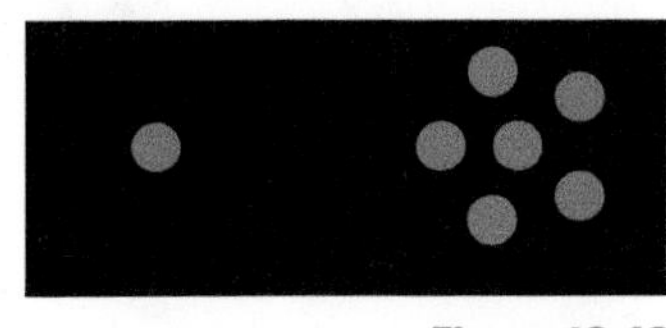

Figure 13-48
This image uses negative space to create emphasis through isolation.

Placement

Emphasis can also be created by placing an element in a particular location on a page. Often, this focal point is in the center of an image (even though that may break the "rule of thirds" discussed below). Returning to Figure 13-15, even though the larger transformers are in the foreground, the center of the image features the two humans. The poster also uses perspective, and the audience's eyes follow the lines of perspective toward this focal point.

If the object is placed at a location that's a focal point for other objects in the images, then the object can become a focal point for the viewer. For example, Alexander the Great and Roxanne in Figure 13-49 gain emphasis because most all of the other figures are looking at them, giving them attention.

Credit: Pietro Rotari

Figure 13-49
This painting creates emphasis by making Roxanne (left) and Alexander the Great (right) the main focal points of the other figures (and each other).

Making Connections

As a Class

Emphasis is used in other visual media, such as video. As a class, watch a television show or film, and note examples that use one of the three techniques mentioned above. As a group, discuss how the technique is adapted for video.

In a Group

Find natural designs, such as the wing of a butterfly, or the abdomen of a black widow. Discuss how you think these elements achieve emphasis. Share these findings with your class.

On Your Own

Find several examples of flyers around your campus or city. Analyze how they emphasize important details and which techniques they use to do so. Besides the three techniques mentioned in this section, do the examples use any other ways to achieve emphasis?

Use of Space

Whitespace

You're probably already familiar with whitespace from writing your conventional academic papers. For example, you probably use one-inch margins on each page, place space between the title and the first paragraph, include space between major sections, or indent at each new paragraph. All of these features of a typed page create whitespace that helps separate the elements from each other so that the audience can more easily read the page.

In creating visuals, whitespace (also called negative space) achieves the same goals. Whitespace is not simply empty space but space that helps to organize, balance, direct, and create an aesthetic effect. Whitespace separates, groups, arranges, and emphasizes the individual elements in the overall visual composition. Whitespace can be divided into two subcategories, micro and macro whitespace.

Micro whitespace refers to the smaller uses of whitespace that you're probably most familiar with. Indenting a paragraph, inserting a break between a header and the section it identifies, the space between columns, and even the spaces in between individual words and letters all constitute micro levels of whitespace. Typically, this level of whitespace will determine how legible your text is to the reader. If letters and words are too close, then the text may be too hard to read. Alternatively, if the letters and words are spaced too far apart, then it may be difficult for the reader to easily scan the text, since large gaps between letters slow the pace of reading.

Micro whitespace may also include the whitespace within a group of elements separated by macro whitespace, such as an image and caption grouped together. Micro whitespace would be the amount of whitespace you use to separate the image and caption, or the title of the image, such as the space used in the examples in this text. You can also use whitespace instead of gridlines when designing a chart, table, or other graphic displaying information in column and row format.

Macro whitespace is used to separate larger elements, such as complete blocks of text, images, and any object that needs separation from the rest of the image. Macro whitespace can be a clean and simple way of highlighting or emphasizing elements. While one option might be to place a box, circle, or some other outline around such elements, these can become repetitive and clutter the overall design of the composition.

Macro whitespace can also be used to show relationships between multiple elements. Smaller areas of whitespace indicate that one element should be read in relation to another, while larger areas of whitespace create more distance and separation, showing what information belongs closer together.

The homepage for Wikipedia (Figure 13-50) uses a mixture of micro and macro whitespace. As you might notice, the brand mark in the center is separated from the language options, while the text itself is separated by smaller, micro whitespace. The text also uses macro whitespace in between some of the more important sections and margins as well as the links at the bottom. The micro whitespace on the page is subtle but important so that like information is grouped together and separated from other kinds of information.

The medium you choose will dictate physical constraints that limit your overall design and therefore limit how much whitespace you can use. You can only fit so much information on a piece of paper, and even though a Web page can be limitless, you generally want a design to fit within typical monitor dimensions (typically 1280 x 768 pixels). In addition, you will have to include certain information on the medium, and doing so might take up every bit of space (consider a newspaper, for instance, which has much less whitespace compared with a magazine).

Finally, whitespace need not be "white" per se but any color devoid of text, images, or other information, and sometimes whitespace is referred to as "negative space," or any space that is empty. In the movie poster for *Transformers* (Figure 13-15), the negative space is black. This "blackspace" is used to separate and bookend the title, framing and separating it slightly from the image above. The black frame also creates the illusion that the transformers are stepping out of the picture, providing a faux 3D effect.

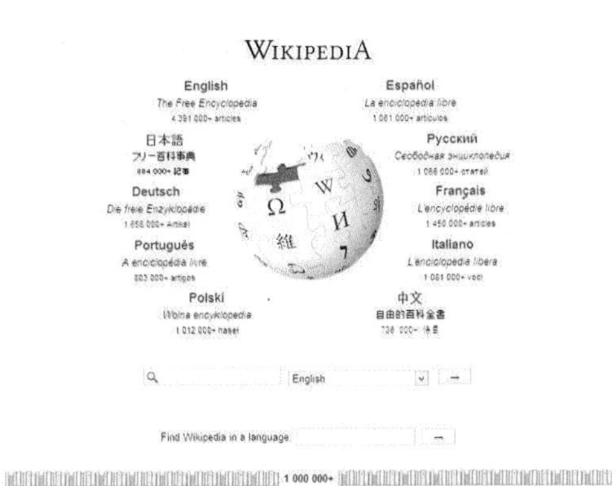

Figure 13-50
This image of the Wikipedia homepage uses both macro and micro whitespace.

Making Connections

As a Class

Gather several documents, anything from books, CD or DVD liners, magazines, instruction manuals, product packaging, etc. Bring them into class, and together discuss how each uses whitespace differently. What rhetorical or design reasons do you think led to the decisions to use whitespace in these particular ways?

In a Group

Choose a publication that has both print and online presences. How does this publication adjust their use of whitespace for each medium? Physical constraints aside, which do you find more enjoyable to read (which produces a better aesthetic experience)?

On Your Own

You might typically think of whitespace as a design element of printed publications. As an alternative, analyze how any videos that you watch use negative space to separate visual elements, create emphasis, or other effects. You will probably do well to think broadly about what counts as negative space in these videos. Share your examples with the class.

Proportion

Proportion names the relationship between different elements in a design, usually regarding the relative scale of those elements. Typically, a good design creates a harmony within this scale, thus creating good proportion.

Several relationships can be shown by varying scale. If two objects appear similar in scale, they're considered more equal than if one object were larger than the other. If you refer back to Figure 13-15, you can see varying relationships of scale. For instance, the two transformers are similar in scale (therefore more or less equal), as are the two humans.

However, the transformer-to-human scale is much greater, showing more importance on the transformers. This poster creates dominance of the transformers over the humans but also offers of focal point by creating diagonals toward the humans, so that even though they are of less importance in terms of proportion, they're still important in the overall harmony of the design (as well as the narrative). The scale between the two sizes also creates a balance between large and small.

Part of this psychological effect comes from the viewer's experience of the human body, the figure from which viewers derive most of their expectations of proportion (Figure 13-51). Generally, if you see a head, you know roughly how big the body will be in relation. When you see Optimus Prime's and Bumblebee's giant heads without their body (Figure 13-52), you know that their body must be equally enormous. If somehow the foreground scene of the poster was removed and you

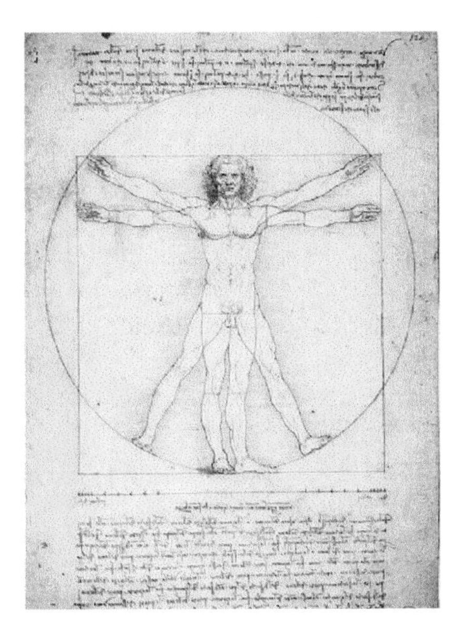

Figure 13-51
Leonardo da Vinci's Vitruvian Man was thought to depict the ideal human proportions.

Credit: ©Paramount/Courtesy Everett Collection

Figure 13-52
Based on our knowledge of the human body's proportions, Optimus Prime's body should be huge, even though he's a robot.

saw tiny robot bodies attached to the heads, you would feel that the proportion was out of harmony and badly designed.

Viewers also react emotionally due to bad proportion. For instance, how would you feel if you opened a 16" pizza box but only found a 4" pizza inside? Or how do you think you would feel if the doorknobs to a house were the size of basketballs, making gripping them very difficult? Such proportions would be annoying if not dangerous for someone who needed to get out of the room immediately.

While viewers generally react negatively (or, at least, immediately notice) when something is out of proportion, especially human proportion, this kind of reaction may be your design goal, eliciting attention or reaction from the audience. A building with extremely high ceilings may create a sense of wonder by making one feel small. However, you also risk offending the aesthetic sense of your audience, which may turn them away from your ultimate rhetorical goals.

Making Connections

As a Class

Find a variety of cartoon characters that have proper and improper proportions. Which characters are in proportion, and which ones aren't? What are the different situations that might have led the artists to design the cartoon characters the way they did? For those characters drawn out of proportion, would the cartoon be as effective or entertaining if the characters had normal proportions? Why or why not?

In a Group

Analyze news websites such as CNN or ESPN. How do these sites use proportion to suggest emphasis or importance? Which elements are largest? Which are smallest? Be sure to analyze not only the images, but other parts as well, such as navigation menus, social media updates, or font sizes.

On Your Own

Locate a flyer or print advertisement. How does it use proportion to make its point? Is this use of proportion effective, or could it be redesigned? How would you redesign it? Share your example and findings with the class.

Rule of Thirds

Typically, you might think that if you want to emphasize a subject, you should place it in the middle of your viewing frame if taking a picture or capturing video. However, asymmetrical designs are often more engaging and dynamic to viewers. When working with space in your designs, one technique you might consider is the "rule of thirds." This rule divides an image into nine segments by virtually dividing the image with two horizontal rules and two vertical rules (see Figure 13-53). Any major compositional elements should lie somewhere near one of the four intersections of these lines.

Credit: Chaky

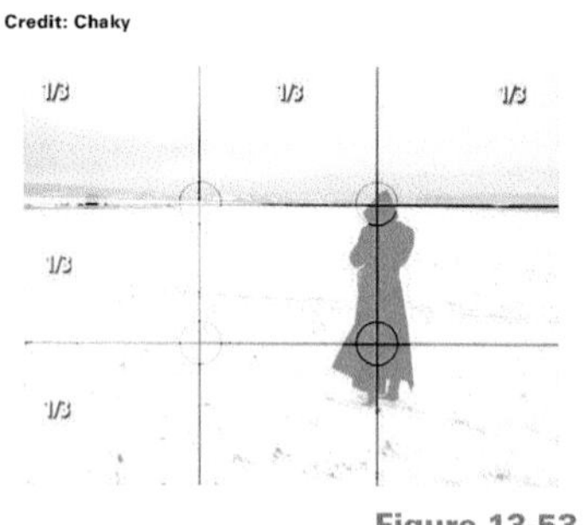

Figure 13-53
The focal point of this image is emphasized through the rule of thirds.

For instance, if you were taking a picture or shooting video, rather than aligning your main object in the center of the frame, you would align it on one of the four vertices. This alignment gives your picture a more dynamic feeling if you're depicting a moving object, or it provides a greater sense of depth and context if you're producing an image of a static object.

The rule of thirds in some ways is a shortcut to creating designs with an aesthetic use of spatial arrangements. A more precise layout follows the "Golden Mean," displayed by the Fibonacci spiral (Figure 13-54). When overlayed on several photographs, notice how the major area of focus aligns with the spiral. Another shortcut to this Golden Mean, then, is to divide the composition into fifths rather than thirds and align your major point of interest along the two-fifths or three-fifths lines in any direction (portrait or landscape). However, the rule of thirds will generally produce good results, and many video cameras have a feature that simulates gridlines in your viewfinder allowing you to align your subject with one of the four intersect points.

Credit: Raiana Tomazini/

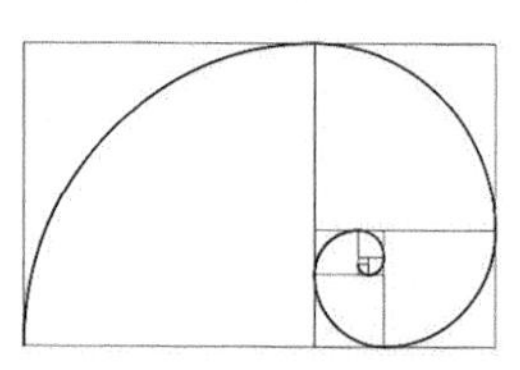

Figure 13-54
Fibonacci spiral.

You can usually notice the rule of thirds while watching television, specifically during interview scenes. For example, this still from *The Office* in Figure 13-55 uses the rule of thirds to position the interviewee's head in the upper right intersect point. If filming your own interviews, you should make use of these upper two points, positioning your subject's face in either of these two spots.

Credit: NBCUniversal

Figure 13-55
Many interviews use the rule of thirds to arrange their shots.

Making Connections

As a Class

Search for stock photographs on sites like corbisimages.com or gettyimages.com, and overlay the Fibonacci spiral onto a few images. How well do the major focal points align with the Golden Mean (or even the rule of thirds)? If not, do you think the image is still effective as those that do?

In a Group

As discussed above, television shows such as *The Office* use the rule of thirds during their "interview" sequences. Locate other instances of television or films that use this technique, either fictional shows or news programs. Share your examples with the class.

On Your Own

Using a camera—either provided by your class or just a cell phone camera—practice taking photos of a variety of objects using the rule of thirds. However, also take a series of photos placing objects in other orientations. In a photo editor, overlay a rule-of-thirds grid onto the images, seeing how well your images align with this principle. Share your images with the class, and discuss which photos are more engaging and whether the rule of thirds improves the composition of your images.

Balance

Credit: Dr F. Nemos

Figure 13-56
Butterflies exhibit symmetrical balance.

This chapter has often referred to the need to "balance" certain design elements, such as balance in proportion, color, or whitespace. However, balance is itself a formal principle and has three main spatial arrangements that you should consider when implementing balance in a design: symmetrical balance, asymmetrical balance, and radial balance.

Symmetrical balance appears when two parts of the design are mirror images of each other when divided in half. This balance can be vertical or horizontal. If you draw a line down the middle of Figure 13-56, each side is nearly the same as the other. Symmetrical balance can be applied to the design of the entire document. If you were to fold in half the *Transformers* poster in Figure 13-15, each element would roughly correspond to a part of the other side.

Asymmetrical balance can be achieved by organizing objects through different combinations of "weight," just as if you were trying to balance a set of scales. The graphic in Figure 13-57 uses asymmetrical balance. Although the single largest arrow appears on the left and dominates the overall design in terms of size, several smaller arrows on the right offset the weight of the larger arrow. If you were to remove these smaller arrows, as in Figure 13-58, then the image might feel "left-heavy" as if it could tip to one side.

Figure 13-57
Note how this ad creates balance through the text's placement.

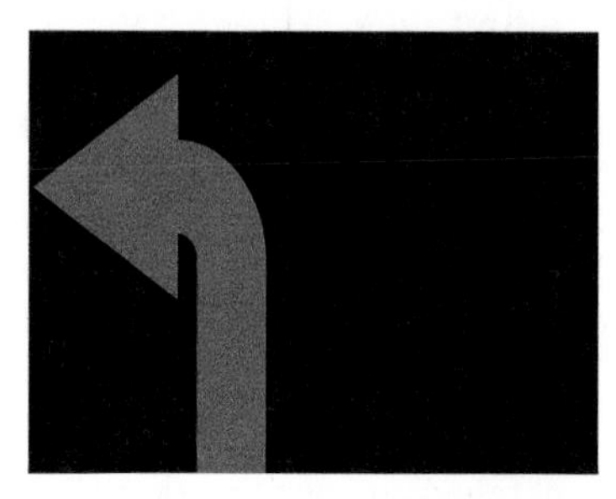

Figure 13-58
Without the text and graphics, the image feels out of balance.

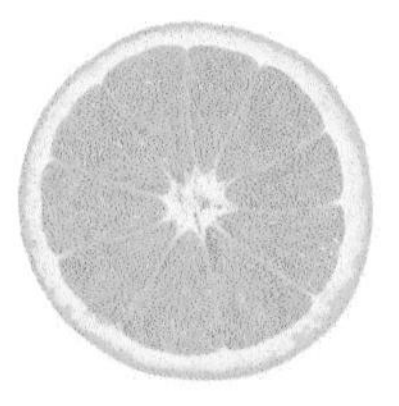

Figure 13-59
An orange displays radial balance when cut in half.

Radial balance occurs in images that can be divided in any direction and still produce mirror images of each other. Radial balance most commonly occurs in circular shapes, such as the orange in Figure 13-59. This kind of design creates balance and draws the eye to a central focal point no matter where on the design you first look.

Making Connections

As a Class

Search online for movie posters of the latest films coming out. Discuss how each poster tries to achieve balance using the above techniques. As an alternative, you might also analyze popular websites, noting how they arrange different elements to create balance.

In a Group

Look through the halls or bulletin board spaces on your campus or community. Find examples that use symmetrical, asymmetrical, and radial balance in their designs. Share them with the class and discuss whether you think the use of balance in these documents is effective both aesthetically and rhetorically. If not, how would you change the design?

On Your Own

In a photo editor, create two designs, each using either symmetrical or asymmetrical balance. Use any objects you want, such as simple geometric shapes or images found online. However, use the same objects for each design and then compare how the meaning of the composition changes as you change the balance between the elements.

Harmony

Figure 13-60
A nut and bolt share the spiral shape of the threads.

Like balance, many techniques can be used to achieve harmony, which—when successful—shows the audience how all the different parts of a design complement each other. While unity (discussed below) uses the repetition of like elements, harmony blends different elements so they work together. As an illustration, you might consider something as simple as a bolt and a nut (Figure 13-60). Separately, each has a different shape, yet they fit together as a structural unit. Visually, they look dissimilar, but they also share the spiral shape (outside on the bolt, and inside of the nut). Harmony attempts to accentuate the tension between these differences and similarities so that their strengths emerge and, like the bolt and nut, hold together as a design.

Figure 13-61
Domino's brand mark includes both squares and circles in harmony.

Credit: Honza Groh

Another common object that achieves harmony is a typical die or a domino. Although the sides are square or rectangular, the dots are circular, and the different shapes balance each other (Figure 13-61).

You can achieve harmony in a variety of ways. For instance, you may link dissimilar objects together by using similar colors for each. A bolt and nut have different shapes, but are often both metallic. Alternatively, you may present different colors within the same shape. A rainbow is made up of different colors but ties together as an arch (Figure 13-62).

Figure 13-62
The different colors are harmonized through the shape of the arch or bow.

A design does not necessarily have to be harmonious. In fact, you might intentionally design a composition so that it is disharmonious in order to capture the audience's attention. Also, a design that has too much harmony may seem monotonous. Some contrast is good and will help keep your audience engaged.

Making Connections

As a Class

Develop a list of examples from the natural world that achieve harmony, as the rainbow example illustrates. You might also consider everyday objects—such as a fork and knife—that look different but work together in harmony.

In a Group

Visit a variety of websites and analyze their various elements. How are they different? How are they similar? How do the elements integrate and complement the rest of the design? Share the website and your analysis with the class.

On Your Own

Look at the *Transformers* poster in Figure 13-15. In what ways does this poster use harmony in its design? Find other flyers or posters that make good (or bad) use of harmony, and share them with the class.

Proximity

Proximity places similar objects together within a design. For instance, if you look at most websites, all the links to other parts of the site are placed together in a menu so that users can easily navigate the site. Or, on a restaurant menu, appetizers are placed together, as are lunch items, drinks, and desserts. In this way, proximity helps to organize information. You can help create proximity by using boxed elements or whitespace to separate elements from each other and group the information that an audience would expect or find useful to be together as a unit.

Credit: Abhijith Jayanthi

Figure 13-63
This flyer uses proximity to group similar information. It also uses borders to help create separation.

The flyer in Figure 13-63 uses borders and images to reinforce proximity. The organization and title information for the flyer appear in a separate section away from the other details of the event. The other information is grouped and placed together using boxes so that the reader can quickly discern what kind of information is located in a particular area. Finally, most of the images are grouped together along the right margin rather than scattered randomly.

Figure 13-64, however, demonstrates bad use of proximity. Even though the author attempts to separate some information through use of color, all the text and images run into one another. Even if the design was limited by the size constraints of the flyer, it could be tweaked at the level of font size, the arrangement of images, and more whitespace to help create visual separation and guide the reader.

By creating a three-dimensional perspective, the *Transformers* poster (Figure 13-15) places like objects in proximity. For instance, the humans are placed together in the center of the poster and "further back" from the two transformers. Optimus Prime and Bumblebee are placed together in the foreground, even though the horizontal space between them seems greater.

Credit: crotonyachtclub.com/

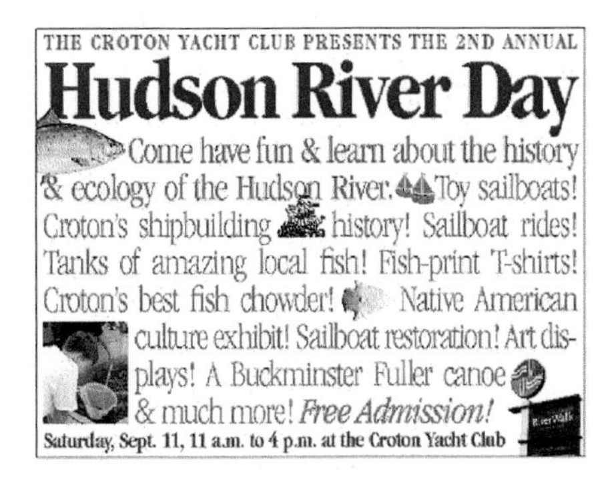

Figure 13-64
This flyer does not use proximity well.

Making Connections

As a Class

Look at a Facebook page. How does the site use proximity to group different kinds of visuals and information? How might you rearrange the site to make similar items more proximate? You may also look at other websites and discuss how each site uses proximity in their designs.

In a Group

Figure 13-64 attempts proximity but could be better designed. Analyze the way that the authors have attempted to place different kinds of information together and what could be improved. Next, sketch out your own design for a new poster that focuses on the proximity of like information. Share your designs, and discuss the choices you made with the class.

On Your Own

Watch one of the cable news stations, such as CNN, MSNBC, or Fox News. Analyze how each station uses proximity to organize the information the viewer sees. Compare this design with their respective Web pages, and write a brief report that explains how the television channels and websites differ in proximity and how they use it in similar ways.

Unity

Unity ties all the different parts of a design together so that the audience understands it as a single, cohesive image. While unity may seem a lot like harmony, unity focuses on creating a like pattern throughout with all objects, making sure the audience sees how this pattern works toward a single idea.

Figure 13-65, a flyer for an annual walking event, uses a variety of arrow shapes, but they're all tied together by the repetition of the arrow symbol. You might say that this image uses both harmony and unity, since each individual arrow complements others via its unique shape while the arrow points create unity.

In Figure 13-66, a series of images runs along the left of the page, but with another image in the upper right corner. One of the ways an audience knows that these images are connected is that they're all bound by a circular enclosure, creating unity among them.

You already use unity in alphabetic writing. Every sentence you write uses different words but ties together in a single, unified message. Likewise, sentences unite into paragraphs, which unite as an essay. A collection of essays can be thematically unified to create a book, and a collection of books can tie together to create a series. In visual design, unity is an attempt to create a single, coherent idea made up of all the different elements of the design.

In the *Harry Potter* poster (Figure 13-67), although Harry and Voldemort are opposed in the movie, within the poster they create unity, demonstrating—via their placement—that they both appear in the film and that there is tension between them. Within the film, the two are opposed; within the poster, their depictions create an overall unity to the design. This unity is a culmination of all the other principles this chapter has discussed already, such as balance, proximity, harmony, and proportion. If you've done well to make use of these principles, then your design will hopefully achieve unity.

Unity can play an important role in creating an overall design cohesion, especially with an image like a brand mark, which must be

Credit: hazencreative.com

Figure 13-65
The arrow shape helps to unify this design.

Credit: Airforce357

Figure 13-66
The circular frame of each image helps to unify them.

Credit: The Everett Collection

Figure 13-67
Unity in the *Harry Potter* poster.

unified with other elements of an organization's brand identity (Figure 13-68). For example, if a brand mark contained geometric shapes, such as triangles, then you may consider using a triangle-based motif for other documents, such as Web pages, business cards, letterhead, flyers, or other professional materials that can double as marketing materials. Each type of document is clearly different, but the design of each should be similar enough to link them together.

Credit: M.Minderhoud

Figure 13-68
Although Unilever's brand mark is made up of many different objects—such as a palm tree, snowflake, spoon, bird, heart, and other shapes—it achieves unity within the shape of a "U" that holds them together.

Making Connections

As a Class

Look again at a popular website. Discuss how the different parts create a unified whole to the site, so that you know they all belong on this page. Consider not just the visual aspects of the site but also the language used in the textual elements. Are there any elements that you could remove that would not disrupt the unity of the site?

In a Group

Analyze short, online videos produced by a single organization, such as Disney, National Geographic, or the National Football League (any source will do). Note how the videos create unity both within a single video but also among different videos. What visual elements help to link the videos and give them a coherent visual identity? Share your examples and findings with the rest of the class.

On Your Own

Choose your favorite sports team, and search online for a variety of documents, images, or objects produced by the organization. These examples should include uniforms, transportation, written documents, videos, etc. Analyze how the team creates an overall unity between all the documents, so a reader or viewer can clearly recognize that all are united.

Movement Through Space

You can create a sense of movement in your design by using different spatial arrangements, even when the composition is still. When a viewer typically looks at an image, the eye scans to the upper left, then clockwise around the image, and then horizontally through the image. A viewer also typically looks from large objects to smaller ones, color to noncolor, or from the unusual to the familiar. By arranging elements to capture an audience's first glance, you can help guide how they view the rest of the design.

Repetition and Rhythm

Just as the repeated drumbeats of a song create rhythm and drive the music, keeping it moving along, repeated elements of a visual composition achieve the same effect. Nearly any element can create rhythm as long as it's repeated throughout the design. Repetition of shapes, colors, objects, or patterns can all create rhythm and guide the viewer's gaze. The eye will pick up on the pattern, follow it, and move along the design space.

Credit: hazencreative.com

Figure 13-69
The matches in this poster repeat and create a rhythm.

Figure 13-69 features a poster for the band Iron & Wine. Notice the repeated use of matches from the match book in the upper-right corner diagonally to the lower-left corner. Typically, the eye will begin with the larger object, the matchbook, and follow the trail of matches. Notice how the designer inserted bits of information (styled in the same colors as the matches) along the trail so that the eye picks them up as it follows the repeated elements. Also, the positioning of the source of the matches (the matchbook) creates a natural sense of movement since viewers know that gravity will cause objects to fall and thus understand the matches as moving from the top of the page to the bottom.

You can also use repetition when writing with words. For instance, when you write a speech you may repeat the use of key words or phrases to make sure your audience receives the particular message you want conveyed. While you should typically try to vary some words in written texts to avoid monotony, you may repeat certain language that the audience identifies with. For instance, if you're writing a cover letter for a job, you may repeat certain phrases from the job advertisement so that your reader clearly sees how your skills connect with the company's needs.

Repetition and rhythm can use alternating elements as well. A series of dots will guide a reader through a page, but if you alter these dots by changing their colors, the audience may become more interested as this alteration keeps the design from becoming too monotonous. Think about how these repeated elements should tie into the overall design, keeping in mind the principles of unity and harmony.

Making Connections

As a Class

Return to one of the websites you've already looked at. What elements repeat and create rhythm for the reader to follow? How do these elements relate back to the page's unity?

In a Group

Look through a variety of magazines. How do these magazines create rhythm through repetition? Pay attention to color, fonts, and other elements. Do you think the use of these repeating elements makes the magazine, or individual articles, easier to read? Share your examples and findings with the class.

On Your Own

Revise your résumé (or write one) by creating rhythm through the repetition of certain elements. For instance, you may use color to highlight specific parts of the document, or you may change font sizes. Create at least three different versions and share them with your class.

Variety

Variety uses many variables—including color and contrast already discussed above—to create movement through a design's space by guiding the audience's gaze through the composition. Variety can also use repetition and rhythm as described in the previous section to guide a reader's eyes and keep a design from becoming too boring. The chief means to create variety include differences in size, color, or shape. However, you should usually only change one variable so that the design still maintains a sense of unity (Figure 13-70).

Figure 13-70
The repeating circles vary in size, creating a variety of rhythm and movement.

Making Connections

As a Class

Examine the advertisements for different Apple products. How do these ads make use of variety, both individually and as a collection? Why do you think Apple used variety in this way? Does variety, in this case, say something about Apple's *ethos* as a company?

In a Group

Create a list of examples from nature that display variety in their visual designs. In these examples, why do you think variety is helpful? Make a list of your examples, and share them with the class.

On Your Own

Look back at the Iron & Wine poster in Figure 13-69. How does the artist use variety to make the poster more interesting? Do you think the artist uses enough variety? Too much? Record your thoughts and share them with the class.

Action

A variety of techniques can display action and thus movement. Some images can create movement simply by the positioning of the object (such as the Iron & Wine example in Figure 13-69). If positioned correctly in the composition, a bird in flight or a skydiver in free fall creates movement because the viewer understands the natural trajectory of their bodies. Such movement is sometimes referred to as anticipated movement, because the viewer anticipates that the figure would move in a particular way if it wasn't a still image.

Movement can also be communicated by giving an object fuzzy boundaries or indistinct outlines. If you've ever watched an object at high speed, such as a pitcher throwing a fastball, or water spraying from a hose, it's difficult to see the ball or water sharply. Instead, viewers experience fast moving objects as more blurry than stationary objects. In visual designs, blurring an image can help show the audience that a particular object is in motion, such as the wings of the hummingbird in Figure 13-71.

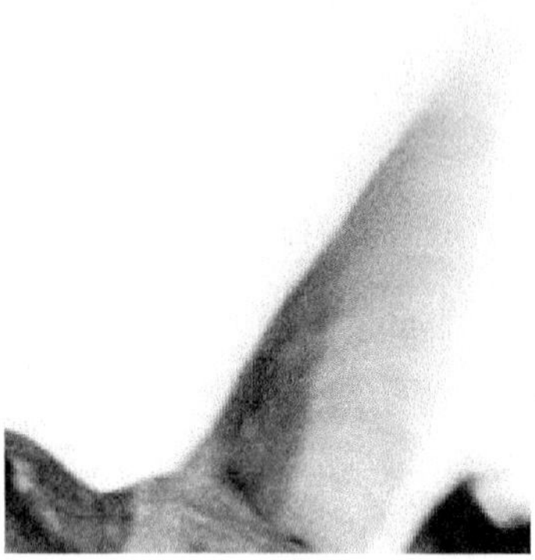

Figure 13.71

The blurred wings of this hummingbird indicate that they were moving when the photo was taken.

Diagonal lines, or objects posed at a diagonal, also create movement. The Heisman Trophy statue's pose creates a diagonal vector pointing toward the way he would move. Actual vectors, such as arrow shapes, also create movement as viewers have become conditioned to following them as movement indicators via traffic signs and other aids. Arrows direct attention, and so move the viewer's eyes along a design. However, the vector need not be an actual arrow. The arm of the Heisman Trophy creates a secondary vector that draws the eye toward the outstretched hand.

Even eye position—where a figure is looking—creates an invisible vector that directs the audience's attention to some other part of the image. A pathway, such as a road, trail, staircase, or aisle can also create movement, as these elements may be physically shaped as diagonals but are also places where one physically moves or where movement occurs.

Figure 13-72, the famous cover of the Beatles' album *Abbey Road*, displays many of these characteristics. The Beatles themselves are actually in movement from left to right, and their gaze straight ahead reinforces this direction. The crosswalk provides an example of a path, yet the vanishing point created by the road they're crossing provides a secondary axis of movement, although dominated by the vector along which the main subjects walk.

Finally, multiple objects can be shown in a single image to convey movement. These objects might appear across several frames, like a comic or the person jumping in Figure 13-73. Here, several frames are overlaid to show the flow of movement, and the viewer understands the full motion of his action. Of course, a single shot of the figure in the air about to fall would also express this to the audience. However, this sequence lets the viewer know that he landed on the next building.

Making Connections

As a Class

Credit: Apple Records/EMI/John Kosh

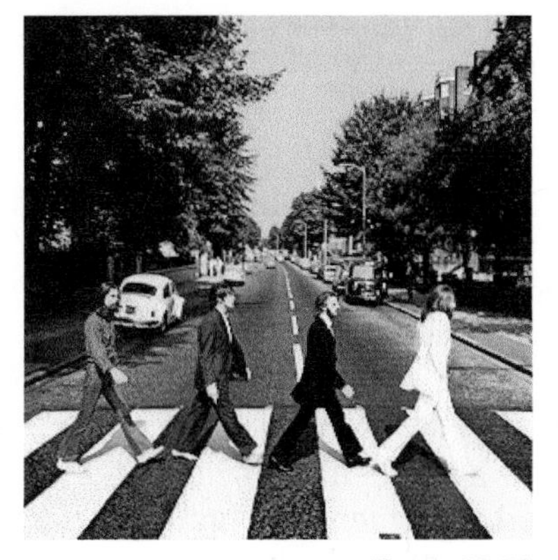

Figure 13-72
The cover art for *Abbey Road* conveys movement in several ways.

Credit: Urban Freeflow

Figure 13-73
This image superimposes several images into one in order to show movement.

Look at a variety of still advertisements for sporting products. Analyze which ads attempt to convey a sense of action and which ones do not. Which ads to you find more effective for the product they're advertising?

In a Group

Look at several comic strips either online or in a newspaper. List all the various techniques that the artists use to visualize movement to the reader. Share your list with the class.

On Your Own

Collect brand marks and still advertisements for organizations that specialize in transport or delivery, such as moving, freight, or mail companies. Analyze if these brand marks or ads use action in their designs. If so, do you think these designs are effective at making a rhetorical point about their company? If the visuals don't use action, are they still effective, or would you suggest revisions? Share you findings with the class.

Sequence

Another way of creating movement within a still image is through sequence. While one method of sequence uses the techniques of comics, isolating individual steps through separate frames, you can also show a progression of movement within a single frame. Figure 13-74 depicts the classic

Credit: José-manuel Benitos

Figure 13-74
This image depicts evolution as a sequence.

evolution sequence that illustrates a movement through time. Figure 13-75 shows a sequence that demonstrates how to exercise by swinging a kettlebell. This image instructs the viewer how to move in a particular way, but does so by conveying a sense of movement.

Figure 13-75
This sequence informs the viewer how to perform this kettlebell exercise.

Credit: Shawn Hazen

Figure 13-76 shows a sequence of the word "UNITED" becoming the word "CHANGE." In this image, each letter "moves" until it has transformed into another. Note that one of the reasons this sequence is successful is that each step introduces only small changes, allowing the viewer to see the transformation. However, the changes are large enough that the designer can fit the entire sequence on a single poster.

If you are composing a sequence to show a particular movement, such as the kettlebell movement in Figure 13-75, then all the other elements of the image (such as the background) should remain as consistent as possible so that the focus is on what changes—the movement itself. Notice in this example, the background consists of a white backdrop so the reader doesn't become distracted.

Figure 13-76
This poster "moves" the letters to change the word "UNITED" into "CHANGE."

Even within moving images, you can still break a scene into a sequence of camera angles to make the scene more dynamic. For instance, you can shoot a single scene from different angles and put them together to present the entire action in a more dynamic way. Changing angles can provide emphasis on different objects in the scene, thus offering rhetorical choices for the director, who might want the audience to identify with a particular character or point of view, or to move the plot in a specific direction.

Making Connections

As a Class

Watch an episode of a popular television sitcom or drama. As you watch, write down how the director distills different scenes into a smaller series of sequences. Note the important aspects of each shot. After the show is over, discuss what you noticed and how the director created sequences to change meaning or emphasis. How do these sequences help move the story along? If the show doesn't use sequences, discuss why you think this might be as well.

In a Group

Choose a simple task that you perform every day and create a sequence of images depicting this task. You can do this with a still camera, taking photos as you perform the task, or you can use video, freezing the footage and taking screenshots. Try and distill the sequence to as few images as possible while still conveying everything that the audience might need to know to complete the action themselves.

On Your Own

Look at your favorite comic book, or find one online that you can use. Analyze how the artist creates sequences between the panels. How do you know that each panel is related to the one before? If the scene changes, what indications does the artist give to let you know that the previous sequence has ended?

Key Terms

action
asymmetrical balance
balance
CMYK
color
complementary colors
contrast
contrasting colors
emphasis
harmony
hue
isolation
perspective
placement
proportion
proximity
radial balance
repetition
RGB
rhythm
rule of thirds
sans serif
saturation
sequence
serif
symmetrical balance
typography
unity
value
variety
whitespace

Output: Flyer

As you may have noticed, many of the examples used in this chapter are various forms of flyers. This section repeatedly referenced the *Transformers* poster (Figure 13-15) to illustrate many of the design techniques you can use to create your own visual documents. For this output, create your own flyer for an event, community organization, non-profit group, a neighbor that needs help, or other purpose designated by your instructor. Here are some suggestions:

1. Approach a community organization such as a homeless shelter, and create a flyer for an upcoming event.
2. Locate a problem, situation, or important event in your community; create a flyer making citizens aware of it.
3. Identify a neighbor or friend who needs help finding a lost pet or who needs assistance advertising some other pressing need, and create an appropriate flyer to meet the exigency.

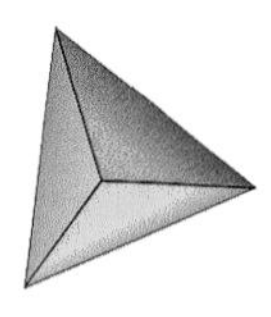

As you think though how you should design your flyer, you'll obviously consider design and genre (a flyer) from the rhetorical tetrahedron. You should also consider the medium on which that flyer will be placed. For instance, if the flyer is in a location where it might get wet, you should print it on waterproof paper. Of course, you must also consider your message and audience, and how *logos*, *ethos*, *pathos*, and *kairos* factor into your design and distribution.

Step by Step

To create your own flyer or poster, you must first consider some rhetorical questions applicable to all writing.

Exigency

What is the situation that demands this flyer? Is this the best kind of document to create for your situation?

Purpose

What is the goal of the flyer? To persuade? Inform? What do you want to accomplish with the flyer? What kind of flyer will be most effective?

Audience

Whom do you hope to reach with this flyer? Who is your primary audience? Can you identify secondary audiences? How will you design your flyer to accommodate all of these audiences?

Delivery

How will you distribute your flyer? On bulletin boards? Online? Through the mail? If you post the flyer in a public space, how will you place or design it so that it can compete for the attention of the audience amongst all other flyers and visuals? Where can you place the flyer so that it will most likely reach your intended audience?

Once you determine what kind of flyer you want to produce, you must also consider some of its physical properties.

Size

What size paper (or other material) will you print your flyer on? This is probably the first question to answer, since it will determine how you design the flyer.

Stock

What kind of paper will you use? Will you use basic printer paper or something more durable, such as glossy card stock?

Font

What kind of font will you use for the most important information? You need to grab the reader's attention, so a large sans serif font will usually work best, but paragraphs of information might be written in a serif font. Also, simple fonts that can be easily read usually work better than a complicated font that is too difficult to make out.

Color

How can you use color to emphasize important information? You want different elements in your flyer to contrast with each other so none becomes lost to the viewer. You might also use color thematically. For instance, if your flyer is about an environmental event, green becomes an obvious choice. If the flyer pertains to your college or university, then you might use the school's colors.

Layout

How will you layout the title, text, and images on the flyer to best organize the information to the viewer while still making it aesthetically pleasing?

Images

Remember, the flyer itself is an image, regardless of whether it contains images. However, is an image important to your argument? Is it ancillary, or the central component, such as a flyer for a missing child or pet?

After you have considered these questions, use the guidelines below to create the flyer.

1. Create a headline or title: This title should be short enough to be read quickly and grab the reader's attention. However, also think of key words that will help make it stand out. For example, using "Sublease Close to Campus" might be more appealing than just "Sublease," since it includes information that might be attractive to a student. Including the price in this title might also be effective. Anticipate and appeal to the reader's needs and wants. If the flyer is for a business, do not include the business name in the title; instead, include what you will do for the reader.
2. Use colorful and emphatic graphics: While your flyer shouldn't look too cluttered with information, it should use color and graphics to make your argument. Use graphics that will get your point across as well as color to help you highlight important information.
3. Focus on benefits/consequences: Ultimately, you need to appeal to the reader, and explain what the audience will get from the flyer's message. In other words, how does the information affect them? You may have lost a pet, but what information can you include to make the audience want to act? An appeal for their sympathy? A reward? If it is for an event, why should they want to attend? If fundraising for a charity, why should they donate? While you might not have space for all your claims, evidence, and reasons, you should at least include some reasons for them to act.
4. Organize boxed elements and contrasting colors: Placing important information into small boxes, using whitespace to separate elements or using colors can help call attention to the information.
5. Clearly identify your main points: In a one-page flyer, you don't have much room to make your argument, so try to stick to the most important information, which typically includes who, what, where, when, why, how. Don't go into too much detail, and make the most important information as clear as possible. As a whole, try to keep the flyer simple, so don't get too complicated.
6. Provide details: You should provide details that let your readers know how to act if they're persuaded by you message. Include contact information, dates, prices, important names, or other information they might need. You can also include URLs or quick reference codes that will take them to online information if necessary.
7. Use the back: Although flyers traditionally only have information on one side, especially if they're posted on a wall, there is no reason they have to be one-sided. Consider if there is any specific or important information that would be useful to print on the backside of a flyer. Perhaps use the space for more images to better highlight or illustrate what you wish to communicate.
8. Proofread: A spelling or design inconsistency in a flyer can destroy an author's *ethos*, especially since it is such a short document. Remember, flyers are meant to be distributed to many people, so this effect is multiplied. You can never know who will really see this flyer,

so make sure everything is correct. As with any document, let your peers review the flyer as well.

9. Delivery: Choose the right medium and placement for your flyer. The delivery medium does not just mean the kind of paper you use when printing but also the overall ecology of the flyer's distribution. To choose the best medium and location, you should screen the environment, taking note of how it will affect your text. Where can you place the flyer so it has the greatest chance of being seen, and thus, delivery to the audience?

Credit: User:Ld

Figure 13-77
Flyers can litter the streets if not removed once they've served their purpose.

Flyers are relatively cheap to produce, and you can easily make a large quantity of high quality flyers using glossy paper and a good color inkjet or laser printer. However, they can also contribute to pollution (Figure 13-77). If you're going to mass-produce a flyer, consider some following guidelines:

- Try to use post-consumer, recycled stock if possible.
- Consider using a stock that is biodegradable, especially for events that will pass and for which the flyer will become obsolete.
- Although an inconvenience, make sure you remove your flyers if you have posted them in a public area once you feel your message has been delivered (or, if for an event, after that event has taken place). Flyers often become detached from their surface and become litter in streets, drains, landfills, and contribute to pollution.

Also, remember that many flyers are exposed to the elements, and that weather, such as rain, can alter the message of a flyer if it causes the ink to bleed.

WORKS CITED

Aristotle. *On Rhetoric: A Theory of Civic Discourse.* Ed. George A. Kennedy. New York: Oxford, 1991.

Badenhausen, Kurt. "Apple, Microsoft and Google are Worlds Most Valuable Brands." *Forbes.* 5 Nov. 2014. Web. 27 Feb. 2015.

Bakshy, Eytan. "Showing Support for Marriage Equality on Facebook." Facebook Data Science. 29 March 2013. Web. 20 May 2014.

Bateman, John. *Text and Image: A Critical Introduction to the Visual / Verbal Divide.* New York: Routledge, 2014. Print.

Block, Brian. Personal Interview. 12 February 2015.

Bruni, Frank. "Is There Any Stopping Donald Trump?" *New York Times*. 21 February 2016. Web. 23 February 2016.

Carr, Nicholas. *The Shallows: What the Internet is Doing to Our Brains.* New York: W. W. Norton & Company, 2011. Print.

Catton, Bruce. *A Stillness at Appomattox*. New York: Doubleday, 1953. Print.

Crowley, Sharon, and Debra Hawhee. *Ancient Rhetorics for Contemporary Students*. New York: Pearson/Longman, 2004. Print.

Darnton, Robert. "Google and the Future of Books." *The Case for Books: Past, Present, and Future.* New York: PublicAffairs. 2009. 3–20. Print.

Fairclough, Norman. *Discourse and Social Change*. Cambridge, MA: Polity Press, 1992. Print.

Fischlin, Daniel, and Mark Fortier. "General Introduction." *Adaptations of Shakespeare: a Critical Anthology of Plays from the Seventeenth Century to the Present.* Eds. Daniel Fischlin and Mark Fortier. London: Routledge, 2000. 1–22. Print.

Florini, Sarah. "Tweets, Tweeps, and Signifyin': Communication and Cultural Performance on Black Twitter." *Television and New Media Volume: 15*(3) (2014): 223–37. Print.

Foucault, Michel. *This Is Not a Pipe.* Trans. and ed. James Harkness. Berkeley: University of California Press, 1982.

Gombrich, E.H. *The Story of Art.* London: Phaidon Press, 1995.

Hutcheon, Linda. *A Theory of Adaptation.* New York: Routledge, 2006. Print.

Isocrates. From *Antidosis.* Trans. George Norlin. Rpt. in *The Rhetorical Tradition: Readings from Classical Times to the Present.* Eds. Patricia Bizzell and Bruce Herzberg. Boston: Bedford Books, 1990.

Jadad, Alehandro, and Anna Gagliardi. "Rating health information on the internet: navigating to knowledge or the tower of Babel?" *JAMA 279.8* (1998): 611–14. Print.

Jenkins, Henry, Sam Ford, and Joshua Green. "Introduction: Why Media Spreads." *Spreadable Media: Creating Value and Meaning in a Networked Culture.* New York: NYU Press. 2014. 1–14. Print.

King, Stephen. *On Writing: A Memoir of the Craft.* New York: Scribner. New York, 2001. Print.

Kress, Gunther. "Genre as Social Process." *The Powers of Literacy: A Genre Approach to Teaching Writing*. Bill Cope and Mary Kalantzis, eds. Pittsburgh: U of Pittsburgh P, 1993. 22–37. Print.

Kress, Gunther. *Multimodality: A Social Semiotic Approach to Contemporary Communication*. New York, NY: Routledge, 2010. Print.

Kress, Gunther, and Theo van Leeuwen. *Reading Images: The Grammar of Visual Design*. 2nd edition. New York, NY: Routledge, 2006. Print.

Kweku, Ezekiel. "What Makes A Person Vote For Donald Trump?" MTV News. 2 February 2016. Web. 23 February 2016.

Lanham, Richard A. "Economics of Attraction." *The Economics of Attention: Style & Substance in the Age of Information.* Chicago: University of Chicago Press. 2006. 42–77. Print.

Lethem, Jonathan. "The Ecstasy of Influence: a Plagiarism." *The Ecstasy of Influence: Nonfictions, etc.* New York: Doubleday, 2011. 93–120. Print.

McCloud, Scott. "Show and Tell." *Understanding Comics: The Invisible Art.* New York: Harper Collins. 1994. Print.

Miller, Carolyn R. Foreword. *Rhetoric and Kairos: Essays in History, Theory, and Praxis*. Eds. Phillip Sipiora and James S. Baumlin. Albany: SUNY P, 2002. xi–xiii. Print.

Miller, Carolyn R. "Rhetorical Community: The Cultural Basis of Genre." *Genre and the New Rhetoric*. Eds. Aviva Freedman and Peter Medway. Bristol, PA: Taylor & Francis Ltd., 1994. 67–78. Print.

Miller, Carolyn R. and Dawn Shepherd. "Blogging as a Social Action: A Genre Analysis of the Weblog." *Into the Blogosphere: Rhetoric, Community, and Culture of Weblogs.* 2004. Web. 20 May 2014.

Mitchell, W.J.T. *Iconology: Image, Text, Ideology.* Chicago: University of Chicago Press, 1986.

Morey, Sean. "Design." *New Media Writer*. Southlake: Fountainhead Press, 2014. Print.

Shakespeare, William. *A Midsummer Night's Dream*. 1593–95. Print.

---. *Romeo and Juliet*. 1593–95.

Sipiora, Phillip. "Introduction: The Ancient Concept of Kairos." *Rhetoric and Kairos: Essays in History, Theory, and Praxis*. Phillip Sipiora and James S. Baumlin. Albany: SUNY P, 2002. 1–22. Print.

Smith, John E. "Time and Qualitative Time." *Rhetoric and Kairos: Essays in History, Theory, and Praxis*. Phillip Sipiora and James S. Baumlin. Albany: SUNY P, 2002. 46–57. Print.

Sontag, Susan. *On Photography.* New York: Farrar, Straus and Giroux, 1977.

——. *Regarding the Pain of Others.* New York: Farrar, Straus and Giroux, 2003.

Swales, John M. *Genre Analysis: English in Academic and Research Settings*. New York: Cambridge UP, 1990. Print.

Tannenbaum, Melanie. "Will changing your Facebook profile do anything for marriage equality?" *Scientific American*. 28 March 2013. Web. 20 May 2014.

White, Brent. "From the Sonoran to the South Loop." @Las Magazine, Fall 2013. Web. 21 May 2014.

Index

E

F

G

H

I

J

K

L

M

N

O

P

R

S

T

U

V

W

Z